TROUBLED CHILDREN
IN A
TROUBLED WORLD

TROUBLED CHILDREN
IN A
TROUBLED WORLD

Edith Buxbaum

INTERNATIONAL UNIVERSITIES PRESS, INC.

NEW YORK

Library of Congress Catalog Card Number: 79–128623

Manufactured in the United States of America

To my husband, Fritz Schmidl

CONTENTS

FOREWORD

This collection of papers is made up of old and new papers Some of the old papers have been revised and for the purpose of continuity rewritten to a certain extent. They represent my experiences and development in the areas of child analysis and education. Having begun my career as a school teacher, I have never been quite removed from education. As an analyst, I have used my observations of children to enhance my child analytic technique.

The combination of analysis and education was not always favorably regarded. In the beginnings of psychoanalytic thinking, it seemed that many symptoms, inhibitions, defenses and anxieties were due to disturbances created by the educating adults who had to limit the child and curb his instincts in order to adapt and fit him into the society in which he would be living. Psychoanalysis, on the other hand, took it upon itself to undo the damages of education. Education and psychoanalysis seemed to work at cross-purposes. In her paper "Psychoanalysis and Education," Anna Freud (1954b) distinguished between two periods in the application of psychoanalytic findings to education—an "optimistic" one and a "pessimistic" one.

The "optimistic" period blamed the child's neurotic development largely on parental education; it was hoped that by eliminating the mistakes of education all children would grow up normally. The "pessimistic" period exonerated the

parents to a large extent and attributed the origin of neurosis to inevitable frustrations and constitutional factors.

Already in the thirties, with Anna Freud's *The Ego and
the Mechanisms of Defense*, it became obvious that education was not the villain it was purported to be, but that it
fulfilled a necessary task in providing the ego with the raw
material for building up its defenses and its structure. Increasingly, the ego and its functions became more important in clinical and theoretical considerations of analysis.

Analytic theory is at its best when it has a clinical basis.
While these theoretical developments were taking place,
analysts and child analysts enlarged their scope of clinical
material by tackling cases which previously would not have
been considered suitable for analysis. They not only treated
neurosis but also behavior disorders and the so-called border-
line cases. In doing so, they followed Aichhorn in his pioneer-
ing work with delinquents: the therapist attempted to trans-
form into neurotics the children and adolescents who were
lacking anxieties and inhibitions, because only when they
suffered from anxieties and guilt feelings would they become
amenable to treatment. The therapist had to be educator in
order to make the child educable so that he could be treated.

In working with these children—who largely outnumbered
the neurotics—the therapist became acquainted with an entirely different population. While the neurotics were over-
educated, these were under-educated. While the neurotics
had often been overprotected, most of these children had
been severely neglected and uncared for. Where the neurotics were unable to separate themselves from their mothers
whom they considered part of themselves, we now became
aware of children who didn't have any constant ties, who
didn't love, relate, or belong, who didn't know who they
were or why. Problems of relationship came into focus as
well as problems of identity. While the clinicians struggled
with these problems, the theoreticians began to set up research projects to observe in detail what the clinicians were

dealing with. Spitz and Mahler worked on their infant observations in this country; Anna Freud, with her co-workers, at Hampstead in London. Their observations in turn are helping the clinician.

The papers in the first part of this book deal with problems of psychosexual development, separation and identity, aggression, ego functions, and related problems of technique. Part II is devoted to a number of case reports which offer more extensive clinical material to substantiate some of the problems discussed in Part one. Part III contains some ideas on education which are particularly geared to the pressing problems of our time, namely, group aggression and violence as they appear in the eyes of an analytic observer and therapist. The paper on problems of kibbutz children deals with an experiment in education in a different society.

I am grateful to the publishers who granted me permission to use the papers in this book. I also wish to thank my friends who helped with the typing and correcting, particularly Mrs. Lucille Worth and Mrs. Nikki Louis, as well as Mrs. Marion Dunsmore who prepared the index.

I. Theoretical Considerations

PSYCHOSEXUAL DEVELOPMENT

When the human child is born, he is helpless for a long time and can survive only with the aid of his environment. This period of dependency, prolonged in comparison with that of other mammals, is of great importance in the child's development. Exposed to the influences of his environment, whether these be good or bad, he must learn passively. Being fed, handled, and taken care of in general, includes being exposed to language, action, food, and drink of certain kinds, at times and in ways chosen, by his environment. This period of prolonged helplessness subjects the child to the customs and habits of the people with whom he lives. Recently, anthropologists and psychologists have concerned themselves more and more with this important period of acculturation (Erikson, 1950; Silverberg, 1952).

THE FIRST YEAR—THE ORAL PHASE

During the first weeks and months, the child needs to be taken care of like any other young animal. He has to be fed and kept warm and he does not care who satisfies his needs so long as they are satisfied. Soon, however, he be-

This paper, originally entitled, "Psychosexual Development: the Oral, Anal, and Phallic Phases," was first published in *Readings in Psychoanalytic Psychology*, ed. M. Leavitt. New York: Appleton-Century-Crofts, 1959, pp. 43-55.

comes somewhat more discriminating. He may show pref-
erence for some foods and dislike for others; he may want to
be fed slowly or rapidly, he may want to be picked up a lot
or infrequently. The mother waits anxiously for the first
smile and is eager to believe that the smile is directed toward her and is intentional and not a chance grimace or
mouthing movement.

The mother is justified in attributing importance to this
expression; although it may not yet be a sign of recognition,
it is, nevertheless, a sign that relatedness is beginning.
Around the same time, the infant learns to direct his hand
to his mouth. He probably finds his mouth by accident the
first time but the action soon becomes deliberate. Both these
developments show beginnings of consciousness. They are
the first actions which the baby undertakes in a controlled
way. The desire to repeat an action is a sign that he remem-
bers a sensation and a feeling. His smiling at the mother
signals a vague kind of recognition and, as such, means that
memory has begun to develop. Unclear and diffuse as these
memories are, they constitute the beginnings of thinking.
From this point forward, the baby is not merely a physical
being whose demands and reactions are exclusively somatic
in nature. These first signs of recognition, memory, and willfulness are related to what are called ego functions.

Physical and emotional well-being are intimately related
—the more so the younger the baby is. When the mother is
absent, the baby feels unhappy, uncomfortable, and may
even react with physical symptoms. He is accustomed to the
touch, voice, and smell of one person. Experiments have
shown that infants do not actually recognize faces, but react
rather to a Gestalt, that is, to a configuration without details.

Once the baby is habituated to his mother's way of handling him, he accepts no other person in her place. We know
this from observing emotionally disturbed children. Such
observations very often can be used to answer questions regarding well babies because they throw into sharp profile

disturbances which occur to a minor degree in all children. Observations of infants cared for in institutions under hygienically ideal conditions, but by a number of people, have shown that these children are retarded in their development, especially with respect to forming object relationships. Sometimes they move their hands and arms peculiarly, stretching their fingers and hands stiffly away from themselves, looking at them but neither grasping nor holding on to anything. Spitz (1945), who has observed, filmed, and described these children, has called this particular syndrome "hospitalism." He has observed that when the children are consistently taken care of by one person they resume normal development. We may say hospitalism is a reaction to the lack of continued contact with one person.

When the infant is deprived for long periods of time of a mother he may become apathetic or cry inconsolably. Spitz (1946b) has called this "anaclitic depression." While the picture of hospitalism shows the baby retarded in physical development with a lack of recognition as if no relations could develop, the baby who is deserted by the mother he already knows regresses to the phase he had reached before she departed. The development of young children is entirely dependent on the relationship with the mother or mother surrogate.

One generally refers to the period of total dependency on the mother as the oral phase, because, although the child's entire body is sensitive, the mouth is the organ which affords the greatest pleasure. The mouth is an erogenous zone. Skin, too, particularly the mucosa, is especially sensitive, as are the eyes and ears. Strong light and loud noises disturb the baby. If the baby is too warm or too cold or too wet, it hurts his skin, and he may even develop eczema. He is also sensitive to the way he is held and to what and how he is fed. His reactions are generally spread out all over his body. When he hurts in one place, he expresses his pain by movements all over his body—kicking, squirming, perspiring, crying, passing stool and wind. His reactions as well as his feelings are undifferentiated.

Possibly the baby's first knowledge of an outside world comes when he feels hungry and food is not immediately available. He is deprived by the outside world, and his source of satisfaction comes from the same external environment. With the conscious recognition of somebody outside of himself who may frustrate or satisfy him, he begins to differentiate between himself and others and develops a rudimentary ego.

With the onset of differentiation, anxiety makes its appearance. The baby does not want to be alone, does not want to be in the dark, cries when a stranger appears and when the mother is not there. Whereas earlier the baby cried as a reaction to physical discomfort, once he recognizes the outside world, he may cry because of some change in his environment. He will still cry and express his unhappiness with his whole body as he did weeks or months ago. However, when the mother appears on the scene, he may quiet down without further ministrations. Although the appearance of anxiety may not seem to be of any advantage to those who are taking care of the baby, it is as important in his development as the first smile.

During the second half of the first year, the baby adds some new achievements. I mentioned as the first intentional movement that of putting his hand into his mouth. Now when he does this, he also looks at his hand or perhaps at something which he wants to take into his hand; coordination of eye and hand-to-mouth movement takes place. He turns his attention to more things as well as to more people; he also learns to control other movements besides the hand-to-mouth one. Foot-to-mouth movement is a further challenge as well as other people's hand-to-mouth and things-to-mouth movements. He becomes better acquainted with his body and learns to control it by holding, reaching, sitting, crawling, and finally walking. With every movement, his ability to do things increases. The more movement control he achieves, the more he is able to do what comes into his mind.

His mouth, the area which we consider so all-important, has a development of its own. Preliminary to teething, sucking changes to biting. He uses his mouth for making all kinds of sounds as well as for spitting and biting. With the advent of teething, the mouth becomes an instrument for aggression and is regarded as such by the environment.

THE SECOND YEAR—THE ANAL PHASE

As a rule, people do not interfere actively with young infants. They may neglect them, but they usually do not harm them intentionally. When the baby becomes a crawling, pulling, biting little animal, the environment feels the need to interfere. People want to protect themselves and their possessions as well as the child. They feel called upon to restrain the baby and interact with him more than before. Previously the baby had no choice but to submit passively, however he was handled. Now he has some movement and activity of his own. He does not submit completely, nor is he entirely passive. All this significantly changes the attitude of the environment. Punishment and praise are introduced into the child's life. He is allowed to do some things and forbidden to do others—with the help of tolerance, praise and punishment. As the parents attempt to curb some of his actions, they also try to curb some of his instincts. The child reacts with anger, aggression, and suppression.

The most crucial interference in the child's life during the anal phase is the introduction of cleanliness education. The right time to bowel train the child is generally considered to be when he can sit alone unaided and when his relationship to the caretaking person is such that he wants to be praised for achievements. If the relationship is not sufficiently matured sphincter control can be established, but at a price. The child may develop constipation or he may after a period of sphincter control start soiling again. When this happens, re-education is more difficult than the original training. However, even when cleanliness education is started at the right time, it usually leads to a battle of wills between mother and child. For most children, this is the first clash with mother and, as a result, many childhood disturbances have their origin during this phase.

To give the impression that the clash of wills cannot happen in other areas as well, and prior to the second year, would be erroneous. It just happens that cleanliness is of major concern to the majority of Americans. We are a bathroom-conscious people with marked hygienic taboos. Our concern for cleanliness makes most of us disapprove of the child's putting into his mouth things picked up from the floor. Fewer of us may object to his eating from utensils which have been used by other people, but some of us object to his using his hands to feed himself. Clothes have to be clean and rooms have to be kept in order. The mother's feelings determine the emphasis in the home placed on clean hands, clean faces and clean bottoms. It is in the areas of washing and feeding that difficulties between mother and child may occur even before toilet training is undertaken.

The mother who is concerned that the baby be well fed may overfeed or force-feed him, thereby creating eating disturbances. Or she may prevent the baby from getting food all over himself, from feeding himself, thus interfering with his enjoyment of food and preventing him from developing independence. Her method of handling the baby makes the bath an experience they may both enjoy deeply or anticipate with dread. Whether the mother promotes or interferes with the baby's development depends on whether she finds his increased agility and motility a pleasure or an annoyance.

Bladder control is usually attempted at about the same time as bowel control. It may be achieved earlier or later, but the problems connected with it are somewhat different from those of bowel control. In the latter area, the child may refuse to relinquish his product; this frequently leads to constipation. Sometimes he is willing to eliminate but wants to keep the product in his diapers; or having consented to defecate in a certain place at a certain time, he may still want to keep it there and refuses to have it flushed down the toilet. These problems are common to both boys and girls. Some boys are proud to be able to urinate standing up. Others, however, refuse to stand up and prefer to urinate sitting down. These preferences illuminate the parents' methods of handling the sexual differences. Holding on to a full bladder stimulates feelings in the genital area. During the toilet-training period, with its preoccupation with the genital area, sexual stimulation by the caretaking person increases. The child has, however, already become aware of his genital area, partly through the mother's normal handling of him. Even babies seek to actively reproduce pleasant sensations once they have experienced them passively. If he is not prevented from doing so, the child uses his genital area to produce pleasant feelings for himself. Children are sometimes prevented from achieving bowel and bladder control because their parents do not want them to get dirty. Such parents often complain that the child touches his excreta; what they are really concerned about, however, is that the child may begin to enjoy masturbation.

Inherent in the cleanliness training is a peculiar kind of contradiction. The mother wants the child to learn how to control his bowels and bladder. To achieve this she demands that the child defecate or urinate when and where she, the mother, wishes. The child's resentment of this process is partly a rebellion against being overly controlled by the mother. If the mother can anticipate the child's need to eliminate and offer toileting at such times, the child may feel less controlled and will perhaps be more willing to comply. It seems, however, that during this period the child's willfulness reaches a certain peak and may easily turn into stubbornness and temper tantrums. He first refuses any demand. It is the child's self-assertiveness which is expressed in this "no." If the mother takes the "no" literally and more seriously than is warranted at this stage of development, the battle is on. Stubbornness and aggressive behavior may become the child's habitual reaction. The repetition of these scenes between mother and child may become numerous, and a fixing of this reaction, generally as well as specifically, may take place. We speak of a *fixation* when a feeling or experience automatically brings on a certain reaction, usually a chain reaction. This prevents a different, more appropriate reaction from forming and therefore interferes with development in the area involved.

During bowel and bladder training, the child's anxiety is centered on toilet activities. Naturally, the person who trains the child has a great deal to do with the anxiety which is aroused. The child may be afraid of using the toilet or the bathroom. He may become frightened when the stool disappears or when the toilet is flushed. He may be afraid that he will fall into the toilet himself. One of the threats which young children like to use against each other is "I'll throw you down the toilet," an expression of their own anxiety (by this time probably overcome). If they use it toward their still younger brothers and sisters, the little ones believe them. They sometimes try to combat their fears by experimenting with a teddy bear or a toy. Usually the person who takes care of the child toilet trains him. If there is more than one person attempting to train the child, the process is prolonged and sometimes ineffective. Anna Freud and Dorothy Burlingham (1943) have described how babies who were taken care of by a number of people did not achieve sphincter control, while those who were taken care of by one person were trained very quickly. When the child who only recently has achieved sphincter control is left by the educating adult, he may relapse and wet and soil again. This is common with young children entering nursery school.

The other great achievement of the second and third year is speech. Vocabulary increases by leaps and bounds and, with it, interest and understanding. Speech development, too, is closely related to the caretaking person. The mother's voice, comforting and promising from the very beginning of a baby's life, is the voice of feeling and of love. In many cases, young children who had just started to talk either stopped talking or made no further progress when their mothers left them to take a job during the day. Whatever function has been acquired is to some degree dependent on a continuation of the relationship to the mother.

Moreover, functions are also interdependent. Speech may become disturbed when cleanliness training is particularly difficult. Closing of mouth and sphincter and opening of mouth and sphincter are connected just as are the pleasures derived from the anal and oral area. Stuttering and stammering frequently occur during the anal period.

As the child learns to love he reacts to praise and punishment. He feels guilty when the mother expresses her disapproval or when she withdraws her love. Should the mother leave the child even temporarily in this period of his life, he is apt to interpret her absence as a punishment for some misdeed—as retribution for his being dirty. The guilt feelings which children develop at this time are still connected with the person who provokes them. They are not independent feelings, but they must be considered as forerunners of the superego.

Another facet of ego development which should be mentioned is the child's relationship to objects. In the oral phase, the child attempts to put every object into his mouth. By the time he is two he has learned that contents of his body may get lost or be retained, just as there are things which do not exactly belong to one's body, yet which may belong to oneself and may be retained. They are possessions; and in the anal phase certain possessions take on a particular value. There is the blanket or the pillow or the bottle, without which he cannot go to sleep. Innumerable toys, cuddly ones in particular, belong in this category. The child is so attached to these objects that he is inconsolable when he is separated from them. On the other hand, even frightening situations become bearable when these things are around. They represent a part of oneself. The child plays with the object just as he plays with himself. He may suck and hold it simultaneously, use it for masturbatory purposes, and even place it between his legs. It also represents the mother and can therefore console the child in her absence; hence its importance at nap- and sleep-time. Children who have been separated from their parents experience a prolonged need for transitional love objects such as teddy bears or blankets. Eventually the transitional objects are given up when the child feels more secure and is not afraid in the absence of the beloved person. Trusting that the person will return, he need no longer hold on to the object. Winnicott considers transitional phenomena a part of normal development. Where the transitional object becomes more necessary than the people it represents, it assumes the psychological importance and meaning of a fetish.

For the child, the transitional object is what a talisman or charm is for some adults. He attributes to it magical powers, since he feels protected by it, most of the time. In his mind, fantasy and reality are not clearly distinguished. In his fantasy the toy animal is alive. It is the friend who protects him, although at times it gets out of hand and frightens him. The cuddly dog or tiger suddenly threatens to bite and destroy his master, particularly at night, whereupon the child develops nocturnal fears and nightmares. Although the object is inanimate and blameless, the child fears losing control over the erotic or aggressive feelings it represents.

Magic plays a larger part in our lives than we are generally aware of or like to admit. The childhood "fetish" is carried over into adult life by means of charms or talismans. The wedding ring is a symbol of marriage, but at times is also an object of magical importance. So are other pieces of jewelry and attire. We find it much easier to detect evidences of magical thinking in other cultures than in our own. We take our own superstitions for granted and overlook the magic which may be hidden in them.

Children's thinking is shot through with magic. Bedtime ceremonies are a common example: the bed has to be arranged a certain way, clothes may have to be put in certain places, doors have to be opened or closed, lights have to be put on or off, a glass of water and a goodnight kiss are requisite. Obviously, all these ceremonies have been originally introduced by the parents. Later on the child takes them over himself and sees to it that they are fulfilled to the letter. Like the prized possession, these ceremonies may become important in themselves. They may become detached from the person who executed them originally. The rituals not only have the purpose of postponing the moment of sleep and loneliness, but every one of them supposedly keeps the evil spirits away. Eventually, the child or the adult may acknowledge that the evil spirits are really his own.

Together with his realization that his parents can do things he cannot do, comes the child's concept of adults, particularly parents, as all-powerful. When these powerful people frustrate him, he feels angry, but helpless. Helplessness, as adults know, leads to panic. And so, as the child becomes increasingly independent in his second and third year, he may attempt to take over this omnipotent feeling for himself. He asserts he can do what he wants when he wants just as the adults have been doing to him. He has, at times, an exaggerated feeling of power, strength and ability. Some children achieve this feeling with compulsions which they force their parents to fulfill for them. Sometimes they merely ask their parents to leave them undisturbed in performing these ceremonies for themselves. They may become unruly and disobedient, maintaining that nobody can tell them what to do. They pretend to be giants or dangerous animals or perhaps adults as aggressive and threatening as their parents seem to be. Children who are alternately overwhelmed by the adult's feelings and their own, and are then neglected by their parents, are those who become unruly and in turn threaten the environment as they themselves feel threatened. Later on, in latency and adolescence, these children, particularly bedwetters and soilers, may become the delinquents who, in their fantasies, control the world instead of controlling themselves. Extreme reluctance in children to ask and accept help from adults, their seeming independence, is usually connected with unruliness and poor relationships with adults. It is a reaction to feelings of helplessness and a denial of them. Because routines are used most frequently in the course of the child's cleanliness education, it seems that this is the period in which these compulsions originate, although they might be based upon similar feelings at an earlier period as well.

THE PHALLIC PHASE

Children experience genital feelings, from very early on. Infant masturbation is expected, its absence is usually a sign of disturbance. In the course of the child's being cared for by adults, cleaned and washed in the genital area, the genitals become stimulated. During cleanliness education, particular attention is paid to this area, and, as the child's attention is focused on it, genital feelings are frequently aroused.

However, genital feelings become stronger and of particular importance between the third and fourth years. The children are now aware of sexual differences. When a new baby arrives, they want to know how babies are born, where they come out; eventually they want to know how they get into the mother, and what the father has to do with it. During this first period of heightened genital awareness, sexual differences are noticed but confused. Little girls insist either that they, too, have a penis or that they are going to grow one, while boys want to have babies and breasts. Both sexes seem to want to have the attributes of the opposite sex, particularly when they are jealous of a sibling of the other sex. Although young children are usually taken care of by their mothers and their relationship to the mother is the outstanding one in their lives, fathers come into their own at this time. The children look forward to father's coming home from work and playing with them. Little boys want to do as their fathers do and to be like their fathers, and little girls also turn toward them with love and affection. Older sisters and brothers become more important; new-born babies, who take priority with the mother, may change their own role significantly.

At this point, identifications with people in the environment take place regardless of their sex which makes it confusing for the child to know his own sexual role. The confusion is usually passing and temporary but may become permanent under certain conditions—especially when the mother wears the pants and the father submits to her.

During the phallic phase, genital feelings are strong and children may masturbate. Sometimes they engage in mutual masturbation. In their uncertainty about sex, masturbation is frequently exploratory and experimental. A child may want to find out what his or the other one's genitals look like and what can be done with them. He may be afraid that something is wrong with his genitals or that something may happen to them. He is afraid that his own sex may be changed, even though he may wish for it.

THE OEDIPAL PHASE

Eventually, when the child has settled with himself the question of his own sex, he enters the oedipal phase. The little boy remains faithful to his first love object—that is, the mother—and promises and fantasies that he will marry her. He is jealous of anyone—sibling or father—who might take her away from him. He wants to have the mother for himself and be alone and undisturbed with her. The little girl turns her love away from the mother to some extent and directs it toward the father. Her feelings at this time are not quite so definite as the boy's. Her sexual role is not as well defined as the boy's role. She has to wait until later on for the fulfillment of her sexual wishes—that is, for her own baby—and vacillates between father and mother as she vacillates between wanting to be a girl or a boy. The disappointment of not getting the baby from the father drives her back to the mother, the disappointment of not getting the penis from the mother drives her to the father. For both sexes, the wish to be alone with one parent is prevalent. The other parent or sibling is considered an intrusion, and the wish prevails to get him or her out of the way. The child may ask the father when he is going to work again, whether he is going to leave again on a trip, sometimes—more directly—when he is figuring on dying. The child wants to take one parent's place with the other. However, the feelings for his competitor are only rarely one-sided. A father is not only the rival, but also an admired and loved parent. Mother, whose place the little girl may want to take, is also the one on whom she is still dependent for the satisfaction of her daily needs.

Children's feelings toward adults are ambivalent and, as such, become the source of conflict. Children feel guilty for their death wishes because, still thinking to a large extent in terms of magic, they do not discriminate between thinking and doing. They are afraid that what they think, may happen, afraid they may bring it about by wishing. Partly for this reason, children often come into the parents' bedroom at night. They want to be near the person whom they love, but they also want to make sure that the other one, the rival whom they want to die, is alive. In addition, of course, they want access to the parents' bedroom to prevent them from having intercourse, for fear they may produce a baby, or because they imagine intercourse to be a fierce battle in which one of the parents may be hurt. The aggressive wishes which the little boy has against his father make him anxious for fear the father might do to him what he is thinking of doing to the father. The father might hurt him, cut him up into little pieces, castrate him, or kill him; all of which the little boy fantasies doing to the father. The little girl's anxieties are usually directed toward being left alone, deserted, unloved, left to die, hungry and cold in a cruel world. Castration or mutilation at this age is not part of the picture for the little girl. In all probability she fantasies that it has already happened to her which is why she is a girl. This in turn gives her further justification for hating her mother.

Children around the fourth and fifth year are known to be more lively than before or afterward. They are in a state of sexual excitement for which they get only partial relief through masturbation. Masturbation is not entirely satisfactory because they are sexually immature; only in puberty can an orgasm be attained. It seems that part of their excitement is released in generally aggressive activity. They move about a great deal, run, jump, fight, yell. Their aggression as well as their masturbatory fantasies, if not masturbation itself, bring about conflicts with the environment, and the child becomes more anxious than before. Castration anxiety reaches its highest point, causing the child to change his ways.

LATENCY

Under the threat of castration the little boy withdraws his direct sexual wishes from the mother; his fear and his hostility against the father diminish; his sexual excitement gradually subsides—he enters the latency period. The little girl, whose anxiety is not so great as the boy's, is less inclined to give up her sexual wishes, since she has less to lose;

however, she, too, enters a calmer phase of existence. Both sexes turn their interests to intellectual pursuits; they are curious, want to learn about things; want to experiment, collect things and knowledge. It is time for them to go to school.

This outline of childhood development represents the ideal. No development ever occurs so smoothly. The younger the children, the more they are likely to be disturbed in their so-called normal (ideal) development through experiences of different kinds: absence of one or the other parent, parental mood swings, their own or somebody else's illness, operations, birth, and death, all the exigencies of life have an impact upon the child, changing the course of his development. Discrepancies between emotional, intellectual, and physical development may cause disturbances. As long as the child continues to develop in all areas, these disturbances may disappear and the child will regain his balance. When he remains disturbed in one area or another, we must consider him emotionally sick.

THE PROBLEM OF SEPARATION
AND THE FEELING OF IDENTITY

———•—•———

Separation from parents is common to everybody. People react to it according to their ages, personalities and previous experiences. The feeling of identity, too, is a universal one. Yet, while the meaning of separation is clear enough, it is not easy to define the idea of the feeling of identity which encompasses feelings of body, emotions, thoughts, actions, as well as one's present and past relations in and to environment. The feeling of identity is always with us. It changes as we change; it can be disturbed, when we are disturbed. When separation is a disturbing experience it necessarily affects the feeling of identity.

In her paper, "Safeguarding the Emotional Health of Our Children," Anna Freud (1954c) discussed as one of the traumatic situations from which children might suffer that of separation of the infant from the mother. She described how the infant reacts with physical symptoms such as vomiting, diarrhea, eczema, crying, sleeplessness, etc. She emphasized that the effects of such separations may be only partly corrected by another person's taking over the mother's role, and that the setback suffered by the infant may persist into later life.

This paper was published originally in Child Welfare, November, pp. 8-15, 1955.

23

I happened to see a six-week-old baby who was on his way to four-hour feeding periods when he had to be hospitalized because of an intestinal infection. Upon his return after a week in the hospital, the parents were first delighted because he was so quiet, then upset because he was also less responsive. After a week at home the child reverted to his previous responsiveness, but he also demanded to be fed every two hours; this schedule corresponded to his four- to five-week-old behavior, constituting a setback of three or four weeks in an eight-week-old child. Whether or not he will make up for time lost would be difficult to ascertain without exact observation.

The baby had been exposed to two experiences, his physical illness and separation from home. His reaction was also two-fold: a physical one—his return to an older feeding pattern, and an emotional one—diminished responsiveness. We do not know for sure how to correlate these reactions. Physical illness in an infant is serious and usually brings with it other disturbances. However, a baby whose mother takes good care of him will ordinarily be even more responsive once the pains and discomforts of the illness are over. It seems to me, therefore, that the lack of responsiveness which this six-week-old baby showed was an emotional reaction to separation. However, the baby's return to a previous feeding pattern might have been a physiological reaction to his illness. Feelings of discomfort in the intestinal tract, the desire to eat when not hungry are some of the physical reactions to separation which Anna Freud, and Spitz, et al. have described.

Children as well as adults may react to unpleasant or frightening situations with physical symptoms. To have a "knot in one's stomach" is a common description of anxiety or upset. I remember a little girl of five who in her short life had too many placements in foster homes. She was afraid, when the social worker came, that she would have to move to yet another home. Every time she saw the social worker or anticipated seeing her, she vomited. Her vomiting was an infantile reaction to separation from a mother figure.

Spitz (1946b) has reported that infants from three to six months or older may react to separation from the mother with severe depression—they cry a lot and cannot be consoled by anyone except the mother; they don't eat, they don't sleep, they only cry. If separation from the mother persists they stop crying and become apathetic; they do not smile, cease to play. They are sad little creatures. When the mother returns, the baby recovers within a day or two, or even perhaps within a matter of hours. These babies have arrived at a stage where they recognize the mother and are attached to her—and only to her. They cannot accept a substitute; their severe suffering is comparable to the reaction of bereavement in adults. For these babies, the mother is lost when she is gone for even a short while, since they do not know whether she will return. This reaction is accompanied by loss of a recent achievement. If the child has already learned to sit up, he may not try to do this any more. An older child may stop talking, or he may revert to soiling or wetting. The most recent achievement, which still takes an effort, which has not yet become automatic, is given up first, but others may follow and the child may regress generally.

The recurrence of wetting and soiling in children, who are brought into a new foster home, is well known. Foster parents assume that the child will get over it in a while after he becomes used to them. It is, as they correctly assume, a symptom of the child's sense of loneliness and loss.

Little children love to play hide-and-seek, a game which symbolizes the great discovery that things or people, including mother, may seem to be lost and yet they will return. In order to accept this idea, the child must be able to remember that the mother who left did return. When this experience is established he can wait for her without falling into utter despair.

But what if she doesn't return? The child's ability to wait depends upon his conception of time. According to his age and development, an hour, a day, or a week can seem an eternity. When he has to wait too long, he becomes angry at the people around him, and expresses his anger and frustration by misbehaving. He may or may not ask for his mother—but whether he asks for her or not, that is really what he wants. When mother finally returns, the child usually directs his anger toward her. Underlying his rage is anxiety lest she leave again. When mother has been away for a week or more, the toddler will follow her around like a shadow, cry when she gets out of his sight, and make incessant demands on her attention. After a bit when he feels secure again, he will relax and trust her to leave and return. The child's ability to express his anger by being naughty, destroying, attacking, biting, running, takes the place of the disastrous depression of earlier months. His increased motility and greater muscular strength make it possible for him to fight rather than to wither away.

When the two-year-old's mother does not return for whatever reason—illness, death, desertion, all are the same to a child—his faith in her, and that means in all mankind, is shattered.

The only possible reasons in the child's mind for mother's leaving him are because she is bad or because he is bad. Usually he thinks both are true. If mother was bad, he is angry at everybody who reminds him of her, and he in turn will be bad too and will punish her in everybody who may take her place. If he was bad (and that is why she left), then maybe he'll try to be good, so good he won't dare move. And so he'll be alternately very good or very bad according to his fantasies.

Eventually, under favorable circumstances, the child may accept a new mother-person and his faith in the world may be restored. But this takes time. The foster parents say the child is "testing" them. He is! He tests how much he can trust them, whether they, too, will desert him. When the child dares to test them, it is really a sign that he has some faith in them. Nobody can be trusted without first being tested. He must feel that he can be naughty without being abandoned. If he is left again after making a new attachment, his capacity for trust will be considerably, perhaps irrevocably, impaired. He will attempt to survive in whatever way he can, by fighting or by submitting, but he will not really love anyone. He may long for someone to love him, someone about whom he fantasies, perhaps the loving mother he first lost long ago, but nobody in real life will ever fill the bill. He has lost the ability to love, as the younger child may have lost the ability to walk, talk, or control his bowels.

In the period of increased muscular control and particularly cleanliness training, the child receives his first introduction to the ideas of good and bad, to prohibition and punishment. He learns to feel guilty and experiences the adult's anger or his withdrawal of love. He is willing to accept certain limitations, that is, precepts of civilization, in order to secure satisfaction of his needs which are dependent on the one he loves. Need satisfaction is still completely tied up with his loving a person. When his needs are taken care of by somebody else, his loyalty goes to that person. When need satisfaction is endangered, the child of necessity has to fight for his life, increase his narcissism, and withdraw from object relations.

When a child has had a normally secure relationship with his parents for the first three or four years, separation and loss of a parent and of his home will still be most disturbing —it remains such throughout life—but he has a better chance of weathering it than he had during his earlier years, when he was totally dependent on his mother for the fulfillment of his needs. When he can move about on his own, talk to people, feed, dress, and toilet himself, when he can express his needs and wants, he can more easily accept another person as a substitute for the one he has lost. The big question of why he was left or sent away will always be in his mind, even when he is told the truth and appears to understand it. When parents are divorced or separated and he has to live with somebody else he will wonder whether he has caused their separation. Maybe he secretly or openly had wanted to have mother (or father) for himself and wished the other parent would "never come back," or "go away," or "drop dead." In a way, he may have gotten what he wished for, but at too high a price, with too much punishment attached. If a parent has to go to a hospital or dies, the child's self-reproaches are going to be even more severe. He may try to be good or may be completely good in order to undo what he thinks he is responsible for. Or he may be naughty in order to get himself punished; he then feels he gets what he deserves: punishment for his great sin, the crime of loving one parent so much that he wanted to get rid of the other. The same process can operate with regard to a brother or sister.

Children's reactions to the trauma of separation depend on their phase of development and on their individual experiences and conflicts. We sometimes speak of "phase-specific" traumata. Separation seems to be a trauma which is always phase-specific. In the phase of physiological needs, the child reacts physiologically; when object relationship and recognition set in, he reacts with impaired capacity for object relationships. At the height of his dependency, when needs and relationship are met by the mother, his reaction is that of depression accompanied by a loss of ego functions. Aggression and guilt feelings will dominate the picture when the balance is upset by the loss of the person whom the child trusts. When he has achieved the ability to love in a sense which resembles adult love, when he has reached the oedipal phase, his reaction to separation will be in terms of these particular oedipal conflicts and fantasies.

Of course no phase of development passes without leaving its traces in the following phase or phases. What I have described is schematic and points out the prevalent features at different times.

The development after the oedipal phase repeats in many ways the development during the first years of life. The child fortifies, weakens, represses or suppresses whatever nucleus of a personality he has with the help and under the pressure of his further life experiences, so far acquired. Separation is an experience which shapes his life, his personality and his feeling of identity.

The feeling of identity changes as the child changes during his development. Right after birth we see the child as a bundle of undifferentiated physical feelings; he feels undifferentiated from his mother as long as his needs are met. Perhaps his first dim realization of body feeling occurs when he first experiences hunger and food is not immediately available. His first sensation of his body as an identity may be closely connected with his first realization of being separated from his mother. These feelings of discomfort interrupt the state of nirvana, or vegetative existence in which the infant lives. They are offset by pleasant feelings during his waking time when he is being fed or fondled. He begins to enjoy his body, begins to enjoy living. He also learns to recognize the mother, who affords him these pleasures, who talks to him. He knows her voice, he hears her calling him. When he reacts to her voice, perhaps there is something more going on than just the expectation of satisfaction; perhaps there is the beginning of a feeling of self. In some ways, the name becomes the carrier of the self. When Johnny begins to talk, he will probably say, "Johnny wants—Johnny likes—Johnny does not want or like." To use the personal pronoun is a later achievement. The infant does not seem to know where his body ends and another person's body starts. He may suck on the nipple or a hand—his own or somebody else's; he may hold his own thumb or somebody else's. He has no awareness of the borders of his body as long as he can suck when he needs to suck or hold when he needs to hold. But gradually he learns that the nipple is not his, that he may have to wait for its return. He will have many similar experiences until he finally becomes aware of himself as differentiated and separate from mother.

Some children do not sufficiently differentiate from their mother psychologically as their physiological dependence on her diminishes. A three-year-old girl refused to accept anything from my hand, but put her mother's hand to mine to take what I offered. She did not talk to me but indicated to her mother what she wanted to say. She used her mother as an extension of herself. Of course she could not stay in nursery school by herself; mother had to be there too.

In the inability to stay alone we recognize separation anxiety; it is one component of school anxiety. Our little three-year-old considered mother as part of herself and felt incomplete without her. The mother, because of her own neurotic needs, had fostered this dependence, and, in order to wean the child properly, we had to have the mother's cooperation. The child's dependence on her mother was a result of the mother's dependence on the child. When the child learned to use her own hands instead of mother's, her own speech instead of mother's, she was able to manage for herself. She learned from mother; she did as mother did; she became identified with her and consequently did not need her as much.

Anna Freud (1954a) has shown that the child's disturbance is his reaction to the mother's own disturbance in a particular area, such as feeding, cleanliness, or genital feelings. Infants gradually discover and learn how to use their bodies. The infant discovers his fingers and hands and learns to put them into his mouth. Gradually he discovers other parts of his body. He feels his full bladder, his rectum, hunger and satiety. Awareness of his body in parts and as a whole gives him a body-feeling of himself as an entity.

The mother of our three-year-old must have disturbed this feeling somewhere along the line by not allowing her child to "feel herself" with "her own hands" in all parts of her body. She preferred unconsciously that the child continue to use mother's body instead of her own, thereby keeping the child more dependent on her than she needed to be.

However, all children are dependent and feel helpless without their mothers until they are physically self-sufficient. One may say the psychological umbilical cord is cut when the child has learned to feed, walk, dress, and toilet himself, when he feels himself to be a person. The learning process leading to these achievements is not a simple matter of learning skills, but one of identifications. The child learns not only to do these things, but he learns from the mother or the person who takes care of him how and when to do them.

When children are left alone much of the time they become retarded; for example, they frequently do not talk. But when they are left alone during the first year of life, particularly during the first six months, as may happen in orphanages or hospitals, they do not learn how to suck their fingers or how to find their toes; they neither smile nor masturbate. No familiar person touches them, so they do not develop feelings toward any one person, and they do not develop any feelings of their bodies and for themselves, except pain. But pain is not enough to create a human being. Pain may push the pain barrier down, which may result in the child's hurting himself deliberately, or it may push the pain barrier up, increasing narcissistic cathexis. At any rate, it distorts the body image and with it, the relations to the world (Hoffer, 1950). Steady contact with one person is necessary in order for the child to feel himself as an entity, a self.

This feeling can be very easily upset. Changes in the environment, the disappearance of the mother or mother substitute, moving the bed into another room, moving from one house to another, all disturb the child. This is even more true when a child's first name is changed after he has become familiar with it, which frequently happens when children are adopted. The child is confused when his routine is upset. When he is accustomed to using a potty he won't function on the toilet seat; if he is accustomed to going to bed in his parents' bed, he won't stay in his own. His feeling of himself is dependent on his knowing where he is and what is expected of him. When environment, routine or name is changed he does not know how to function: a part of his ego identity is temporarily lost.

Children like to play dress-up. In a way, they learn constantly by playing dress-up. They imitate father coming home from work, mother talking on the telephone, big brother throwing a ball, and little sister throwing a temper tantrum. Attitudes, behavior, characteristics and occupations, positive and negative, are constantly imitated. This period of indiscriminate imitation is one in which a great deal is being learned, provided there is a certain amount of consistency in the environment. If the people the child imitates, from whom he learns, are themselves consistent in what they do in the child's presence and in what they demand of him, he can learn and imitate them until he has made these traits a part of his personality. To what degree personality is hereditary or constitutional we do not know; but we do know that environment and experiences do contribute to its formation.

What happens to a young child when he is boarded out? When he is removed from his environment he does not know where his bed is, or his toys, or the bathroom; not only are routines changed, but everybody around him is changed too. He cannot look to mother to see how she reacts; he does not have brother who may help him in a fight or perhaps beat him up. His whole system of orientation is upset, he is without direction like a skipper without a compass. Only when he attaches himself to somebody in his new environment, when he finds a new pivot of orientation, a new object to

imitate, will he regain his functions. This takes time. Before
he gets to that point he feels very lonely and frightened and
often holds on tensely to one object from the past—a doll,
perhaps, or a stuffed animal, coat, hat, or bottle. Whatever
it may be, it is the only thing he knows and loves in a strange
world. He may become frantic without it. It is a part of his
past and therefore part of himself.

The continuity of the past is another point of orientation
for the child. He has to remember the house, the people, the
pets, the toys he used to live with. When we forget what we
did during a certain time, where we were, what the people
looked like, what their names were, we are bothered. We
feel as if we "weren't all there." The child feels that way too.
Not to remember one's past is like losing a part of oneself.

During the period of adjustment to the new environment,
the child has to learn new attitudes and behavior and to
unlearn old ones. The direction in which his personality
started to develop is being changed inasmuch as the people
after whom he had patterned himself are gone. Not everything and everybody from his past, however, are just for-
gotten; they still exist in his memory, in his habits, in his
thinking; new forms are superimposed on the old ones—and
they don't always fit very well. It will take some time for
him to feel he "belongs," for his new family to feel he is "like
their own flesh and blood," until he can relinquish that doll
or stuffed animal.

Children who are repeatedly taken from place to place
cannot develop characters of their own. They can only re-
flect the characters of others; they will lack reliability and
"backbone." Never having learned how to love or trust anybody, they can survive only by a process of adaptation
wherein they change character with the environment, as
chameleons change their colors. They are unhappy children
and develop into unhappy adults. They have been deceived
and disappointed and they in turn are deceitful and cannot
be trusted. Every time they thought they were loved and

tested this love, the people they tested were found wanting. If this is the only experience after which they can pattern their characters, no wonder so many of these children become delinquents—later criminals—or psychotic.

The length of time a child is given to develop relationships and to establish behavior patterns is extremely important to the stability of his character. Only when he can live free from the fear of losing his home again, when he does not have to fight or submit in order to survive, can he begin to form his own identity. He must have time to learn to love people and to trust them; he must be allowed to become dependent on them, as a young child is dependent on his mother. Only then will he be able to develop in a "normal" way the feelings which a child in a "normal" family would have.

The identifications developing out of the love, jealousy, and competition implicit in the oedipal conflict become a permanent part of, and build personality. The solution of the oedipal conflict will determine to a decisive degree with whom the child makes his predominant sexual identification, whether he will be homosexual, manifest or latent, or heterosexual. Only a child who has passed through the oedipal phase in relative security can develop his own identity. The chances of his achieving this successfully are slim if he has been subjected to too many changes before reaching the oedipal phase. It is difficult for him to hold on to his newly developed identifications when the family constellation is interrupted during or even shortly after he has passed through the oedipal phase; he needs time to consolidate his identification. Only when he has developed a character of his own, can he preserve it, should he have to be separated from the people after whom he has patterned himself.

There are other people besides his parents who are important to the child, whom he loves, fears, hates, and after whom he may pattern himself and with whom he may identify. For the young child, older sisters and brothers, adults of any age who are part of the immediate environment are an influence. When the child is able to go out on his own into supervised or unsupervised groups of children, many more influences enter his life. He may pick up certain characteristics or behavior from them temporarily. These group or gang influences may become permanent either because the group is more satisfactory than the home or because its attitudes are essentially those of the home. Group influences remain important throughout our lives and enlarge the scope of possible identifications.

During adolescence, groups are of particular importance. We often hear about adolescents who are in trouble as part of a gang. Frequently they are under the influence of some member of the gang with whom they identify, or the adolescent may be the leader of the gang, impersonating some common ideal of the group. Sometimes the groups are socially acceptable, sometimes not, but apparently many adolescents need groups as a part of their lives. If they are living with their families, the group helps them break away; if they don't have families, the group offers a substitute. The group helps them toward independence by offering support during an essentially lonely period.

Of course, there are many adolescents who have no use for groups. They may form intense friendships instead or perhaps worship some older person as a shining hero, or develop crushes, or fall in love. But whichever it may be, these intense relationships become the basis for new identifications—some of them temporary, some permanent.

The identification process continues throughout life, as long as we remain flexible. When we come to a new country, even as adults, we learn to identify with the new group and the new environment. What we call our identity is a rather complex phenomenon. E. H. Erikson has described it at length in his paper "The Problem of Ego-identity" (1956). The feeling of identity is different in different phases of development: for the infant it is a body feeling, a feeling in relation to his mother and her manipulations of his body. For the toddler it means having a name and a place, his bed and his toys; his ability to do things, to function increasingly by himself. When ideas of good and bad enter the child's consciousness, he identifies himself as "I am a good boy" or "I am a bad boy," both said and felt with conviction and pride. Relations to individuals and groups become part of the child's identifications from the oedipal phase on into adulthood. The identity feelings change from phase to phase and become a record of the person's past; his memories are part of his identity. Separations are disruptive to the feeling of identity and to its development. The earlier they happen in the child's life, the more disruptive they are.

ACTIVITY AND AGGRESSION IN CHILDREN

The meaning of the term "aggression" was clarified by Lowrey et al. (1943), who pointed out two interpretations: one by which we understand aggression as an act of unprovoked hostility and destructiveness; the other, in common use, as taken to mean "self-assertiveness." Common language, which is at times the expression of common sense, agrees in this instance with Freud (1915) who, in his early concept of instincts, discriminated between ego instincts or instincts for self-preservation, and sex instincts. According to this concept, aggression is one of the manifestations of the instinct of self-preservation, meaning that as long as we live we are aggressive. Destructiveness and hostility in this concept appear as only one form of aggression.

The theories on the origin of aggression vary. The main point of contention is whether aggression in the destructive sense is a reaction to experiences, or whether it is a constitutional, original drive (Fenichel, 1945). However, all schools and theories agree that even hostile and destructive aggression can be converted to useful and constructive ends; it can be redirected. For practical purposes, the question of whether aggression was originally destructive or not seems

This paper was published originally in *The American Journal of Orthopsychiatry*, 17:161-166, 1947.

unimportant; we must work with the fact that aggression is an instinct which can be used for either constructive or destructive ends. Our interest is in finding out the conditions which are favorable in bringing out one or the other aspect.

The activities of infants are usually accepted with approval. The baby is permitted to suck his fingers, make noise, spit and make bubbles with his mouth; he may wet and soil, kick and pull as much as he likes. He is praised for holding onto fingers, breast, bottle, or any object he can grasp, and he may handle it any way he likes. He may sit, stand, crawl, or walk. Whatever he does is appreciated as progress in his development. This period is truly the child's paradise, where nothing is forbidden. As he grows older and stronger, more skillful and able to move about on his own, he meets with disapproval from his surroundings. Just when this happens depends on individual and cultural factors, but happen it must. The amount of anger expressed by the adult's words, actions, or facial expressions makes the child aware that his action is naughty. Whether the child will comply with the adult's wishes by dropping the behavior altogether, only the naughty part of it, or continue in the old way, will depend on a number of factors.

Every phase of libidinal development has its own form of aggressiveness. The child's activities, which are expressions of his libidinal drives, can be turned into aggressive ones: he learns to bite, hold tight, pull, tear, rip, kick, run, spit— all of which he needs to be able to do in order to achieve his purposes, one of which is expressing aggression. We can discriminate between three different stages in the development of the child's activities: (1) the experimental stage, in which he discovers a new activity and tries it out; (2) the practicing stage, during which the child learns through innumerable repetitions; (3) the stage when the activity is at his disposal and he can call upon it when he needs it.

During the process of learning, until the child has achieved control over his vital activities and his body, his relationship to people is of greatest importance. The younger the child, the more tolerant are the parents. The older he becomes, the more he is subjected to demands and restrictions which will influence his relationship to people as well as to his own activities. Inadvertent destruction, interpreted and reacted to as deliberate aggression, may turn the particular activity into an aggressive one to the point where it loses its original meaning and becomes stigmatized as aggressive action only. The child's relationship to people, especially to the caretaking person, will influence his ability to express and control aggression which, in turn, affects the development of his activities in general. At what stage in the development of a certain activity the interference from outside sets in is of great importance.

Levy (1944) and Greenacre (1944) have made some observations on the reactions of animals and infants to movement restraint. Levy finds that modifications of activities *before* they have been fulfilled may be easily achieved. Greenacre does not think that simple hampering of motion brings about any aggressive, ragelike behavior in the infant. It seems to her that, during the first year of life, the child reacts with rage only when the angry attitude of the restrainer is added to the imposed restraint. She also calls attention to the custom of swaddling, which is common to certain peoples but does not produce the general effect of marked aggressiveness in infants. Both observers agree that friendly restraint of motion at an early age, when the child is in what I have referred to as the experimental stage, does not provoke aggression. It would seem however, as Greenacre shows in one of her adult cases, that early and deep repression is to be expected.

Interference in the practicing stage seems to have quite a different effect on children. Levy observes that hyperactivity, both in animals and humans, is a reaction to early movement restraint. He states that after a child has experienced creeping or walking, a restriction of these activities will be felt as restraint. This is in agreement with Lauretta Bender (1936) who attributes the aggressiveness in children, hospitalized between the ages of 11 and 18 months to severe physical restrictions as well as maternal desertion or neglect. As soon as these motherless children are consistently handled by *one* person—a mother substitute—and find opportunity to form a relationship with that person, they respond by developing new habits and playful activities. With this progress, their extreme aggressiveness diminishes, thus clearly proving it to have been a reaction to both physical restriction and lack of relationship.

The observations which have been made by Levy, Greenacre, and Bender are particularly concerned with the restraint of motility. Levy points out that restraining the motion which the child has the need to develop, provokes his aggressiveness; Greenacre and Bender see it as a combination of restraint with a lack of a positive relationship. However, it would seem that restraint *per se* would hardly occur at this point without a hostile or neglectful attitude on the part of the caretaking person. It would seem that the child who is deprived of using his muscles constructively, uses them destructively instead. When he is given a chance to use them in accordance with his stage of development, he can display his aggressiveness in activity.

The ideas presented in the following pages are largely theoretical conclusions, drawn from the analyses of older children. It would be desirable to follow them up with direct observations which, unfortunately, are rarely at the analyst's disposal.

It seems significant that another reason for uncontrolled aggressiveness in children occurs as a result of failure in habit training. Habit training is, similarly, restraint in motility, an outside interference with the muscular apparatus. The adult who confines the child to his crib or prevents him from crawling, walking, sucking, or masturbating, prevents him from using his muscles in accordance with his needs. In habit training, the adult demands that the child use his muscular control according to rules imposed from the outside. The aggressiveness of some of these children appears in temper tantrums; they are disorganized and unable to concentrate on any activity. A brief example will serve as an illustration.

The case is that of a boy of ten. Because it is rather complex, I shall confine myself to those aspects pertaining to the topic under discussion. This boy felt unloved, inferior and guilty, all of which kept him in a constant state of self-assertiveness and self-defense, expressed in the form of aggression directed particularly against his mother. Temper tantrums alternated with enuresis. He was dry at night if he had a temper tantrum the evening before going to bed. The connection between aggression and enuresis became even more obvious when he started to wet the blanket, pushed it to the foot of the bed, and slept on the dry sheet. As a next step, he got out of bed and urinated on the rug. He admitted to enjoying the idea of his mother cleaning up the mess. He knew she would do this because, although she generally neglected him, she felt embarrassed to have others know about her child's fault for which she felt responsible.

When the aggression expressed in the bed-wetting became conscious, he gave it up and found other means to control his mother. Whereas he had forced her to care for him as if he were a baby by wetting his bed, he now forced her to help him with his schoolwork. When he was a baby, mother had left him frequently at night, to which he reacted by wetting the bed; now he tried to discourage her from going out evenings by waiting with his school work until she came home. For him, this had the significance of controlling her and, at the same time, of controlling himself. Simultaneously, he also learned to control his bladder. The temper tantrums were an open attack against mother both consciously and unconsciously. To some extent, they constituted an anticipation of the mother's attack against him should he wet the bed. He punished her in the same way in which he expected to be punished. Having punished her that way, and by playing the mother's role himself, he was able to forego wetting the bed. For a long time, it was the only way he could control both his mother and himself.

Children of this kind, whose symptoms are derived from a failure in habit training, differ from those previously mentioned. The frustration is not as terrifying; they are not as badly threatened as the children described by Bender. They are not completely thwarted in achieving control of their muscular apparatus, nor as severely lacking in human relationship. The restraint imposed upon them was introduced at a later period in their life and concentrated on one particular field, that of sphincter control. They resented this particular interference and protested against it with temper tantrums. Later, the temper tantrums became divorced from the immediate source and occurred whenever somebody or something interfered with their wishes. The relationship with the mother became disturbed at this point. In every case, the children whom I treated for wetting and soiling had compulsive mothers, who reacted violently against their children's difficulty. They reacted against the baby's dirtiness before the question of habit training ever came up. Undoubtedly, they had a share in the symptom of enuresis as well as in the development of aggression.

The inability to control his body is continued in the child's inability to control himself in general. As soon as some of his aggression is turned into the mastery of his sphincters or of an outside object, as soon as he achieves in one area, he makes progress in others; aggressiveness turns from destructiveness to constructiveness.

Another case deals with a disturbance in speech. A mother of a two-year-old boy consulted me because her child started to stammer. It turned out that the little boy had picked up a forbidden four-letter word and had used it constantly. The mother forbade the use of the word; he could not understand why, since he never before had been forbidden to use words. He reacted by continuing to use the word teasingly. A battle ensued, and the mother finally punished him. He gave up using the word—but started stammering. The mother was advised to tell the child he might use the forbidden word and that she would not punish him. He played with the suggestion provocatively for a while, then lost interest in the word. The stammering disappeared.

The mother's punishing attitude connected with talking had disturbed his speech altogether. It was necessary to reverse the process which had led to the disturbance in order to restore his ability to speak. The child was unable to understand that just *one* certain word was forbidden; for him, it meant that the activity of talking was dangerous and prohibited. Fearing to lose his mother's love, and fearing to do wrong, he was willing to give up talking which he was in the process of learning. It was the *timing* of the prohibition which had this undesired effect. Had language already become established as a means of expression, the prohibition would not have resulted in a stammer. This child developed a symptom in which his love for his mother and his aggression against her were combined. There were no other indications of aggression and hostility.

The outcome of speech disturbance in the practicing stage is obviously different from those in other areas. While the children who were disturbed in using their muscular apparatus reacted with hostility and destructiveness, this child developed a symptom confined to the oral sphere. This kind of speech disturbance has a parallel in certain eating difficulties. Children who are beginning to learn to feed themselves are sometimes disturbed in eating altogether when they are forbidden to use their hands or the spoon as they would like to. The eating disturbance may remain an isolated symptom. In contrast to children restrained in motility who become aggressive, these children tend to develop inhibitions.

In summary, the disturbances created in the children described here are due to interference in the practicing stage of activities. They become fixated at the phase of their development in which the disturbance occurs. This is expressed by hostility which that particular phase of development puts at their disposal. When the disturbed activity is restored, the particular from of aggression diminishes or disappears. In this connection, the positive or negative relationship to the caretaking person is of paramount importance in bringing out hostility and destructiveness, or inhibition. Interference in the practicing stage of children's activities may be responsible for disturbances in eating, sleeping, or habit training. A future neurosis may easily make use of these points of fixation.

AGGRESSION, VIOLENCE, AND CRUELTY IN CHILDREN

Diderot said in *Rameau's Nephew*, "if the little three-year-old boy had the strength of an adult, he would be a murderer." An adult patient expressed the same idea when he said, "Nobody has to be taught to kill. We all know how to do that. What we don't know without being taught is how not to kill."

Whether we speak of aggression as an instinct or as a drive, we know it is inherent to all species. Man, unlike the lower orders, has both an ego and a superego which can be deployed to control or modify aggression. When subject to these modifications, aggression is used contructively to master both activities and the environment. As stated by Hartman, Kris, and Loewenstein (1949):

> We no longer assume the existence of an independent "instinct of self-preservation" or drive for survival but stress amongst factors contributing to survival the functions of the ego, which in order to assure the individual's safety, reacts to a large set of signals . . . uses all available human equipment from the reflex organization to the most highly differentiated processes involved in reality testing, and coordinates these varied means and functions [p. 13].

Fusion with libido also modifies aggression. The infant's relationship with his mother is crucial to the establishment of this fusion. When there is empathy between the two, the infant learns to read the mother's feelings as she reads his. He gradually identifies with her. He smiles when she smiles, is cranky when she is cross. He learns to curb his aggression so as not to lose her love and approval. Wanton aggression, violence, and cruelty in children can usually be traced to an unsatisfactory early mother-child relationship and the lack of fusion between libidinal and aggressive drives (A. Freud, 1949, 1951).

Whenever reason does not substitute for instinct, when the aim of the aggressive drive is not modified by libido or when, through faulty development, libido and aggression are not fused and when the ability to sublimate breaks down, the destructive aspect of aggression comes to the fore and manifests itself in outbursts of rage or cruelty.

Lorenz (1966) shows that "the small servants of species preservation" have a tendency to be active regardless of immediate need. The hunting dog hunts when he is not hungry, the cat lurks, the starling circles. Each one of these activities has its own spontaneity and needs to be exercised. Cage the animal and its restlessness immediately increases. People, when confined, react in much the same way. The more severe the restrictions, the more severe their reactions. Aggression must have an outlet, and it finds this outlet in the motor apparatus. Hyperactivity in children can often be traced back to severe early restrictions. The reactions, in these cases, have continued long after the original cause was removed. I remember a four-year-old girl who constantly ran through the schoolhouse and up and down the stairs; when we tried to stop her, she had a temper tantrum. We learned that the child had spent more than a year before starting the school term in a body cast.

I have already described (this volume, p. 39) how interference with children's activities during the practicing stage produces frustration and aggression. In addition, any activity, when restricted in an aggressive, punitive, or violent manner, may become combined with aggressive feelings and become in itself an expression of aggression. Toddlers are difficult to handle because their hyperactivity goes hand in hand with an ignorance of what is dangerous. If the toddler runs away from his mother, into traffic, or plays with electrical appliances, her attempt to protect him may be experienced by the toddler as an aggressive restriction of motility. A struggle between the two ensues and the child may get "hooked" on the forbidden activity as a form of counteraggression.

Similarly, because control of the excretory functions is much more important to the mother than to the child, toilet training often becomes a battle of wills, with the child using urination and defecation as weapons of aggression.

Every healthy young child has a urge to be active, to practice his growing strength and his skills. His increased mobility and curiosity, when it conflicts with other people and the environment generally, may be interpreted as aggression. But the activity is actually serving to develop independence and is in itself an expression of independence. As Bender (1953) says, "Actually this thrust of activity is not an increase of aggression, but an intensive process of adaptation." It serves the purpose of growing independence and is in itself an expression of independence. These are what Lorenz (1966) calls "small servants of species preservation." However, aggression is increased when its necessary outlet in activity is blocked.

The ability to be active and to function by himself is in itself satisfying to the child. As I describe in the paper on learning disabilities (this volume, p. 85), children who are tied to their mothers in partially symbiotic relationships are given to violent temper tantrums when the mother, their subsidiary ego, is not available. They feel omnipotent with her and helpless without her. The helplessness makes them feel like an infant who is unable to express his feelings in any way except by yelling, kicking and flailing about. When these children learn to function by themselves, their relationship to the mother changes and their outbursts of temper diminish.

What we see in pathological cases is true for the normal child as well. A child may throw a temper tantrum because he is unable to do something, whether it be to lift an object which is too heavy for him, ride a bicycle or draw a picture. If he cannot make himself understood because he cannot express himself in words, he may become furiously angry; when he learns how to say things his anger becomes goal-oriented and his temper tantrums subside. The satisfaction which children show on accomplishing a difficult task is unmistakable and is commensurate with the feelings of frustration when they cannot.

Adults, too, get angry when they feel inadequate or helpless. If the rage is intense, it has a disorganizing effect and interferes with the ability to function reasonably. The inability to use aggression in the service of the ego brings about a regression to the infantile stage of development when rage and panic were undifferentiated and were expressed in random, disorganized movements involving the whole body.

The ability to function has an ego-building, integrating effect. When the child becomes able to control his body functions and when he achieves in school, he calms down. This happens not only because he is less frustrated, but because his aggressive energy is deflected onto other areas. It takes energy to control one's sphincters, but also to control one's impulses. The aggressive drive is used in the building and functioning of the superego.

While children learn, they are engrossed in the learning process; they are happy while they are learning successfully. The result is, of course, very pleasant, but the process is the important thing. To achieve mastery in anything is tied to the use of attention, concentration, muscle and brain; it is dependent upon the use of diverted sublimated aggression.

Children, and adults as well are not always able to work when they are physically restrained. They may play with pencils, doodle, chew gum or suck on tongue or hands, tap their feet, walk around, rock on chairs, etc. When such movements are performed in a rhythmic way, they remind one of autoerotic activities which may lead to a climax; when they occur in situations of physical restraint, they probably contain an element of aggression as well. Teachers know it is necessary to allow children to move about after periods of study. They are frequently not understanding enough to allow them to move while they are studying.

Aggressive energy is flexible and when modified can be used in different ways. Whether it can be modified depends on a number of factors as e.g., impulse control, mobility of aggressive energy, admixture of libido. One of the modifications of aggression is sublimation. The ability to sublimate, i.e., to use aggressive energy as brainpower, varies with the individual. It seems to be particularly easily disturbed, as we find in children with learning disturbances.

The following cases illustrate some of the dynamics of aggression and violence and their interaction with the environment.

Bobby, a five-year-old boy in kindergarten, had temper tantrums without apparent provocation. The only way to prevent him from hitting and kicking the other children was to remove him to a far corner of the room. It was difficult to control him without using force, and force made him even more furious.

When I observed him in his schoolroom, he began to play with some blocks and clothespin figures. He started peacefully enough to build a room in which he placed a mother and a boy. Then a man approached with heavy steps, entered the room and beat the boy and the mother. As Bobby played out his story, he became wilder and wilder and ended up throwing the blocks and dolls in every direction.

I learned from his mother that the game reproduced a

common family occurrence—the father would come home drunk and beat her and the child. Bobby's aggression could now be understood as both a defense and an imitation of his father. Afraid of being beaten, he defended himself automatically, using the precept of offense as the best defense. He may not even have known he was afraid.

Inasmuch as he played the game when he was alone, his goal at the time was not communication but a repetition of an experience. He actively did something which had been done to him. The change from passivity to activity and mastery afforded him a certain relief from tension and anxiety. His game provided an outlet for his aggression. He was both the aggressor and the attacked.

The little boy would be a murderer if he had the strength of an adult. Sometimes he does later become a murderer. When we read in the paper of adolescents killing the drunkard-father who abuses the mother, we understand the motive. We sometimes do not understand when the interaction does not take place between the offender and the offended but between the beaten child and some other, quite innocent person. When the son who has been beaten in turn beats his brother or a boy on the street, when he fights the teacher or a policeman, we call him "delinquent." We refer him to legal authorities. We subject him to further violence . . . "right is the might of a community. It is still violence, ready to be directed against any individual who resists" (Freud, 1933, p. 205).

The psychological reasons for the child's aggression derive from his hatred of the father. Because he dare not retaliate against him, his rage is displaced onto another person.

This example may imply that if the father would not brutalize his child, if no adult would brutalize any child, the child in turn would not become a delinquent. In some instances this may be so, but it is not that simple—with Bobby either.

Up to a certain point the play served Bobby successfully to build up defenses against his anxiety and pent-up aggression. However, the play ended in destruction beyond the play; why this was so we can only guess. In reality the aggressive scene ended, most likely, in a sexual one. Bobby's growing excitement during the play contained this sexual excitement, which he could not express in any adequate way. It reinforced his aggressive feelings, which he could not control any more, and his defenses—i.e., the play—broke down and destruction prevailed.

We turn now to Harry, a thirteen-year-old boy who lived in a children's institution. Harry stole. Nothing very big or valuable, just inconsequential things such as food, cigarettes, paper or pencils. After he stole, he provoked the other children by teasing them. If the house staff interfered, he grew angry and swore at them. When they did not react, he attacked them physically, forcing them to defend themselves. When removed from the group, particularly when removed by a man, he went completely wild.

We had only the barest outline of Harry's history. His parents were divorced. During the early years, he lived with his mother, a promiscuous woman who had married five or six times. When he was eight, his mother suddenly sent him all the way across the country to his father whom he did not know at all. The father, too, had remarried and, although he had had no previous contact with the child and had not even contributed to his support as required by law, accepted him into his family. While with the father, Harry set a number of fires. One day he set fire in school and was apprehended by the janitor. The janitor threatened to tell the authorities unless Harry agreed to have homosexual relations with him. Eventually, remanded by the court, the boy came into the institution.

Why did Harry steal? Why did he set fires? Why was he so upset at being taken away from his group, even though the educator assured him he would not be hurt? Information gleaned from the boy during his course of treatment allowed us to make some tentative constructions.

Harry was upset at having stolen. He expected to be found out and punished. The tension while awaiting discovery was so strong he found it unbearable, and he had to commit another crime in order to call attention to himself and be punished. He was apparently asking to be punished in order to be relieved of anxiety. The situation in which he was apprehended by the educator evidently reminded him of the time or times he had been apprehended by the janitor. The homosexual contact had not only frightened but also attracted him. His actions were calculated to bring a repetition of the experience. His wild behavior was both a defense and a provocation for the educator to repeat the seduction with him.

We can surely assume that Harry had been neglected and rejected by his mother who sent him all alone, at the age of eight, to an unknown father some 3000 miles away. Nor did the father, with a new wife and other children, care about him. Perhaps Harry stole because he didn't know how else to get what he wanted. The things he did steal in the institution, he could have had for the asking; but perhaps he did not know how to ask; perhaps he didn't believe he would be given what he asked for. Harry was starved for affection. Food and cigarettes, both connected with the mouth, symbolized that affection. Cigarettes, in addition, were the possessions of privileged people, such as the house staff, and therefore doubly attractive. In his frustration, Harry reached out with anger and aggression. He knew he would be spanked eventually when he was caught. But perhaps he preferred to be spanked to not being noticed at all.

Fire-setting and playing with fire is something we usually connect with sexual feelings and sexual excitement. When children make a fire they excitedly jump up and down and grasp their genitals; when they fantasize about fires they masturbate or wet as they frequently do when they dream about fires. Smoking affords both oral and sexual satisfactions. In smoking as well as in fire-setting, the forbidden aspect provides satisfaction for aggressive feelings.

Harry showed sexual excitement and behavior by provoking adult men to manhandle him and seduce him. His teasing of children also had that purpose; he actively seduced children of both sexes, younger than himself when he could get them. He had lived with his promiscuous mother for eight years. During those years he had witnessed sexual scenes many times and had been frightened and excited by them. He may also have been seduced genitally by men and by his mother. He had experienced sexual feelings and excitement without being able to get any satisfaction because he was too young and physically incapable. He was frustrated and angry, excited and frightened. Playing with fire—by seeing the flames outside of himself—helped him to express some of the feelings that burned him up inside. Sexual play, in all its ambiguity, was another outlet for doing to others what had been done to him. His provocative behavior with men served all of these wishes and was an attempt to repeat the experience with the janitor who had provided the sexual excitement which, in turn, represented his life with mother.

Harry's wild behavior was defensive, aggressive, and strongly interlaced with sexual feelings which made him repeat a pattern in which he experienced some sexual satisfaction. The amalgamation of aggression and sexual feelings was clear.

The story of the peasant woman who complains that her husband is no longer interested in her because he doesn't even beat her up anymore provides an illustration of the interrelationship between aggression and sexual feelings. We may wonder why a wife puts up with her husband's abuse although he does not pay any attention to her or provide for her materially. The usual story is that first he beats her and then they have intercourse. The beating is the foreplay for sex. Eventually he forgets about the sexual part, but the beating meted out and received is still a pleasure. Both partners are engaged in a sadomasochistic relationship where cruelty is an essential part of their sexual relationship, whether it leads to genital satisfaction or not. Sadism, which is cruelty directed against a person with the intent to hurt "can be viewed only in the context of an already developed and complex object relation" (Hartmann, Kris, and Loewenstein, 1949, p. 27). It is, however, not less likely to be finally destructive. The man who beats his wife has sexual and aggressive feelings toward her which are mixed in the wrong proportions; however they are still mixed. Somehow, it is more understandable than unmitigated destructiveness and therefore less frightening.

Dostoevsky says in *The Brothers Karamazov*, "I know for a fact that there are people who at every blow are worked up to sensuality, to literal sensuality, which increases progressively at every blow they inflict." He points to the sensuality, which is produced by cruelty and which may have a climax-like sensual activity. Hartmann, Kris and Loewenstein (1949) assume that aggressive discharge per se may be experienced as pleasurable. In fact, they consider it "unavoidable to assume that the very fact of discharge of aggressive tension is pleasurable" (p. 27).

Konrad Lorenz (1966) shows impressively the connection between aggression and sex, aggression and friendship and love. With some fish and birds aggressive gestures become "redirected" and change into gestures of greeting and wooing. Sometimes, however, the friendly gestures may revert to the aggressive gestures from which they are derived. "The great instincts," aggression and sexuality, have a tendency to be active and to mix so that aggression may become sexualized and sexuality gets tinged with aggression. Lorenz believes there can be aggression without sex, but no sex without aggression.

The adult's reactions towards curiosity and cruelty towards animals seems to vary according to size; when children pull out wings of insects, cut worms, fish, there is very little objection from adults; if they do similar things to birds or small wild animals, it is considered fair game—because they are game. When children are cruel and curious towards dogs, cats and other pets or domestic animals, adults object according to their own attitudes towards these animals. However, what is acceptable or unacceptable with regard to cruelty towards each other or towards animals varies widely among different peoples, classes and cultures at different times. Not until 1866, was the American Society for the Prevention of Cruelty to Animals (A.S.P.C.A.) founded; it was preceded by 40 years by the Royal Society P.C.A. in England. The A.S.P.C.C. (Cruelty to Children) followed only some years later.

Cruelty, an exacerbation of aggression, is common among children and may be either intentional or inadvertent. The infant who pokes his fingers into another person's face, pulls at spectacles, jewelry or hair, is not being deliberately cruel. He is merely curious and enjoys the activity of exploration. Later on the same motives will cause him to pull out insects' wings, cut up worms, or maul the family pet. The child has to be taught not to hurt other people or animals. He learns through the other person's reactions. At first he perceives this only as a prohibition and frustration. Only when he learns to recognize signs of pain in others, only when he can empathize, identify with others, can he inhibit his impulse to hurt. His reaction formation develops through empathy. And empathy exists only when his early relationship with his mother has been satisfactory.

The empathy which starts with the mother gradually extends to other people. Hostility and cruelty are accepted feelings when they are directed against the enemy and the outsider. They become unacceptable when they are directed against a person or animal with whom we identify. A child may hit another child because he is angry with him; he may also cry when another child has been hurt and is crying. In the first instance, he sees the other child as an enemy; in the second, he shows his capacity for empathy. Without empathy, the child who impulsively does what he pleases may be cruel and destructive.

The child who grows up without a satisfactory early mothering experience does not identify with an adult except in aggression. He develops no libidinal tie, no empathy with the other person. Nothing prevents him from expressing aggression in any form because he doesn't love anybody and is not afraid to lose anyone's love.

The most frightening aspect of destructiveness is the one turned against the self. Anna Freud (1951), in writing about manifestations of autoaggression, discusses the similarity between head-knocking and autoerotic practices in infants and young children and points to a common factor in both which consists of "a rhythm which may lead up to a point of climax," which in the former case may be one of self-destruction. She suggests that if head-knocking is an "early manifestation in behavior of aggression and destruction turned against the self," then it "might gain a place of importance in analytic theory as one of the rare representatives of pure destructive expression where fusion of the drives is incomplete or defusion has taken place" (p. 28).

Other manifestations of aggressive behavior against the self in young children are hair-pulling, biting, and scratching. Hoffer (1949) says, "we might say that the child that likes himself will not bite himself" and considers this "the first principle of primitive narcissism over a partial instinct" (p. 54), enabling the child to protect himself against his destructive instinct. When adults in great pain dig their fingernails into their palms, bite their lips or pull their hair, we may say they are regressing to previous modes of dealing with pain. When they can hold somebody else's hand, they can divert their aggression to the other person. The "bad mood" of people in pain, which they may vent upon doctors and nursing people, helps them deal with their discomfort. The infant or young child in pain will use whatever means of expressing aggression he may have towards the person with whom he is in physical contact, instead of attacking himself. Discomfort unrelieved by a caretaking person may lead to self-destructive activity.

It seems that the child who is unloved is in danger of destroying himself. It is impossible for an infant to survive without the presence of an outside, caretaking person. There must be at least a minimum of mothering in order for any narcissism to develop. In the absence of any satisfactory mothering, the child does not develop a protective barrier of libidinal investment in himself. Bender (1953) describes a number of cases of suicidal children. Most of them are unwanted children who identify with their rejecting parents. Beres (1952, p. 247) describes an eleven-year-old boy who was extremely aggressive against others and himself; he bit himself, jumped off roofs of cottages, hit his head against the wall, squeezed his neck, put a rope around it. He had been rejected by the foster parents with whom he had finally, after many unsatisfactory placements, begun a tenuous relationship. His suicidal impulses appeared after this last rejection.

In cases like these we are faced with our own helplessness. All our explanations and therapeutic efforts are insufficient when we find ourselves vis à vis with this powerful destructive force. A. Freud (1951) describes how, in the Hampstead Nursery during World War II, extremely destructive children could not be diverted and controlled until an adult succeeded in establishing a relationship with them and they made a libidinal tie to that person (p. 24). The children who turn their destructiveness against themselves are even harder to reach; their relations to people are not durable. When the person with whom they have established any kind of relationship leaves them, even temporarily, they regress and revert to their previous self-destructive behavior. It takes the constant presence of the person who provides care for these children to keep the self-destructive force in check. The fusion of drives has not taken place; the libidinal object is not introjected, and the child cannot protect himself from himself.

While suicide among children is not too frequent, suicidal attempts are quite often made. In a way, these children draw attention to themselves with their desperate actions and in some instances may get help. There are, however, a great many children who are less ostentatious but still self-destructive; they scratch themselves until they are bloody when they are infants and use knives when they are older; they run out into traffic when they have just learned to run, and use bicycles and cars when they are adolescent. Some children frequently get sick; others fall and break skin or bones. None of these children take care of themselves because they never learned how from a caretaking adult. They do not care whether they get hurt because nobody else does either. They are accident-prone or prone to be sick, but do not intentionally attempt to kill themselves. Perhaps the difference between them and the suicidal children is more quantitative than qualitative.

CONCLUSION

Aggression which is uncontrolled by reason or libido is potentially destructive. There are, however, a number of ways in which it may be modified and not only made less destructive but constructive. Aggressive energy is employed in all physical and mental functioning. In that sense, it is life-preserving. Freud said in Why war?, (1933) "there is no use in trying to get rid of man's aggressive inclinations—it is enough to divert them." Some of these modifications of aggression have come about in the course of evolution (as Lorenz shows); others are the result of civilization (as Freud shows) which demands that the instincts be controlled by the ego. The person who is taking care of the infant has an essential part in bringing about the modifications of aggression. The fusion of aggression with libido is the most fundamental modification of aggression which, in addition to the physiological pain barrier (Hoffer, 1949), protects the child against self-destruction. It allows him to use aggression against an object while preserving it. The relationship which develops from these beginnings offers the motivation for restriction of aggression and its displacement, as well as for internalization of object relations in the formation of the superego. The ability of the child to use his aggressive energy in constructive ways, through learning and sublimation, is largely dependent on this early development.

Not only the ability of the child to absorb and become part of a society and its culture depends on the modifications of aggressive energy, but his humanization as well. The development of human relations and empathy with people make it possible for him to forego cruelty and violence. Therein lies our hope for the survival of mankind.

THE PARENTS' ROLE IN THE
ETIOLOGY OF LEARNING
DISTURBANCES

I

In the course of working with school-age children who suffered from learning difficulties of varying degrees, we had the opportunity of studying not only their relations to their parents but also their parents' relations to them. There are only a few references in the psychoanalytic literature to the parents' active and continued contribution to children's learning difficulties. Koff (1961), reviewing the psychoanalytic literature on a panel on "Learning Difficulties in Childhood," summed it up in the following way:

It seemed to me that the greatest agreement and understanding has been in the areas of the content of the fantasies of people having a disorder of learning. The nature of the conflicts, the dynamic tendencies and counter-tendencies, are most clearly described. Starting with Freud's concept of inhibition of function, the id-ego-superego conflicts are elaborated and related to instinctual development on oral, anal, phallic, and genital levels. Regressions to early types of mental operations are described.

The next point of view is the consideration of the nature

This paper was published originally in *The Psychoanalytic Study of the Child*, 19:421-447, under the title, "The Parents' Role in the Etiology of Learning Disabilities." New York: International Universities Press, 1964.

of the ego itself, especially the quality or mode of the energy utilized in the learning process. The essence of learning is in the process of abstraction, or conceptualization, and the ego utilizes a sublimated form of energy, as well as a shift of aim to accomplish this. Regression to sexualized and aggressivized modes of energy is characteristic of learning problems.

Finally, there is the huge puzzle about the nature of language itself. Learning problems in children most often seem oriented about learning to read and write a language, because words are the symbols by means of which we communicate. Some authors believe language is originally derived from a symbol-forming tendency inherent in the human mental apparatus. Likewise, speech is said to be genetically determined. There must exist some point in development where the need to communicate is the organizing principle which joined the originally separate symbol-forming tendency with speech to create language (unpublished ms.).

Thus, the literature on learning difficulties is almost exclusively concerned with intrapsychic processes and conflicts. The interpersonal conflicts of childhood are only implicitly considered as contributing to the symptom of learning disability. Yet, for some time analysts have been aware of the fact that parents participate in a most important way in the etiology of learning difficulties. Spitz and Wolf (1946), J. Robertson (1962), and E. Kris (1962) have described and discussed the interaction between mothers and infants that may delay the smiling response, the desire to be held, to touch, or to grasp which are expressions of the first social contact. Vocalization may be promoted or delayed by the mother's response. Preverbal communications and subliminal perceptions on the part of both mother and child are intricate and complicated; only prolonged observation and contact allow some understanding of them.

Ego functions, like flowers, require certain climate and soil conditions for growth. They may develop normally, subnormally, or hypernormally. As is generally true, it is easier to study conditions connected with abnormality than those which assure normality. The delayed and retarded development of infants as described by the above authors seems to be owing to a deficiency in the relationship between the mothers or their substitutes and these children. Lack of stimulation as well as unrelieved pain and frustration are the rule for those infants whose mothers are unable to read the signals with which the children communicate their needs.

Another type of retarded development has been described by Mahler (1952), who has coined the term "symbiotic relationship" to describe a relationship between mother and child which results in making each the other's prisoner. They seem to be unable to live with each other and unable to live without each other. Hellman (1954) has made similar observations on mothers of children with intellectual inhibitions.

Analysis makes it possible to understand, and often to dissolve, the noxious tie between mother and child. I have found that such mother-patients often develop a strong, overly dependent transference. They are unhappy at any interruption of treatment, afraid to be left alone by the therapist; silence on the part of the therapist is hardly bearable for them; they are afraid that they or the therapist might die at any separation. They expect that the therapist will fulfill all their needs and often think that their troubles would be over if only they had a penis. They expect fulfillment of that wish, too, and are angry and disappointed when the reality is pointed out. At times they show an inability to express themselves adequately—but they expect that the analyst will understand them without words.

The relationship of these mothers to their children shows the same characteristics, only in reverse: the mother insists that the child stay with her lest one or the other, or both, might die. The understanding between mother and child must remain wordless, as it was in infancy, in order to ensure their insoluble oneness. Such more or less complete symbiosis of mother and child leads to severe, massive disturbance of the child, usually of a psychotic nature, which Mahler (1952) has described.

I consider partial symbiosis to be the etiological basis for functional deficiencies which encompass not all areas of behavior and functions but are confined to specific ones. Among these is inadequate speech. Such children may say just a few words and mostly indicate their wishes by gestures. The mother, and sometimes siblings, understand these gestures and fulfill their wishes, thus making speech unnecessary. Or the children talk baby talk, which again is understood by somebody in the environment; this baby talk then serves as a secret language between two people from which everybody else is excluded. The mutual dependency is upheld in the area of speech. An example of the mother's investment in her child's deficiency in speaking was a mother who brought her four-year-old boy into therapy because he spoke very poorly and only to her. She did not bring him back, however, after he had talked to the therapist the first time in whispering tones—and had said within the mother's hearing, "I don't want to go home!" She found the child's speaking problem preferable to his loving somebody else; she was afraid he might leave her.

Eating is another of those areas. The child refuses to take food from anybody except one person and, in addition, is extremely selective about the kind of food he will eat. Very often he eats only two or three kinds of foods. Again, the mother is concerned and upset, but secretly she is delighted to be the only person from whom the child will take nourishment. This reveals itself in her visible disappointment when the child eventually likes somebody else's food.

Another instance of such partially symbiotic mother-child relations occurs with regard to sphincter control: in one way or another, the child whose mother is preoccupied with his and usually her own, defecation remains dependent on his

mother in defecating. Some children soil, some are constipated, but they all cling to their mothers' ministrations, by
demanding enemas, others by wanting to be wiped, to be
asked to go to the toilet, to be asked whether they have
to go to the toilet, or to be asked whether they have had
a bowel movement. The same holds true for control of urination. The child needs to be awakened or reminded to
urinate long past the time when children normally are able
to control themselves. He insists that his mother participate
in this function. The mother, on the other hand satisfies
her own needs as much as those of the child; the genital
or anal area of the child is touched, looked at, cleaned, and
fondled, allowing the mother direct and vicarious satisfactions of old, infantile, forbidden pleasures, which have been
repressed for a long time. The mother who wants a penis
of her own insists on participating in the handling of her
son's penis in order to fantasy that she owns it.

The child's reluctance to dress himself or to play by himself or with another child often results from the same kind
of relationship with his mother which tends to keep him dependent exclusively upon her.

The child who suffers a functional deficiency of the kind
described will have trouble learning when he goes to school.
His inability to function independently carries over into the
academic area. I consider an all-pervasive learning difficulty
a disturbed ego function which is based upon a partially
symbiotic relationship between mother and child.

The child whose academic learning difficulties are perva-
sive is disturbed not only in the area of learning. He is always a behavior problem. He is unable to tolerate any pressure, for example, to sit on a chair longer than he wants; his
attention span is extremely short; he cannot tolerate any
frustration, but bursts into tears or temper tantrums at the
slightest difficulty. He won't let anybody teach him anything.
He is engaged in a constant love-fight with his mother; he
clings to her desperately to the point of being unable to

separate from her for any length of time. His school attendance is apt to be poor. He is often sick or is kept at home for other reasons. The mother herself is desperate; she alternates between tolerating or promoting the child's demands, and losing patience and punishing him in wild outbursts of temper. She participates excessively in the child's school performance. She considers his success or failure her own; she checks his work, tests him, and bribes and threatens him, carrying on the old fight in a new field. The child in turn feels unable to function alone in his work, as in other areas of his life. The ability to learn in school—or to study in any situation—has become another area of a partially symbiotic relationship.

All-pervasive learning disorders differ from circumscribed, symptomatic learning disorders. All-pervasive learning disorders, like primary behavior disorders, are the result of a continuing conflict with the mother. Symptomatic learning disorders are to some degree the result of internalized conflicts, although here, as in other neuroses of childhood, the battle with the environment continues and shapes the child's behavior.

II

We had an unusual opportunity to study the interaction between parents and children with regard to their learning difficulties in the Northwest School, which was housed by the Northwest Clinic from 1953 to 1963. The school was intended to teach the children between the ages of six and twelve who were unable to attend the public schools because of their psychological difficulties and who were in treatment. All of these children showed learning disabilities of varying degree, which were treated by either the therapists of the Clinic or by outside therapists. The proximity of therapists and school allowed for a degree of cooperation between teacher and therapist which went beyond that of the regularly scheduled individual and staff conferences. Sidewalk consultations between teacher and therapist proved to be most helpful because it was possible for each to keep the other completely posted from day to day. Cases treated by outside therapists served as an unplanned control group: their progress was slowed down by the lack of immediate communication.

The school consisted of one schoolroom which could be subdivided by movable walls. There were two teachers. The number of students varied from three to eight, eight being the largest number the teachers could handle.

Most children in the Northwest School were two or three years behind in their grade achievement. They had been promoted in the public schools, despite their difficulties, as a result of public school policy based on the philosophy of making social promotions. With these particular children this policy had failed. The children did not fit into their classes socially, although they were kept within their peer group. They did not play with other children, nor had they attained their academic achievement. Social difficulties had been added to their academic difficulties so that many of them had been expelled from school.

We considered it the role of the Northwest School to keep the children in school and on their achievement level. Many of them had been frequent truants from their other schools. We found that truancy practically disappeared in the Northwest School. In public school these children had at times been sent out of the classroom or sent home for punishment, but to little effect. In contrast, at the Northwest School the children felt punished and deprived when they were asked to leave the school temporarily or for good. The school represented a kind of guarantee against failure and saved them from being ostracized by other children.

The combination of school and treatment in one building created a type of relationship comparable to that which patients develop in a hospital setting. The school may be compared to a six-hour-a-day hospital which enhanced and facilitated the psychotherapeutic process. Frequently we found the children would linger at the clinic before and after schooltime. Everybody in the building, from secretary to janitor, including all the doctors, had a part in the relationship. There were certain limits which had to be maintained, and these were consistently enforced by everybody.

In the schoolroom, minimal standards of behavior and of academic achievement were permissible. The teachers reduced their demands to the point where the child could produce. From this level on, demands were made vigorously and it was expected that they would be fulfilled. Failures to produce in any one subject or in general were constantly brought to the awareness of the student and of the therapist, who then could deal with them as he saw fit.

The possibility that a child could slide through without learning or with cheating of any kind was excluded. Thus the school served as a means of differential diagnosis, as did the nursery schools discussed by Katan (1959). At the same time the school was an adjunct to treatment, since it could either insist on, or dispense with, certain performances.

The teacher held conferences with the parents, calling their attention to actions and attitudes adversely affecting the children's progress. These included not bringing the children to school on time or bringing them irregularly; calling for them late and keeping them waiting; forcing them to come to school or go home alone or preventing them from doing so; participating in their children's homework too much, and also preventing the children from doing their homework by deciding that they should use their time in other ways.

In addition to the conferences between teacher and parents, most of the parents were seen by a therapist, either for their own difficulties or in connection with their children's difficulties. Whatever was discussed with the teacher could eventually be continued in discussions with the therapist.

The following cases will demonstrate the interaction between parents and children and their therapy.

III

AN ALL-PERVASIVE LEARNING DISABILITY[1]

Henry, age nine, was a shy, quiet boy, who was unable to function in school, had no friends, and did not play with other children. He appeared younger than his age, in size as well as in behavior. Both parents were in psychoanalytic treatment and denied, as long as they could, that their son was in need of help. Henry was skillful in drawing. He was inventive with paper and wood, Tinker Toys, and plasticine. Psychological tests revealed that he was of "at least average intelligence." He did not read, write or do any number work. He said and demonstrated that he could not remember. He did not know his street address, his birthday or his age. His mother brought him to the Clinic and called for him. He was the youngest of three children. Before he was born, an older brother had drowned at the age of five. Supposedly, he knew nothing of the death of this oldest son.

Henry started analysis by setting up a scene: a house in the woods. There were no animals and no people. At the end of the session he quietly dismantled the whole thing and put it away. He repeated this performance on succeeding hours, gradually adding animals and people to the scene. The people were in their beds; it was night. The beasts stood quietly in the woods, their heads directed toward the house. Nothing was ever said, nothing ever happened. At every session he dismantled the setting. The dismantling, however, became more and more violent. Although it was

---

[1] Therapist: Edith Buxbaum, Ph.D.

timed to happen at the end of the session, it became the climax of the play; it was staged as a sudden, frightening outburst of impersonal destruction—a catastrophe that destroyed everything and everyone. Gradually the catastrophe moved from the end of the session into the session itself. The people rose from their beds and started to fight; the animals moved toward the house and attacked the people. The setting became less important than the fighting and eventually gave way to another fantasy.

It was clear at this point that Henry represented himself as the wild animal who observed quietly what was going on at night in the parents' bedroom. He saw every action, his own as well as those of others, as utterly destructive. The masturbatory quality of the fantasy as well as Henry's anxiety were obvious.

This fantasy was followed by that of the "Superbaby." The Superbaby could conquer and destroy all people, animals, and monsters. He was almighty. As a last resort he drowned his enemies and eventually drowned himself; however, he came to life again but his enemies died. Of course, once he had come back to life, the fight would start all over again. He never got older and never died.

When the therapist asked Henry about the boy who had drowned, he knew all about him—the family had talked about the accident, and Henry had heard. He thought of himself as the boy who had drowned when he was five years old. The brother had gone to school but had not learned to read and write. He lived eternally in his and other people's fantasies. So Henry did not want to go to school. He did not want to read or write or learn, in order to remain magically five years old and continue the fantasy of living his brother's life.

Henry could not swim and refused to learn. His refusal was a mixture of the fantasy of magically being able to swim and his fear of drowning. When he could admit his fear, he gave up his fantasy of being the Superbaby who did not die and who, since he was omnipotent, never had to learn anything. The first thing he learned was swimming—and he became an excellent swimmer. Moreover, this resolution of his conflict and fantasy with regard to swimming opened the door to an interest and desire to learn other things as well: he now wanted to go out alone in order to play with boys with whom he had made friends. He did not want his mother to take him everyplace—he found it embarrassing to be treated like a baby and wanted to be like the other children. In order to be able to use the bus, he had to know his address, how to read the numbers on the bus and the street signs and how to make change. Knowledge of reading and arithmetic became necessary in order to get away from his extreme dependency on his mother.

When Henry gave up the Superbaby fantasy, his various anxieties became more apparent. His fear, lived out in the Superbaby fantasy, was fear of dying, which he denied by his fantasy. It was also fear of destroying his parents, which he acted out in his repeated dramatic play. Kill and be killed was what he saw in the world around him: this was what his parents did to each other, what they did to him —or to his brother?—and what he wanted to do to them.

Feelings of revenge pervaded his fantasy of the Superbaby. Another fantasy revealed this more clearly: he played at being a dentist with the therapist as patient. Out of plaster of Paris, he made two models of jaws with teeth. He then proceeded to drill through the upper teeth into the brain, and through the lower teeth all the way through the body into the penis. His fantasy demonstrated what he was afraid of at the dentist's, and what he held his parents responsible for. At one point he casually said, "See my finger? My mother smashed it in the car door." This had occurred when he was two years old, and one finger was shorter than normal. The finger, which was crippled in reality, to him represented far more than a finger: it was his penis, his masculinity, his ability to function.

Henry's not learning was a response to parents who had crippled him in mind and body. At the same time he punished them by remaining the (drowned) Superbaby, who would take revenge for his death. Helplessness and omnipotence were thus mixed in his fantasies, and both were represented in his learning disability.

The parents' part in creating, promoting, and prolonging Henry's inability to learn in school was considerable. Although the family lived within ten minutes' walking distance from the Clinic, the mother insisted on bringing the nine-year-old boy and taking him home. When I suggested that she allow Henry to come alone, she burst into tears, saying she could not face losing him, too, in an accident, as she had lost her oldest son. The problem was compounded by the fact that the Clinic is located near a lake. Eventually the mother, through her own analysis, overcame her fear and allowed Henry to learn to swim, to come to the Clinic alone, and to go other places by himself.

Henry's father referred to him as "the little guy" and gave him whatever he desired. Once when Henry was working on a model boat with a motor, the father brought home for him a bigger and better boat, already put together. He saw no reason for "the little guy" to work so hard if he could buy him a better boat. He also saw no reason to give Henry an allowance, since he could have as much money as he wanted any time. He thought nothing of taking Henry out of school to accompany him on fishing or hunting expeditions, or on a vacation. When the therapist and the teacher protested, he told them that it was quite unnecessary for Henry to be a student because he would inherit the family business and fortune anyway. Even if he could not read or write, other people would do the work for him—so why shouldn't his father go on a vacation with him if he wanted to?

Henry did not know the value of pennies, nickels and dimes; he never bought anything. Once, when he wanted to make model ships or airplanes, I bought them for him in order to work on them during his session. Henry was concerned that I be reimbursed; since he had no money, he would have to ask his parents. When I raised the question of an allowance, Henry was not interested—he said he did not need any money because his parents bought him whatever he wanted.

The question of money came up again at Christmas time. The idea of giving anybody a present had never occurred to Henry. But when the children in school started talking about it, he told me that he thought of giving his mother a wristwatch. I asked how he would manage, since he did not have any money. Henry replied that of course his father would buy the watch, but it would be his present. Making distinction between what belonged to his father, his mother, and himself finally led to his wanting to give a present that came from himself. He asked his father to give him some money to buy his mother a present. The father thought this was a "cute" idea but suggested they would go shopping together and buy mother something "really nice." At this point, Henry gave up and was satisfied to fall back into his role of the "cute," dependent, little boy.

I then discussed the matter with the father. It developed that the father was opposed to giving an allowance of a quarter or a dollar a week because that was not enough to buy what the boy might want and "he could get anything he wanted by just asking for it." On the other hand, the father did not want to give Henry five or ten dollars a week because he had no idea about the value of money and would probably lose it. Henry's father's reluctance to give him an allowance was in part the product of his need to keep exclusive control over money, on which he based his position in the family. He felt threatened by the idea that his son might not need to ask him for something, by the possibility of being considered expendable.

Eventually the father saw that his attitude was preventing Henry from learning how to deal realistically with money. He decided to give him fifty cents a week, a sum appropriate to his age and the same as the other school children received. After a short time, Henry learned what he could buy with his allowance; he learned to make change, and his arithmetic skill took an upward swing. But, even more important, he felt more independent and grownup because he could go places on the bus with his money if he wanted, without having to ask somebody for transportation, and he could save money and buy presents for others.

Each parent had a different reason for keeping Henry "a little guy." Both of them used magic means to keep him alive. Both parents used this unrealistic overprotection for ambivalent reasons. Henry, in his refusal to learn, lived out the fantasy of the Superbaby, which they supported. One or the other blocked every attempt on Henry's part to give up the role of baby. It took the therapist's intervention and the parents' therapy for Henry to relinquish it. The parents' reluctance to allow realistic gratifications appropriate to Henry's age made it unnecessary and even undesirable for Henry to seek them. The pull toward unconscious gratification in fantasies of magic and omnipotence was reinforced by the parents. To mature against his own infantile wishes and against those of his parents was not possible for Henry: he stood still in his development. This, too, was represented in the eerie scene at the beginning of his analysis—time was supposed to stand still, as in "The Sleeping Beauty," keeping the strivings of life in abeyance together with the powers of the bad fairy.

Henry's analysis shows how the partial symbiosis with his mother can be considered as the basis for his reluctance and inability to grow up, which would mean separating himself from her. One part of his learning disturbance was an aspect of his partially smybiotic relationship with her. Another part of his learning difficulty was related to his father's attitude and Henry's relationship with him. This will be discussed at a later point.

A SUCCESS NEUROSIS OF CHILDHOOD[2]

Martin was brought for treatment by his parents because of severe anxiety—his learning difficulties became known shortly after the beginning of treatment. Martin was nine years old, shy, small, and of average intelligence. He suffered from nightmares and was afraid to play with children in the neighborhood or in school. The public school teacher liked him, but said he was too quiet and a poor student; however, since he did not give her any trouble, she was not concerned.

Martin was seen three times weekly; his mother was seen once a week by the same therapist. Martin dreaded going to school. Every day, when it was time to go to school, Martin refused to go. His mother drove him to school because he refused to walk. When they arrived at school he refused to get out of the car, and this resulted in a lot of pushing and pulling. When his father took him to school, he went without offering any resistance.

One of the reasons for Martin's fear of going to school was his inability to do the work. He could not read, spell, or do any arithmetic, although he was in the fourth grade. When this state of affairs became known, it was decided by the parents and the therapist that Martin should attend the Northwest School, where he could get tutorial help, in order to catch up to his grade level.

Martin's difficulties with going to school continued for a while after he came to the Northwest School. In guidance work with the mother and in therapy with the child, the idea was developed that the fight about coming to school was a game in which both participated. The mother decided not to play the game any more, and she was able to convey this

[2] Therapist: Adolph Gruhn, M.S.W.

decision to Martin so that he soon began to come without difficulties, and even to come alone on the bus.

The teacher drew Martin's attention to his reading mistakes and reported them to the therapist. They became understandable in the course of his therapy. Martin was not really unable to read, but he read hesitatingly and made peculiar mistakes. He stopped completely when he came to a word with any kind of aggressive connotation or which he associated with aggression. An example was the word "tank." In the particular context, the word referred to a water tank. Martin, however, took the word in its military meaning and refused to read it either to himself or out loud. It was obvious from his behavior that his difficulty was not in reading but rather in his refusal to pronounce words with aggressive connotations.

Martin's father was a reserve officer, absorbed in the study of weapons of all kinds; he had a private arsenal in a locked room. Martin was extremely interested in these weapons, but he was forbidden access to them. He was not allowed to enter his father's armory, much less touch the weapons, which were father's toys. Martin carried over this prohibition against handling aggressive weapons into other areas and consequently was unable to fight or compete in any way, to express aggression in words, even to read any aggressive words.

Martin's difficulties with arithmetic were similarly meaningful. Most of his mistakes were miscalculations by one, either one too many or one too few. They were connected with his mother's lack of one finger, a disfiguration she concealed so skillfully that it was not immediately noticeable.

It also became obvious that Martin always left his work unfinished or made at least one mistake in otherwise perfect work, and this troublesome behavior proved to be most difficult to understand and to handle. In observing his working with models, which he wanted to do very much, we began to understand the meaning of his need for imperfection. As long as a model was not perfectly finished, it had to be left in the school or in the therapist's office; this was one of the rules in school and one of the rules the therapist had set up. Martin managed never to take anything home by never finishing anything. His fear that his younger brother might destroy his models was discussed, but apparently this was not the decisive reason. What seemed to bring about a change was the analysis of the following situation.

The father worked in a store that sold models, among other things. He sometimes brought models home for Martin and, when Martin had finished one, took it back to the store where it was displayed as an advertisement. If Martin wanted to keep a finished model, the father demanded that he pay him part of the cost. This meant that an unfinished model remained Martin's, while a finished one cost him either the model or some money. He never knew exactly how much money, since his father's prices were somewhat unpredictable. (This, too, had something to do with Martin's difficulties in arithmetic.) But, even worse, Martin considered it dangerous to finish any work, for if he finished anything, he would lose it. That he did not know what he would lose made the danger even greater. It could be anything—something he cherished, e.g., part of his body like the finger his mother had lost, or perhaps even his life.

Discussions with the father revealed that he saw no harm in taking things such as airplane models from the store. He did not think that he ought to pay for them, although he did not think that Martin should have them without paying for them. His armory also contained things that he had kept from the army; his reason for keeping Martin out of that room was not only that he feared for Martin's safety, but also that he did not want Martin to question his ownership of the weapons.

When the father came to recognize the inconsistency and dishonesty of his petty thievery, he decided it was not worth the trouble it caused Martin or the money it cost him in therapy. He modified his handling of the situation to the extent of allowing Martin to keep the models and to setting a fair price on them if Martin wanted to buy one.

But the private armory remained a closed room for Martin until one day he burglarized it, stole the stolen goods, and distributed them among his friends. His courage scared him almost to death. Fortunately, his father felt guilty enough himself not to punish him severely.

When Martin's fears became clearer, his reasons for not finishing or for making mistakes became conscious, and making mistakes became a willful act instead of an involuntary one. As often happens with people who suffer from one type of anxiety or another, Martin was not yet willing to give up his defense without help. The teacher had to insist that Martin finish his work without mistakes. Only then could Martin realize that it was possible to be successful without danger to life and limb.

The teacher's observations provided clues which enabled the therapist to look for certain relationships between Martin's learning difficulties and symptoms he was already familiar with, or which made the therapist aware of connections not previously known to him. In this way the teacher's observations became an important stimulus for the therapeutic work, which was considerably accelerated by this close cooperation.

When the therapist and the child came to an understanding of the reasons why Martin could not learn in certain areas, the teacher offered a proving ground for the validity of their conclusions. The teacher and the school represented a reality situation that did not yield to Martin's fantasied anxieties. Omitting words helped him to avoid dangerous fantasies; making mistakes in numbers was a symbol of his castration anxiety, as was his attitude of voiding success. None of these devices—defenses in the dynamic sense—was accepted by the teacher. Failures in reading, as well as not finishing or avoiding perfect scores, were at first unconscious; later on they were conscious forms of avoidance and denial. The teacher's insistence that Martin did know, and that his mistakes be corrected and a perfect score be achieved, proved to Martin that he could risk the achievement of perfect scores upon the insistence and with the approval of authority. Eventually he was able to achieve perfect scores without this means of ego support; he learned to work up to his capacity and enjoy success; he could play with other children and be openly aggressive when necessary.

DISCUSSION

Martin's learning difficulty was a symptom of his success neurosis. The success neurosis of children is to be differentiated from symptomatic learning disorders, which can be resolved by the analysis of the particular symptom. Martin's making the specific arithmetic error of one was a symptom that yielded to the connection made with his mother's missing finger. His success neurosis, however, caused him to continue to make less definable mistakes. He had to fail. Teachers meet many such children. They may do creditable work in general, but spoil their scores during tests: leave their work incomplete or lose part of it, forget their assignment or do the wrong one, continually failing in small ways so that their teachers are forced to downgrade them.

The picture these students present is similar to that of adult patients who complain that they have just missed a promotion, or that they are afraid of promotion because they may not be able to do the job. Even when they have already been doing the job in an acting capacity, when they get the actual title or are offered it, they either collapse or fear that they will collapse. This symptom has been described by Freud (1916).

The children do not want to be promoted either. The American school system of today makes it extremely difficult for them to achieve their goal. Children get promoted for "social" purposes which prevents teachers, parents, and children from recognizing their particular difficulty for what it is. As in Martin's case, such children get into treatment largely because of difficulties in other areas than in learning. Martin's father contributed to his learning difficulty. He rationalized keeping his arsenal for himself and forbidding Martin to use any part of it by pointing to the danger of the weapons. Similarly, other fathers find more or less valid rationalizations for forbidding their children the use of tools ranging from pencils to power saws. Obviously it is necessary to forbid children the use of dangerous objects. There is also something to be said in favor of allowing fathers a certain amount of private ownership. Yet these possessions are overdetermined in the minds of men; they are regarded not only as useful tools but as symbols of status and masculinity, and it is for just this reason that the sons desperately desire them. The sons need to identify with their fathers in the area which they consider a masculine prerogative. As we have seen, another area Martin's father considered his prerogative was money. That Martin did not know how much money he could call his own, or how much his father would take from him, was reflected in his arithmetic mistakes and in a deeper sense symbolized his castration anxiety.

Martin's reluctance to go to school was associated with the love fight between himself and his mother. It afforded them both a certain amount of body contact—enough to make Martin feel extremely guilty and afraid of his father. Martin had to give up this physical relationship with his mother before any further progress could be made.

We can see in Martin's case that the area of failure was determined by the interaction between father and son. The son backed away from an area the father had staked out for himself, symbolized by a room containing all the father's instruments of aggression and symbols of manliness, a room from which Martin was excluded. Henry, too, was forbidden to learn the value of money, the area of his father's strength and authority.

Martin and Henry could not resolve their difficulties with the help of therapy alone as long as their fathers continued to oppose their sons' attempts to compete with them. An isolated learning difficulty may be considered a symptom, i.e., an intrapersonal conflict, and as such may be resolved in analytic therapy. When a child's symptom is being created and maintained by a parent, the child needs the parent's permission—manifested in a changed attitude—in order to give it up. In learning difficulties it is necessary, as a rule, to explore the possibility of such adverse parental influence and to deal with it.

It is a general accepted truism that great men do not bring forth great sons, but that, on the contrary, well-endowed sons are likely to be handicapped by their great fathers.[3] A study made of certain geniuses has suggested that they had fathers who devoted all their knowledge, time and love to their gifted children while they themselves remained in the background, making no claim to fame except that of being the father of a successful son. Eissler (1959) has described this kind of relationship in his study of Goethe. The examples of John Stuart Mill, Mendelssohn, and Mozart might also be cited. The corollary to the idea that a father plays a role in bringing out his son's abilities is our clinical experience, which shows that he can also significantly disturb his son and prevent him from using and developing his abilities. And unused abilities, like unused limbs or tools, deteriorate.

A father who says to his son, "When you finish this airplane model, either I will take it back to the store or you will have to pay me for it," implicitly forbids his son to accomplish what he set out to do.

When another father says to his son, "I never went to col-

[3] There are exceptions: Bach and his sons; Breughel, father and sons; but perhaps these exceptions are in the fields of art, music, and artisanship, areas where family traditions and schools are involved.

lege, and if you don't get to college you'll have the money anyway," and when, in addition, he takes his son out of school to suit his own convenience, then he is actively preventing his son from striving to be better than he is.

Only rarely do we find the father's feeling expressed so clearly outside of analysis. However, analysis of fathers makes us aware that the father's feelings toward his son are just as strong and rivalrous as the son's feelings toward his father. They are, in fact, derived from the father's own oedipal conflict. In a renewal of feelings, the father sees his son as dangerous, as he used to see his own father. Now that the father is stronger and more powerful than the son, he can do to the son what he could never do to his former rival and he wins at his son's expense.

E. Kris (1955) has said that the learning process functions best in the conflict-free area. Both Martin and Henry bore this out by their inability to learn. For Martin, the learning process was laden with conflict and anxiety, pertaining to his rivalrous competitive feelings toward his father. To some extent Henry's disability had a similar genesis. Both boys were so intimidated by their fathers that they were unable to function normally in the areas in which the fathers were relatively strong—areas the fathers had reserved for themselves. These boys resolved their oedipal conflicts by avoiding competition and aggression in the areas of their fathers' strength. They gave up their ability to function by becoming passively aggressive in these areas. They surrendered to their fathers by not exercising those ego functions they considered aggressive and competitive, and which their fathers acknowledged as threatening to themselves.

Success neurosis has been discussed in the psychoanalytic literature beginning with Freud. Such patients, as adults, may fail when they meet with success in their work, and also when they have succeeded in obtaining the love of a desired woman. They are very often, if not always, impotent. The surrender to the father occurs not only in their ability to function in their work but also in their ability to function as men. In children, this impotence is expressed in castration anxiety, which forbids them to function in areas their fathers have reserved for themselves, and which prevents them from being normally aggressive and competitive.

IV

In recent years, ethologists have pointed out that the development of imprinting occurs during a critical period in the early development of the organism. This critical period seems to terminate when the organism shows fear of responsiveness (Salk, 1952; Kaufman, 1960). Learning, too, can progress best at "critical times"; i.e., when an organism is ready for action. Kris (1962) remarked in his paper that a function that has matured, but was not being used, led to retardation. When a child suffers severe deprivation and lack of stimulation in early infancy, as in the example described by Spitz (1945, 1946a), irreversible retardation and eventual deterioration of constitutionally normal capacities take place.

Most of the children with all-pervasive learning disorders as we have seen them at the Northwest School were amenable to therapy and able to learn. It is significant that they were children tied to their mothers in a partially symbiotic relationship. They were not physically deprived or left without stimulation. On the contrary, they were overstimulated and overprotected.

When the kitten or the puppy is ready to feed itself, the mother does not insist on continuing to nurse it. When the human infant is ready to be weaned, however, the mother may or may not adapt herself to his needs. Many difficulties connected with weaning are caused by faulty timing. The readiness of children to take in knowledge may be compared to food intake in more ways than one. We talk about people who "devour books," who "drink in everything." One of the children in the Northwest School refused to learn from a white teacher, but accepted a Negro teacher; she reminded him of a nurse who had fed him when his mother had deserted him for the birth of his sister. He had refused to take food from his mother when she returned. Henry insisted on going home for lunch to be fed by his mother, although the other children stayed in school. Only when his mother packed his lunch, telling him that she would not be home, did he stay in school and eat with the others—and he also began to learn with them.

When a function has matured, the child feels the need to use it. If he is thwarted, a conflict develops between the child and the person who is imposing the restriction. Children thus restricted become frustrated and express themselves in various forms of aggression. Those children whose learning disturbances were all-pervasive were often openly aggressive toward their mothers, from whom they were inseparable; all of them were preoccupied with fantasies of destruction of others as well as of themselves.

As long as the child is prevented from functioning by another person, his anger is directed externally. Only when outside intervention is removed, do anxiety and inhibition become apparent as signs of the ongoing introjection. What used to be on the outside is now on the inside, e.g., Henry's fear of drowning became apparent after his mother no longer prevented him from learning how to swim.

We think of inhibitions as the result of phase-specific traumata which disrupt the progression of libidinal phases and bring about regressions to previous fixation points. We expect that, once an inhibition is removed, recovery will occur. This is true in those cases where normal development has taken place. For example, a child who has learned to walk, talk, be continent, may give up one of these accomplishments because of a traumatic experience, but he recovers it once the experience has been mastered. It is otherwise with the child whose functional development has been disturbed through the repeated intervention of the mother or her substitute.

Ego functions that have been stifled at their inception and have never been established independently from the mother can be severely impaired, leading to retardation or distortion in libidinal development. In Giovacchini's (1963) words: "If the external world does not supply the gratifying experience that leads to learning at a time when the physical apparatus has acquired the ability to master certain skills, a defect occurs which is reflected in the structure of the ego and later in character" (p. 405).

Anna Freud (1960) says: "Where the neurotic symptom, the conflict, or the regression of a child is anchored not only in the young patient's own personality but held in place further by powerful emotional forces in the parent to whom the child, in his turn, is tied, the therapeutic action of analysis may well be slowed up or, in extreme cases, made impossible" (p. 379). The disturbing factor is not so much the mother's active and conscious interference as a general attitude, which she displays toward the child. Henry's mother was afraid to lose him, as she had lost her oldest son. By overprotecting him she prevented him from becoming oriented in place and time as well as with people. She prevented him from thinking and doing for himself. As is the case with inhibitions and phobias, the affected area has a tendency to spread so as to encompass other areas.

The partially symbiotic relationship between mother and child prolongs the child's feeling of helplessness. If he cannot function alone and is left alone he becomes anxious. On the other hand, when he is with his mother and has her at his disposal, he feels wonderful, inasmuch as his feelings about himself include her. She functions as his complementary ego. So long as they are together, he feels big, powerful and capable. In either case, his attitudes concerning his ability to function (expressed by Henry in his fantasy of the Superbaby) are unrealistic. Nor are these unrealistic attitudes restricted to the area affected by the partial symbiotic relationship. They are carried over into all other areas: if the child cannot perform, his rage and anxiety find expression in a temper tantrum; if mother fails to rescue him, he gives up. He can assess neither his own ability nor his own strength and therefore cannot gauge that of others. His view of the world is distorted; he cannot adapt himself to it, he cannot learn.

Mothers who were afraid of their own mothers when they were young transfer these fears onto their children. The demanding, aggressive child threatens his mother as she was threatened in childhood. The child who threatens his mother feels powerful and reduces her to helplessness; when he demonstrates his helplessness and dependence, she feels indispensable and powerful. His belief in her power supports her own fantasies which is why she continues to play the role he assigns her, however inconvenient it may seem to be.

Mother and child are bound in a relationship wherein each expects and demands miracles—both wished-for and feared —from the other. This brings about an extremely ambivalent relationship in which mother and child are afraid to let go of each other for fear that they will be mutually destructive. The child feels all-powerful as long as he dominates his mother. When the mother is removed from him, he feels threatened by the world onto which he projects his own aggressive fantasies. He now feels as helpless as he felt almighty before. The child who feels all-powerful cannot learn, because learning is itself an admission of not knowing —an admission of weakness. It presupposes logical thinking and an acceptance of reality, not in accordance with the fantasy of omnipotence.

Freud (1911) wrote about the magical thinking of the infant. He discussed the child's inclination to believe that fantasying something makes it come about. He goes on to say, "Since the later care of children is modeled on the care of infants, the dominance of the pleasure principle can really come to an end only when a child has achieved complete psychical detachment from its parents" (p. 220). The transition from magical thinking to reality-oriented thinking is a long drawn-out process, which at best is resolved together with the resolution of the oedipus complex. However, children who are arrested in a partially symbiotic relationship do not reach the oedipal phase; they remain in the pre-oedipal phase, and their thinking remains largely magical. Unable to progress toward reality, they regress further into magic and fantasy.

The child's all-pervasive learning disability is a derivative of a partially symbiotic mother-child relationship. Because he depends on his mother to interfere with reality on his behalf, he is unable to judge it, deal with it, or adapt himself to it; he cannot think, and he cannot learn. His learning ability, one of his most important ego functions, has been crippled.

Learning difficulties which are rooted in the relation to the father are usually limited to certain subjects. They are success neuroses—failures resulting from the child's fear of competing with a powerful adversary. This was the way it appeared in Martin's case with regard to his reading, which was connected with forbidden aggression; his arithmetic, which was connected with money; and his inability to finish a task. His castration anxiety was displaced from his genitals to his ability to function intellectually.

As it happened, all the cases with this particular syndrome were boys. The corollary would be the woman who refrains from making herself attractive to men because of guilt feelings toward her mother. Sprince (1962) has described a patient, an adolescent girl, who "avoided success" in the intellectual field because her mother claimed it for herself. Grunebaum et al. (1962) discuss a number of cases in which sons, in obedience to the unconscious wishes of their unsuccessful fathers, developed specific learning difficulties. The onset of Martin's learning difficulty occurred during the oedipal phase and was a symptom expressing his conflicting feelings toward his father. The inability to learn was his way of foregoing aggression and submitting to father. This adversary, however, is potent in reality; the relationship is based upon existing power, however distorted by anxiety and ambivalent feelings. The threats posed by Martin's father were real ones. Martin's anxiety was partially justified.

CONCLUSION

The cases presented here indicate that boys who suffer from success neuroses are "little Oedipuses" who fight their fathers—unsuccessful though they may be—from the vantage point of the oedipal-genital developmental phase. Realistic concepts are in the foreground. In both aspects they differ from children whose learning disabilities are all-pervasive, whose libidinal position is preoedipal, and who are preoccupied with fantasies of magical power. The success neuroses of children differ from those of adults in that they involve the active participation of the parents in the child's neurosis. In the case of adults, the parents' roles have been internalized in the demands and prohibitions of the superego.

TECHNIQUE OF CHILD THERAPY
A Critical Evaluation

During the last few decades, interest in methods of therapy for emotionally disturbed children has greatly increased. This development is due to Freud's discoveries and theories, which have gradually penetrated the fields of psychiatry and psychotherapy as well as education. By and large, the wide range of ideas on child therapy and the tremendous effort put into the realization of these ideas, especially in this country, are to be considered a wholesome development.

At present, the student of child therapy is faced with a multitude of techniques for prevention and cure of emotional disturbances in children. We have child analysis, play therapies, relationship therapy, release therapy, counseling, child guidance, group therapies, and a few others. Many of the proponents of a specific technique offer more or less impressive case material as evidence of their success.

Enthusiasm for their own ideas and successes causes many child therapists to think that their particular technique is best and should replace all others. Most presentations, however, fail to relate the use of a certain technique to the characteristics of the cases in which it is effective. Yet, this seems to be one of the most essential problems. When we

This paper was published originally in *The Psychoanalytic Study of the Child*, 9:297-333. New York: International Universities Press, 1954.

know *which technique is best suited to a particular disturbance*, we will be able to make optimum use of the constructive ideas on child therapy produced under the influence of psychoanalysis.

How should this problem of relating the appropriate technique to the particular case be studied? During the last few years there has been a widespread feeling that such questions could be decided only after thorough research on success and failure of different techniques in different cases. Theoretically, such research may offer the most reliable solution. Practically, however, this type of research may not bear fruit for years to come because of the enormous number of variables to be considered and the amount of time, money and effort required. What should be done in the meantime? I am reminded of a father who, when consulting one of my colleagues on problems of his four-year-old son, commented that he was an ardent student of child development, very eager to treat his child according to the most recent findings of science. But his trouble was that his son grew faster than he was able to read up on child development! If child therapists should decide to wait with technical decisions until all the studies, projected or now in progress, are successfully completed, they might find themselves in a similar quandary.

Another way of approaching the problem is to evolve technical procedures from psychoanalytic theories on child development. Undoubtedly the student of psychoanalytic literature will be influenced by these ideas; however, their direct application to technical procedures is not feasible because of the individual differences in each case. I prefer a third way, namely, to examine successful techniques and procedures in an attempt to understand which elements have been instrumental in bringing about a change. The critical method commonly applied tends to place emphasis on finding out what did not work and thus fails to shed sufficient light on what did. I want to try the reverse approach.

Anna Freud developed her technique of child analysis for

infantile neuroses, which comprised phobias, obsessional, hysterical symptom neuroses and anxieties, neuroses comparable to adult "transference neurosis," which Freud found eminently suitable for the application of the so-called "classical" psychoanalytic technique. For cases which deviate from these clearly defined transference neuroses, modifications of technique are necessary. The point beyond which we no longer wish to call these techniques psychoanalysis proper is outside the scope of our immediate problem.

Anna Freud (1952) observed that "Less well-defined and fluctuating developmental disorders are on the increase at the expense of the real infantile neurosis which was more frequently recorded and treated by the analytic workers of the past" (p. 50). Modifications of technique in child analysis became necessary to secure therapeutic success with cases showing deviations from the "real infantile neuroses" for which the technique originally was developed. I shall take child analysis as a starting point in exploring the effects of other therapeutic techniques in relation to it; borrowing K. R. Eissler's term (1953), I shall explore "the parameter" of the technique of child analysis, as presented by Anna Freud (1936, 1946a).

CONTACT BETWEEN CHILD–PARENTS–THERAPY

Anna Freud (1926) used to say that child analysis should be limited to children whose parents were analyzed themselves. Even so, the child analyst should maintain contact with the parents. In a later paper (1945) she states that whether or not a child should be analyzed is usually decided for him by his parents, ". . . frequently enough on inadequate reasons" (p. 72). However, child analysts of the Vienna school do analyze children of unanalyzed parents. The analyst sees both the child patient and his parents.

In contrast to this approach, followers of Melanie Klein work only with the child, a procedure based on the idea that the superego is developed during the first year of life and that the baby is threatened by aggressive fantasies from within which are independent of reality (Rickman, 1936; Waelder, 1937).

A third method of contact has been developed by the child guidance movement through the use of the clinical team. Witmer (1946) traces this method to Adolf Meyer's interest in gathering information about the patient from many sources. Here the role of the social worker was limited to the gathering of historical information. Through the influence of psychoanalysis, the mere collection of data became secondary to a dynamic, interpretative—i.e., treatment—approach. The clinical team now functions in a new form: one therapist works with the child and another with the parent. The new meaning of the team approach has been emphasized by Allen (1942), who says: "Thus, the first seeking of help by the parent and the subsequent coming together of parent and child, with the separation and reunion that takes place, has in it the essence of the entire therapeutic process" (p. 64). This definition of the therapeutic process is based on Allen's philosophy, derived from Rank, who stated as early as 1909: "The detachment of the growing individual from the authority of the parents is one of the most necessary, but also one of the most painful achievements of evolution" (p. 67). According to Rank and later to Allen, failure to achieve this detachment (Allen calls it "differentiation") results in neurosis, a repetition of the trauma of birth.

These are essentially the three most important ways in which therapists may handle their contacts with parents and child. I think that diagnostic and dynamic considerations rather than philosophies, which assume *a priori* causes of neuroses, should be introduced in order to select the best therapeutic procedure for specific cases. I shall attempt to do so in the following discussion.

The closest approximation to the psychoanalytic treatment of adults is the psychoanalytic treatment of a child while he continues living in his usual environment. His independence in treatment is but a seeming one, for children are always dependent on their parents' willingness to tolerate the treatment. Even when treatment does not cost money, children frequently need transportation, which offers the parents sufficient inconvenience to necessitate at least their tolerant participation. Moreover, when changes occur—and we hope they do—they may not always be to the parent's liking. At such times parents may interfere by expressing their objections, or criticizing the child and the therapy. This circumstance might already be regarded as an indication that we cannot work with the child alone. We shall come back to this point later.

Before a therapist starts working with a child, he needs to know a great deal about the child's history and something about the parents. When the parents first contact the therapist, they are prepared to talk about the child's symptoms and their concern or complaints about the child's behavior. Despite their willingness to talk about the child's history, we frequently encounter some difficulties in this area: sometimes they do not know what to say, and sometimes they do not want to say what is important. Sometimes they do not remember important facts in the child's life, and sometimes they forget things which occur everyday. For example, they do not remember that the child had been upset when the new baby arrived—they remember only that the child was "delighted." Or they forget to say that the child still wets the bed. They are reluctant to speak about their own histories—after all, they came because of the child, not for themselves. Only after the therapist has established a relationship with them can he get the material he requires. Sometimes the analyst is in a better position to ask direct questions after he has worked with the child for a while, because the parents, having acquired a better understanding of the connection between their own lives and that of the child, are then more willing to answer. A ten-year-old girl's persistent cursing, for example, led me to ask the mother where the child might have heard such language. The mother, a widow, then told me of an affair she had had some time ago with a man who cursed precisely the way her child did. She had not given this information previously because she had not considered it important, nor had she thought that the child remembered the swearing. The additional information obtained from the parents while the child is in treatment can then be used as one sees fit.

Although in cases such as the one mentioned above, information could be secured from the parents, in the following examples the parents only contributed their tolerant permission to the process of therapy.

Mary, age ten, was brought into treatment by her mother, who told about Mary's truancy, stealing, temper tantrums and disobedience. After a few weeks, Mary said to me rather abruptly, "I wet my bed; can you help me so that I won't?" This was her way of telling me that she wanted help for enuresis, and not for the reasons her mother had described. With this request she set her own treatment goal, which differed from that which her mother had in mind. The mother had not even mentioned Mary's enuresis.

At times Mary excluded her mother from the treatment process; at other times she wanted me to include her and to tell her certain things. But it was Mary who really determined what she wanted treatment—or me—to do for her. The mother played only a secondary role.

Eva, age nine, was brought in for treatment because of compulsions and terrific rages if they were interfered with. When the mother brought her to see me, she said she could not bring the child as often as I wanted because she could not find the time and the child was afraid to go any place alone. During my first conversation with the child, I told her about this difficulty and asked her what we could do about it. Eva said she would come alone. I was surprised and wondered whether she was not afraid, whereupon she said that she was not afraid, that it was her mother who was afraid to go any place alone.

As it turned out, many of Eva's compulsions were the result of interreactions between mother and child. The treatment consisted of disentangling them from each other. I had entertained some doubt as to whether this could be done without the mother's entering treatment. Eva, however, showed with this first step which direction she was going to take.

Neither her mother nor her father contributed to my understanding of the situation, telling me much of their own or the child's history, but they were sufficiently troubled by Eva's behavior to allow her to continue treatment. I saw them in order to get information about everyday occurrences which I could put to use with Eva. Eva continued treatment by herself, for herself, as she had indicated by her first step in taking responsibility for getting to my office, excluding her mother from participating in her treatment.

Robert, a child with temper tantrums and a tendency to hurt himself, had, according to his parents greatly improved after a few months of treatment. They did not want him to return to treatment after the summer vacation. Robert, at this time six years old, asked to see me. His mother said he could telephone me if he wanted to. He repeated that he wanted to come and see me. She amiably said that he could tell me over the phone that he wanted to visit me. He retorted angrily, "I don't want to visit her; I want an appointment." At his request, his mother dialed my number. He did not ask to speak to me but arranged an appointment with my secretary. In spite of the parents' reluctance to continue his treatment, they finally acceded to his wishes.

I think one may say that all of these children were treated "alone." However much or little information their parents gave when I saw them occasionally, the children determined the course of their analyses by the material which they brought to me in actions, words and play. I saw the parents with the child's knowledge. I always told them the content of my conversation with the parents so far as it pertained to the child. Problems which arose before or after my seeing the parents were taken up with the child: whether I would or should tell the parents about things going on in the treatment situation; whether the child trusted me or not; his fear that I might side with the parents against him; his hope that I would help him against the parents, etc.

These parents wanted their children to be treated; they were not particularly anxious and did not, even unconsciously, disturb the treatment process significantly. Even Robert's parents, who wanted to terminate his treatment prematurely, gave in to the child's determined wishes to continue therapy.

What made these children available for help was their suffering, and their state of emotional development: they were either in different stages of the latency period or, like Robert, at the height of the oedipal phase.

Children who are at the height of their oedipal phase or already in the latency period, who suffer from their disturbance, and whose parents are not significantly disturbed themselves so that they do not interfere with treatment— these children can be treated by themselves with a minimum of contact with, and information from, the parents. The suffering child either is aware from the beginning that he is disturbed or acquires this awareness without great difficulty in the course of treatment. Anna Freud's technique of child analysis is thus applicable to him.

A different technical procedure will be used with children who are either chronologically or emotionally in the preoedipal phase. Procedures must also be modified if parents, because of their own emotional reasons, do not permit us to work solely with the child. Various therapists have described different methods of working with children in the preoedipal period. With the exception of Melanie Klein's English school, which works only with the child, regardless of his age, all these therapeutic methods somehow include the parents in the treatment process. Sometimes therapists even go to the extreme of working exclusively with the parents.

Children in the preoedipal period—we can say roughly under five years—present a wide variety of psychopathology. A child may suddenly refuse to sleep, eat, or defecate; or he may suddenly develop fears—e.g., of dogs, airplanes, noises, darkness, being left alone. In the beginning, such disturbances may be isolated and do not affect any other areas of the child's functioning. Wulff (1951) calls this state of isolated disturbance a "monosymptomatic neurosis." A number of authors have reported on the treatment of such disturbances (Bonnard, 1950; B. Bornstein, 1935; S. Bornstein, 1933; Burlingham, 1951; Fraiberg, 1950; Schwarz, 1950).

A boy of three was brought to me by his mother because he had suddenly developed constipation and refused to use the toilet. He demonstrated in his play with dolls that he thought he made a baby when he defecated. He therefore wanted to save his feces in order to make a nice big baby. I explained to him how babies grew, where they came out and about his being a boy. He pretended not to hear me. At last he turned to his mother and demanded, "You tell me!" He repeated the demand and insisted that she repeat verbatim what I had said, showing his disapproval when she deviated and demanding that she repeat the story again and again, as he did with other stories he liked. He refused to take the explanation when I gave it; it had to come from his mother.

In another instance, Peggy, age four and a half, in treatment because of a phobia about bees and consequent refusal to go out, had shown some anxiety about getting herself dirty. One day she started to paint but did not get very far because the time was up. We postponed it for the next session. Although she had come alone into the office thus far, the next time she insisted on bringing her mother, and we all painted. She observed her mother while we painted and only when she saw that her mother got herself dirty did she relax and enjoy herself too.

These children show their need to have mother's approval and permission for their feelings and thoughts. They have no judgment themselves, but accept only what mother says is right. Conflicting ideas expressed by people whom they like are extremely disturbing to children of all ages; but children who are past the oedipal phase can bear some disagreement with adults or between adults. Not so the child in the preoedipal period, who is still strongly dependent on the mother. Therefore, unless the mother is in agreement with the therapist, the child cannot accept therapy.

This dependence of the young child on the mother makes it necessary to include the mother in the treatment process. In addition, we need to get information about what is going on between treatment sessions when we do not see the children. The communication between parents, therapist and child must be free and easy. The therapist must be allowed to use what information he has about the child, and the mother must be able to use with the child what the therapist has conveyed to her and to talk about the therapist. It seems natural to the child that sometimes he plays alone with the therapist and sometimes mother may join them; and also that therapist and parent may talk without the child present, as grown-up people do. In this way the therapist can make use of a variety of situations.

If the child's particular anxiety is aroused by separation from the parent, the therapeutic approach will have to be adapted accordingly. In all phobic conditions, treatment must have progressed to a certain point before the patient can be induced to renounce his specific technique of avoidance. With a child who is afraid to be separated from his mother, treatment will first aim at enabling the child to stay with the therapist without his mother. Although some apprehension in meeting a stranger may be considered normal in a young child, I do not believe "separation anxiety" is the core of all neurosis in children, as maintained by O. Rank, Allen, and their followers.

Parents have different ways of expressing their need to be included in the treatment process. They may worry because they do not know or understand what made their child disturbed, or what they may have wittingly or unwittingly contributed to the child's pathology. They do not want to continue to make the same mistakes. They may be jealous, feel guilty or defensive. We must not neglect their feelings. It is "their" child. They decide whether the child should be treated, and their willingness to cooperate with the therapist might well be a decisive factor in the success of the treatment. So long as the child is dependent on his parents for socioeconomic reasons and is exposed to their influence, the therapist must rely on their cooperation. If the parent is not too disturbed, or if the child's disturbance is not identical with the parent's, we can limit our contact with the parent to that just necessary for his assistance with the child's therapy. The same applies if the parent is in treatment with another therapist.

Should the parent react to the child's treatment with such apprehension, jealousy, or guilt feelings as to affect the child, the amount of time spent with the parent must be increased. We may have to allow the parent, usually the mother, to be present in the treatment situation until she is able to leave the child alone with the therapist. If the mother cannot bear to leave the child, the child cannot stay without conflict. The situation may demand that the therapist deal with the mother alone until she is able to allow the child to be treated. The degree of the mother's disturbance will determine whether the therapist can work with the child and use the mother's help, or whether the mother may need therapy herself.

If both mother and child need treatment I think it preferable that each be treated by a different therapist. It is too difficult to keep the problems of child and parent separated so as not to be influenced in one direction or the other. Moreover, since I wish to use information given by the parent in the treatment of the child, I feel handicapped when the discretion imposed upon me by the parent's treatment situation prevents me from freely using that information. Sperling (1950), however, treats mother and child simultaneously or in successive hours. She claims that the deeper insight into the mother's disturbance can be directly applied in the therapy of the child.

I find the use of separate therapists most successful in cases where the parents have obviously made a major contribution to the child's problems. I refer here to children with long-standing behavior disorders. They resist toilet training, are difficult about their food, refuse to dress themselves, won't go to bed and are generally disobedient. The parents submit to this until some outside observer, perhaps the family doctor, a teacher, relative, or friend suggests that the child needs help. There is further delay while the parents weigh the merits of the suggestion. The child senses their resistance to the idea of therapy. Consequently he reacts to the parents' belated efforts with anger and resistance, and often new difficulties are added to the old ones.

Sometimes the therapy of the mother alone changes her attitude to the child in such a way that the child's difficulties disappear. A common factor in these cases is the supporting role which the therapist assumes. In discussing the child's problems with the parent, one treats the child like a symptom of the parent, taking the child's problems as the focus of discussion and going into whatever the ramifications may be, whether marital problems, recent and past conflicts with parents or parents-in-law, sibling rivalry, etc., yet always returning to the child. Thus, the parent's own conflicts are discussed only in connection with the parent's attempt to learn to understand the child. The therapist has to listen patiently to all these problems, and should be sympathetic and tolerant. The woman who feels harassed by the manifold demands made upon her in the role of wife, mother and housekeeper, and sometimes even of breadwinner, thus encounters someone who offers her help instead of making demands on her. We have observed that such mothers who felt put upon, exhausted, and angry, after having been given support by the therapist, are able to adopt a supportive role at home. Perhaps they feel relaxed after having talked about their problems; perhaps they obtain some satisfaction and can therefore give satisfaction; perhaps they identify with the therapist and can now do what they could not do before. In any case, the mothers begin to function better in relation to the child.

All kinds of occupations are used in child therapy. Skills are developed largely through play. It often seems to the observer that a lot of time is wasted. Yet, the relationship to a friendly adult has a stabilizing effect upon the child who has a period free from fear, anxiety, and uncertainty. If he needs to test limits, he may do so without the need of having a temper tantrum. This is what one may call a "corrective experience."

It is not quite clear what the therapy consists of that could not be done by the mother herself, except that she obviously could not do it. Then why could it not be done by some other person—a teacher or some other friendly adult? Why does it have to be a therapist? Usually because the mother would not allow another person to be a "better mother" to her child than she is herself. She would not allow it to happen with the therapist either if she did not receive some help herself which enabled her to allow it.

The child's therapy is often the means by which the mother can accept therapy for herself without losing face. When both child and mother are in therapy, the mother's attitude may change, but so does the child's. The mother may be more able and willing to continue at home the "corrective experience" started by the child's therapy. In this kind of therapy the child is seen usually only once a week; it will be effective, therefore, only when the atmosphere of the brief therapeutic contact is sustained by the attitudes of both parents at home.

Habit disorders—soiling, wetting, refusal to eat, resistance to going to bed or staying in bed, to dressing or undressing, general disobedience and difficulties in getting along with children—are largely reactions to the parents' inadequate pedagogical procedures. When parents learn how to handle the child differently, the preschool child, who is flexible and easily influenced, responds comparatively quickly. With older children, they become serious defects. Habit disturbances never stand alone, but are always part of a more general developmental disorder, characterized by impulsive, asocial behavior, and lack of control, frequently combined with an oedipal period that is unduly prolonged and does not flatten into latency (Buxbaum, 1950).

These children are hard to manage. They are willful and seem to live solely according to the pleasure principle. They cannot tolerate postponement of satisfactions, and attempt to control their environment instead of their desires. Such a state of affairs could not have come about unless their parents had allowed it to happen. Often, neglect is responsible for the children's lack of socialization. However, habit disorders occur in children who are by no means neglected, but who have been handled inconsistently. The parents assure the therapist that they did everything recommended in a book, or in many books. We know that these parents would have been inconsistent with or without books, with or without advice. Their inconsistency will focus on an area or activity that has a special unconscious significance for them. For instance, some parents who were enuretic themselves promote enuresis in their child despite visible efforts to the contrary. In one case a ten-year-old boy was sent to be treated for his enuresis, but the mother left the wet sheets on the bed, did not air them out and did not clean the room because she was disgusted. The fact that she herself used to be enuretic gave us an understanding of the reasons which made her work against therapy despite her obvious efforts to the contrary.

The secret wishes of parents are no secret to the children, who understand signs and actions better than words and act accordingly. For example, a father describes with delight the tricks his little boy plays on everybody including himself. Admiringly, he says that he would not have dared to tell off his father or mother the way his nine-year-old rascal does. Obviously the son fulfills the secret childhood wishes of his father. The father punishes him every so often, but the boy knows that his father would rather have him be naughty than good. Johnson and Szurek (1952) and Bettelheim and Sylvester (1949) have described such acting-out children as suffering from superego lacunae. The parents must undergo therapy—and we wonder whether anything short of analysis would be effective—before the children can give up the behavior patterns which both gratify their parents' unconscious wishes and provide easy satisfaction for themselves. If the parents are not willing to undergo therapy, the treatment of the children will not be successful so long as they remain at home. It will therefore be necessary to place them in an environment where the parent substitutes do not have the same tendencies as the parents.

If these parents accept treatment for themselves, they should not be treated by the child's therapist. If parents try to promote the cure of their child on the conscious level, while unconsciously they aid and abet his acting-out behavior, they need to understand their own unconscious motivation for so using the child. Treatment by the same therapist endangers this understanding by providing the opportunity for parent and child to unite in resistance to therapy, i.e., the treatment situation becomes an arena for their unconscious interaction.

Mrs. N. had brought her nine-year-old boy for treatment

because he was disobedient, attacked her physically, and was cruel to his younger siblings. The boy's behavior was, to some extent, a reaction to a cruel father. Hating his father, who allowed no expression of hostility against himself, the boy displaced his feelings onto the mother and his younger siblings. Since the father refused to consider even counseling, much less treatment, it became necessary to remove the child from his home. The parents agreed, but the boy refused to leave home. We were at an impasse and, as a last resort, requested that the mother see a male therapist for herself, which she reluctantly did. In the transference with him, she revealed an unconscious wish to fight with her son as she had fought with an older brother who had died as a young man, whom she had loved, and who had seduced and beaten her. Before long, she registered the boy at a private boarding school to which he went without difficulty. The boy's inability to leave home was produced by the mother, who unconsciously wanted to continue the fantasied relationship with her brother. When she was given a chance to transfer her feelings for her son (brother) onto the therapist and to become conscious of their meaning, she could release her son. Her husband's cruel and aggressive personality attracted her because of her previous incestuous relationship with her delinquent brother. The son, at the time closer to the image of the brother, was a less dangerous object for the repetition of this relationship than her husband, of whom she was afraid. She used her son as a protection against her desire to provoke her husband's attacks on herself by exposing the boy to father's punishment, which she then watched, unharmed herself. Although the father refused to take any part in the therapy, he was willing to pay for the boarding school and for the treatment of his wife and son. His refusal may also have been influenced by the mother's wish to keep him as he was. But because she discontinued her therapy as soon as the boy was placed in the boarding school, we can only speculate about that aspect. She might have been afraid to lose her husband as she had lost her son, or to lose her masochistic satisfactions if she continued therapy.

In most cases where removal of the child from home becomes necessary, treatment of parent and child may be helpful in achieving such a goal. If the same therapist works with child and parents, the therapist necessarily identifies with both sides, and the parents identify with the therapist. This situation is much more conducive to holding the family together. The parents may find themselves competing with the therapist for the love of the child, wanting to be as good as he is. If different therapists are working with parents and child respectively, it will be easier to disentangle the interests of each party and, if necessary, achieve a complete separation.

All therapy with children takes into consideration the relationship between children and parents. This relationship takes on a special meaning when the child is physically sick. Even when a child is sick for only a short while, he needs more care than at other times. Usually it makes him more dependent on the mother than he was before his illness. When illness is prolonged, the child may easily regress to a stage of dependency, which he has left only a short time before. This is particularly evident in illnesses which require care and restrictions for a period of years, such as rheumatic fever, poliomyelitis, or heart trouble. Whenever children are chronically ill, either from birth or early in life, their relationship with the person who takes care of them is peculiarly intensive and dependent. Yet it is not only the child who becomes dependent on the mother, nurse, father, or other relative. The reverse situation is equally true. Mahler (1952), in this connection, speaks of the symbiotic relationship. In all these cases there is an interrelation between psychological and physical factors which has direct bearing on the physical well-being of the sick child. This is strikingly true in epileptic children. Some parents cannot bear the idea of their child being epileptic and consequently deny the existence of obvious symptoms. A mother who came for therapy in her own behalf, complained of general anxiety. Eventually she mentioned how annoyed she was with her five-year-old boy who constantly fell and got all bruised, "and why wouldn't he watch where he was going! He was even falling down staircases, and some day he'll break his neck, the little fool!" She thought that perhaps he, too, could profit from therapy. Examination revealed that he was epileptic. The mother's anxieties were considerably reduced once the condition was recognized and treated. Her anxiety had been displaced from the child onto herself. In another case, a mother who was responsible for giving medication forgot about it and thus, for needs of her own, produced seizures in the child. The child, too, can produce seizures for unconscious reasons. A girl, age nine, threatened, "I'll be dizzy" (her expression for seizures) whenever her parents scolded or frustrated her. As a result, she dominated her whole family. The parents, in turn, hating her for forcing them to give in, frustrated her unnecessarily and thus produced the feared seizures. They switched from one doctor to another, changing medication so quickly that no results could be obtained.

The mother who denied the illness of her child was able to handle the child with the help of her own therapy. In another case, mother and child were treated by different therapists, and in yet others by the same therapist.

The same considerations that are valid for organically sick children apply also to psychosomatic disturbances. M. Sperling (1949) has reported on a number of cases in which she analyzed both mother and child in succession. She describes how the mother's disturbance has direct bearing upon the child's symptom, how the child in turn can unconsciously use his symptoms to satisfy or attack the mother. Other workers, e.g., Sylvester (1945b), were able to work with the child when he was entirely separated from the mother. Apparently both approaches are valid.

The techniques used in the treatment of children who are called psychotic or autistic are as controversial as those used in cases of psychosomatic disturbances. All of these children apparently have no object relationships. Treatment in these cases cannot be done on an hourly basis; it must be environmental. This is easier in an institution where everything is geared to children than in a family where the adults wish to pursue their own interests. Institutional treatment which can provide adequate therapy and care is, however, extremely expensive. Unfortunately, the number of such places is limited, and public support for them insufficient.

Some autistic or psychotic children who have been treated in institutions show a great deal of improvement. Tony came to an institution at the age of four and is now nine years old. His speech had been unintelligible, whereas now he enunciates well; he stopped his constant whining and crying; while previously he could not sleep, he now sleeps through the night. First he ate only very few things and lived mostly on milk; now he eats almost everything he is given. Toileting has been accomplished. He was able to form attachments to only one person when he was admitted. Both house staff and therapists changed during the years, and each change was traumatic for Tony, who thereupon relapsed into previous mannerisms and unrelatedness. Eventually, however, he accepted the new person and slowly worked up to his previous accomplishments. Children and adults at the institution are fond of Tony; they are kind to him and play with him as one would a pet.

Tony's parents lived hundreds of miles from the institution and could not visit him more frequently than once a month. In the beginning of his treatment, these visits were most disturbing. He reacted unhappily to their coming as well as to their leaving. It was then decided that they should not come so often, but only every three or four months. During these periods Tony made progress, but the parents were unable to notice this when they came to visit. They were disappointed because, during the time they did not see the child, they had built a fantasy of how much he had changed, whereas really he had changed only a little. At the request of the institution, the parents consulted a therapist in order to talk with him about their own relationship with Tony, their disappointment and their hopes. In the course of this therapy they resigned themselves to his illness and to his absence from home; they allowed themselves to admit that life without Tony was much more comfortable and simple. Tony was recently placed in a foster home where he maintains the level reached at the institution. The foster home is near enough to make possible frequent visits between the two places for both Tony and the staff. This arrangement also allows for supervision, if necessary, in the form of supportive treatment for the foster parents.

The foster home which has been chosen is socially, economically, and culturally far below the standards of Tony's parents. However, Tony, too, is far below his parents' standards, nor will he ever be able to meet them. It is to be hoped that he will fit into this new environment or perhaps into another one of a similar kind. Tony's condition forced the therapists to find an environment into which he would best fit, since he could not adapt to, nor be accepted by the one into which he was born.

Francis, age seven, resembled Tony in many ways. He too was a "psychotic" child by clinical appearance, history and psychological tests. Yet his therapy took an entirely different course. When he entered the institution, he was out of contact with reality, hallucinating, attacking poeple unpredictably, and refusing to talk. He had no father and lived with his mother. She worked while finishing her education at the same time. She had no time for him, and always left him in the care of other people during the day. The institution was therefore a decided improvement in his environment. Since his mother refused to participate in the therapy by coming for regular appointments and did not want to be bothered, contact with her was dropped; she rapidly lost interest in the child, visiting only rarely. Visits were disturbing to the child; therefore she was asked not to come at all if she could not come more often and stay longer. This, however, was the turning point. The boy became worse, withdrew into himself and finally refused to eat. The situation became so alarming that attempts were made to hospitalize him, but facilities were not available. As a last resort, reversing previous treatment plans, the mother was called in. She was given financial support, and arrangements were made for her to live near the institution, thus enabling her to take the boy home at night. During the day he stayed at the institution which then actually functioned as a day care facility. The mother was grateful for the help and accepted therapy for herself in connection with the everyday problems of the child, later on revealing more and more of her personal problems. Francis resumed eating as soon as he saw his mother. Continuing in therapy with a male therapist, he improved steadily. He stopped hallucinating and was able to go to school. The mother received supportive treatment in which she used her therapist, a woman, as a mother substitute.

In this case, it seemed the mother could function to a certain extent as a mother as long as she herself was taken care of by a mother substitute. It is significant that she could accept therapy only after she had received financial help. The child was unable to live without the mother. It could be argued that this assumption was incorrect and that, if a different course had been followed, the child might have overcome this critical point and accepted the situation. Yet, I think his improvement at this point indicates that the forced separation was more than he could tolerate, whereas being with his mother, however neglectful she may have been, had a therapeutic effect.

Only rarely do children express need for their parents in

this dramatic fashion. Generally, it seems to me that long-lasting separations between severely disturbed children and their parents tend to be permanent. Parents who do not see their children regularly cannot appreciate the change their children have undergone; they see no need for changing themselves or for seeking therapy. When the children are ready to leave the institution, either they are not welcome at home, or they return to find the same unsympathetic environment; thus they cannot maintain their gains. If his eventual return is planned, it is necessary to maintain the contact between parents and their psychotic child during the child's absence from home. One can do that the way the Boston Day Care Center does, by taking care of the children during the day and letting them go home at night, with mother and child in therapy. Or, if the child lives in an institution, the parents must be kept in contact with him, as is the practice at the Langley Porter Clinic in San Francisco. The contact can be varied as to frequency, place, and duration, according to therapeutic needs, but gradually it should be increased in order to prepare for a return to the home. Such contacts will provide the necessary incentive for the parents to accept therapy, which in turn may enable them to accept the child.

Working with psychotic children in their home is extremely difficult. It entails therapy of the parents, of course. But if there are other children besides the patient, the differences between the children make for constant disappointments and frustrations, and progress is constantly endangered by the repetition of old traumatic situations. Temporary removal from home may be necessary, either during the day or totally, while contacts with home are maintained.

In short, there cannot be any uniform or standard procedure in therapeutic work with children and their parents. The specific nature of the relationship between child and parents should, in each individual case, determine recommendations for the extent of contact to be maintained, and for the therapeutic method to be used with the parents. While the neurotic child, from the height of the oedipal phase on, may be able to sustain treatment by himself, all other disturbances need a higher degree of cooperation on the part of the parents. Separation of parents and children is at times unavoidable; however, only with simultaneous treatment of the parents will the child be able to resume living at home without the danger of regression to his previous difficulties.

INTERVIEWS WITH CHILDREN

So far, I have discussed the part which the parents play in treatment and have tried to show that it depends on the child's type of developmental disturbance, on his age, and on the parents' character structures and their emotional difficulties.

In discussing interview techniques, I shall start with some devices which Anna Freud (1926) has worked out for the child with a "classical neurosis" and then examine the modifications which become necessary with children who have other developmental difficulties. I shall discuss the following types: (1) childhood neurosis; (2) symptomatic disturbances in children under five; (3) behavior disorders in (a) children under five, and (b) children over five; (4) behavior disorders versus neurosis; (5) children unable to relate.

Childhood Neurosis

The child whose development allows for the procedure of child analysis usually can stay alone with the therapist after the introductions are over. In the first interview the reasons for treatment given by the parents are mentioned to the child and he is asked to tell us what he thinks about them: whether he agrees or not and whether he has other reasons which differ from those of his parents.

Ben, brought to me when he was nine years old, had been an alert, happy child, friendly and well behaved. Now he had no friends and did not know how to occupy himself. Over the last three or four years, according to his parents, he had been subject to spurts of malicious and vicious behavior, episodes which seemed to be recurring with ever-increasing frequency. After an outburst he would leave the house for about an hour. When Ben was five, his mother had a miscarriage. He had been told about the expected arrival of the new baby and had been rather disappointed when it failed to make an appearance. He now had a little two-year-old sister.

He came willingly to see me. When I asked him why he wanted to come, he said sadly, "I could not get any clothes yesterday." Those which mother and the saleslady wanted him to take were for "a kid seven years old!" and those for nine-year-olds were "much too big" for him. While we talked, we also played checkers, a game which he chose. He told me he liked to play; his little sister was too dumb, and nobody else had time. He did not play with the kids—they did not like him because "I have an ugly face." The game proceeded amiably and peacefully, though he soon became bored with it. After a few sessions he began to cheat; when I remarked on it, he accused me of cheating, hit me, kicked me, shouting that I was a cheater and that I hurt him and he would "throw [me] in the garbage can!" He ran out of the office, but after a few minutes he stuck his head in and said with tears in his eyes, "But next time I'll really leave and I'll never come back."

These first sessions offer considerable material. We can understand Ben's complaint of being small. He really is smaller than children his age, but he is in no way ugly, and we do not understand why he believes his "ugliness" to be the reason for his not having any friends. The cheating and the scene that followed it give us a sample of the kind of scene he makes at home, and we realize how unhappy he is.

When he shouted at me, I remained friendly but warded off his physical attack. After he returned, I told him I did not mean to hurt him and did not know how I had. I also added that I had to defend myself, because I did not like to be hurt; it made me angry and then I could not help him as well. I did not expect, nor ask for, his explanations but rather invited him to help me understand his behavior. We continued to play whenever he wanted. A positive relationship developed in these hours which found its expression in his coming punctually and trying to prolong the sessions. While he swore at me often enough he referred to me at home as "my friend Edith."

The repetition of scenes following the pattern of those enacted with his parents was a sign that a transference had developed. He behaved this way only at home or with me. His attack was a defensive move against an expected attack; he always accused me of attacking him, even when I had not budged. The threat, "I will throw you in the garbage can," was at the time a fashionable expression among children, but the affect with which he said it seemed to me disproportionate.

Much later in his treatment the meaning of his threat with the garbage can became understandable. One day Ben said, "My mother had a baby once. She was hit by a car and the baby died. But she got a lot of money for it." He referred to his mother's miscarriage, which had happened when he was five years old. He wondered what she had done with the baby, adding, "she probably threw it in the garbage can." We could understand now that he was afraid to be "thrown in the garbage can" himself if his parents did not like him. He regarded himself as "small and ugly" like a fetus, which he had seen in pictures. His ambivalent feelings toward the unborn baby as well as toward his little sister were thus threatening him.

When we talked about these matters, neither of us knew exactly how his mother happened to get money at the time of the miscarriage. Ben thought his mother did not care for her children if she could so easily be consoled by money. The fear that his mother valued possessions more highly than children was acted out repeatedly in vandalistic attacks upon her possessions or mine. Ben did not know what had happened to the fetus. At my suggestion he asked his mother about it. She told him that she had received money from the insurance company, because she had been hurt in the accident. She also told him that the hospital disposed of the fetus and that she was very sick and grieved by the loss of the baby. This information clarified things for Ben and greatly relieved his mind: his mother was not a bad mother; she loved her children!

Ben's behavior, which we had understood as defensive action against an unknown danger, changed markedly after he had been given the following interpretation: "You think that mother will be angry and throw you out as you thought she had done with the baby."

This fragment of a child analysis may serve as an example demonstrating the dynamics of therapy: I started with a statement of the child's disturbance in the words of the parents—which was followed by the child's complaint in his own words. What he presented could be understood, in the course of the analysis, as an essential part of his unconscious anxieties and fantasies. He was unhappy and wanted to change, conditions essential for analysis.

Games or other occupations, general conversation supplemented by candy or other food established a relationship between the child and the therapist which soon developed into a transference relationship.

I confronted the child with his repetitious and irrational behavior, and he learned to look at it objectively. When he had become able to do so, he often said, "It was the Gremlin —not me!" This expression showed that he regarded his behavior as strange, not belonging to him; it was like another person acting in him. The "Gremlin" was that "ugly, little boy" whom nobody liked, the fetus, whom he hated. He was in conflict with this part of himself, even when he apparently made use of it.

Three approaches were adopted in utilizing the material: (1) confrontation; (2) clarification (Bibring-Lehner, 1947), i.e., getting the facts straight as they are in reality; and (3) interpretation, i.e., explaining irrational behavior in terms of fantasies and past experiences. Transference interpretations were made in the same way; reality and fantasy with regard to the therapist were separated.

There were also some educational aspects to Ben's treatment. One was my attempt to protect myself from his attacks; the other was my encouraging the mother to do the same. She had not done so, thinking that Ben could not help himself. However, to allow such attacks was tantamount to inviting them.

Ben had an anxiety neurosis accompanied by some acting-out. He was, by age and development, in the latency period with defensive mechanisms well established. He developed a transference which at times strongly resembled that found in an adult neurosis and which made him amenable to the procedure of analysis with a minimum of active participation on the part of his (analyzed) parents.

Symptomatic Disturbances in Children Under Five

In treating younger children with symptomatic disturbances, I find it necessary to have the parents participate actively. In my example of the three-year-old boy with constipation, I have described how I had to explain things through the mother. The explanation was a clarification of his ideas on childbirth, namely, that children were not hedged in the intestines and were not born through the rectum. Clarification of misconceptions is one of the most important techniques with young children.

Peggy, four years old, was afraid of bees. It turned out that, to her, bees were "bugs" which she confused with "cold bugs." Having had some unfortunate experiences with illnesses which were called "colds" and for which she received "shots," she was afraid to get sick from the bugs, that is, bees. A bee had stung her mother; airplanes and motor boats hummed like bees—she was afraid of all these things. She had caught a cold in an airplane, and from there was taken to the hospital and consequently separated from her mother.

Peggy let me know about her fears through dramatic play into which pieces of conversation were woven. Whenever one or the other of these topics was mentioned, I asked the mother what the story behind it was, which the mother usually could supply. I could then talk about it with the child or the mother would; sometimes we both did.

Earlier in this paper, I mentioned that Peggy insisted that her mother participate in painting, which meant to her that mother should be there and let her know whether it was really all right to get herself dirty. When she had this assurance, she proceeded to show me that she masturbated. The mother was not in the room at the time. I had a talk with the mother alone about masturbation. After some hesitation she remembered that Peggy had stuffed sand into her vagina. The mother had scolded her about it and had washed her vigorously in the bathtub. Stuffing sand into her vagina had been preceded by a catheterization by the doctor in order to have a urine examination. Peggy had demonstrated this catheterization to me on many occasions in playing with the doll, but I did not understand because the doll was not correctly built anatomically. Fortified with this fresh information, I could now offer a clarification with regard to sex differences and also tell her that, although it was not good to stick things into her hole, it was all right to touch it. This explanation, and particularly the revocation of the previous punishing attitude about masturbation, had to come from the mother as well, in order not to confuse the child. This procedure is essential whenever a command or prohibition given by the parents needs to be revoked for therapeutic reasons; it must be taken back by the person who first pronounced and enforced it.

Sometimes, when one part of it is being restricted, the whole area of an activity is disturbed.[1] In the course of therapy it may be necessary to promote regressions and to revoke previous prohibitions. The purpose is to allow the child to return to a point which precedes the disturbance in order to be able to re-educate him. Our aim is to remove obstacles to emotional development by means of drive control, rather than inhibition.

Clarification, revocation, or modification of parental orders are technical devices of importance with young children. They can be effective when a misconception has to be corrected. We are dealing here with suppression rather than repression. With the help of the person who gave it, a command which has led to inhibition of an activity can be revoked as long as it has not been introjected into the personality but is dependent on outside threat.

Similarly, activities such as smearing during therapy sessions, which express aggression, should not be condoned without the active cooperation of parents, unless they are in parallel treatment and are prepared to go along with the child. Outright contradictions of the parents' orders, I think, cannot be used therapeutically without their knowledge and participation.

Many child therapists, following the English school of child analysis, use symbolic interpretation with the idea that translation of symbols is easy for children, particularly young ones, because they are "so close" to the unconscious. It is true that children will play with a stick and call it a penis or make mud pies and eat them, calling them by whatever their word for feces may be. Similarities in shape, color, or consistency lead to associations of this kind before repressions are fully effective. During our first session, four-year-

---

[1] See the case of the two-year-old boy who stuttered, in my paper on "Activity and Aggression in Children" (this volume, pp. 37-44).

old Allan picked from among the toys an alligator with a broken tail, brought it to me, and demanded that I fix it. His trouble was bed-wetting. It was easy to talk with him about his concern that something might be wrong with his penis—but we did not know what he thought was wrong or why he thought so. Symbols indicate the general direction of the material, but they do not help in finding out specific fantasies or experiences. Since repression in young children has either not yet taken place or is not very deep, the children do not show the resistance to talking about such topics that we find in older children or adults. Their readiness to talk directly about everything is mistaken for "knowledge" of symbols. Anna Freud (1936) says, "By translating symbols we may reveal the contents of the id without really gaining any deeper psychological understanding of the individual with whom we are dealing" (p. 17).

Children with Behavior Disorders

The counterpart to the treatment of children who are inhibited is the treatment of children who are uninhibited: preschool children with behavior disorders caused by faulty training or lack of training. In discussing the treatment of such cases, I mentioned that success depended essentially upon the parents. One may even wonder whether the term treatment is in order. Actually treatment in such cases consists of supplying a piece of education which normally should have been given by the parents. If it seems advisable that the child be seen by the therapist, a positive relationship is the basis upon which the child will be able to accept education: he will learn to exchange love and praise for restrictions and frustrations; having given up old satisfactions, the child will look for new ones and thus progress in his development. Lack of training, like inhibitions frequently results in general retardation of development. Children who are not bowel-trained but are kept in diapers longer than necessary may be equally retarded in speaking, eating, ability to dress, etc. As soon as this lack of training is remedied, development in other areas may follow.

The treatment of behavior disorders in older children is, as I mentioned before, a much more complicated matter. For one thing, the child does not feel any need for treatment; it is the suffering parents who want to get help. The first part of treatment then must be devoted to promoting motivation for treatment in the child, usually a rather complicated and time-consuming process.

When Mary, age ten, was brought for treatment, her mother was concerned about her truancy and stealing. Mary, who was willing to try treatment, was quite friendly during the first session. She tested me in various ways—investigating the room, the desk, taking cigarettes, stuffing herself with candy. When I asked her whether and why she wanted to come, she wrote down, "I don't like to live because I am not liked a bit and I make so much trouble. Mary." This looked like a good start but we were a long way from being able to use it. After the first session, Mary deployed her full arsenal of resistive devices. She came thirty to fifty-five minutes late; she cheated at play. When I told her that I noticed it, she accused me of cheating, swore at me, withdrew to the door and, watching me, slammed it shut and left. When she returned the next session as if nothing had happened, I asked her why she had run away. Did she think I would hit her or punish her, was she afraid of something like that; had it ever happened to her? After a silence she asked, "What would you expect a little girl two years old would do when she is very much afraid of a little dog that barked at her?" I said she might cry or run away. She scornfully said, "That's what you think! But I, because I was the little girl, I barked at him!"

Her statement was helpful in letting me know that she attacked when she was afraid. This type of behavior does not differ from that of a neurotic child—as a matter of fact, we found it in Ben.[2] When Mary felt guilty about something she had done e.g., when she had stolen or had gone to the movies instead of to school, she was afraid of being punished. Sometimes she told me herself, when I guessed right; sometimes I was informed by her mother, as for example when Mary had pilfered her mother's purse or when they had had a major fight. She really made a lot of trouble, but she did not want to change—except for one thing, which was her bed-wetting. She said, after a few weeks, "I wet my bed. Can you help me so I won't?" There was a sequence from her misdeeds to her attacking me, her mother and other people, to her bed-wetting. My first attempts to show her this connection did not work because to understand required too much effort. And Mary could not make a sustained effort or be patient. She had to be shown how to do things repeatedly. She was intelligent, but did no school work; whenever she thought she would be caught at not having done her lessons, she truanted. I offered to help her with her school work; I asked her to help me with it; I did it for her. Anyway, she had it done by hook or crook—went to school—and the bed was dry—to her amazement and my relief. Then there were Mary's white rats. Neglected, dirty, hungry, and sick, they smelled—just as Mary had once smelled. The mother, who was in analysis herself, gave Mary more of her time and attention and did more things for her —so did I. Eventually Mary began to take care of her rats, became anxious and concerned about them—and again the bed was dry for a few days. Every bit of progress she made appeared in reaction to some satisfaction she had obtained in other ways. She drove a hard bargain and never gave up any gratification before she knew what she would get for it.

The analysis of the neurotic parts of her behavior became possible in the second year of her treatment, after her delinquent behavior had largely subsided and when she had be-

[2] See this paper, under "Childhood Neurosis."

come genuinely concerned about her persistent temper tantrums and her inability to control her bladder. From then on, her treatment was more like the treatment of a neurosis. The problem of bed-wetting had made Mary amenable to treatment, while her other behavior disorders had not bothered her. But somehow it was possible to bargain with her. She had to give up her delinquent behavior if she wanted to keep her bed dry. One could say that, in the end, the bed-wetting saved her from delinquency.

Mary represented a type of behavior disorder first described by Aichhorn (1925). She was a neurotic delinquent. Her treatment required efforts in three directions which did not follow chronologically but were interwoven: (1) Motivation for treatment had to be induced. (2) She had to be helped to dissociate herself from her delinquent behavior, which she was unwilling to give up because it allowed her gratification without effort. She had to learn self-control, to work instead of cheating, to go to school instead of truanting, to dress and work instead of running around like a ragamuffin. This was done with much active participation on my part as well as on her mother's. These are what we may call ego-building devices. Gradually Mary substituted my values for her own, accepted my judgment over her own, and became more civilized. (3) Her neurotic symptom, namely the bed-wetting, had to be treated analytically.

The treatment of older children who have behavior disorders without neurotic symptoms or with little anxiety is extremely difficult. They do not suffer and therefore have no need for treatment. They have so far not become educated. Most probably this is a failure on the part of their parents, who may have been inconsistent or may have unconsciously favored their child's delinquent behavior. The child is used to easy satisfactions and is not willing to give them up. If we succeed in finding a chink in the armor and can make the child feel uneasy, guilty or anxious—that is, if we can find traces of hidden suffering, we can work with the child in individual therapy. Mary's desire to get over her bed wetting, for example, made her accessible to treatment.

Richard, age eight, illustrates delinquency without neurosis: he stole, truanted and set fires. After one year of unsuccessful treatment while he continued living at home, he was admitted to an institution. His behavior made it difficult for the house staff to abstain from manhandling him. When the adults did not fall in with his provocation, the children did. This gave Richard justification for treating them as he had been treated before; he hit them and hurt them as much as he could. Therapy consisted of repeatedly confronting him with his provocations of others and his punishing them. Somewhat later we observed that Richard, after having succeeded in being beaten by a boy, would attempt to engage this same boy in sex play. When his therapist confronted the child with this sequence of behavior, Richard recognized his need for help. Finally he revealed that when he used to misbehave, his father had spanked him with sadistic pleasure and ceremony and followed the procedure by petting him, loving him, and playing with his penis. Richard responded to the father's sadistic and seductive handling by repeating the delinquencies in order to get masochistic and sexual satisfactions. It became clear why treatment had not worked as long as the boy had remained in the parental home. He had no need to give up his delinquencies and the masochistic satisfactions which followed. But above all, he would not reveal what was going on between himself and his father as long as he was living with him.

The wish to change his behavior pattern was to a large degree brought about by the change of environment which removed previous masochistic and sexual gratifications, and substituted more acceptable ones. Richard began to like the people with whom he lived and wanted to be liked by them. When he did not feel accepted, first he blamed them for rejecting him, but later he began to realize and to admit that he himself, through provocative behavior, had made it difficult for the people in the new environment to like and accept him. This step in the direction of a more correct evaluation of reality forced the child to face his projecting, paranoid mechanisms, thereby strengthening his ego. Ego-building and strengthening devices are of paramount importance in all cases of behavior disorders (Buxbaum, 1950; Redl and Wineman, 1951, 1952). In the young child, educational measures set controls from without which eventually become introjected. In older children controls from without are useful only when they can be taken over almost simultaneously by the child himself. If mastery of a situation is required, the older child wants to do it for himself. He cannot tolerate domination from the outside. This is why such children usually respond better in groups than in a foster home; they can accept criticism from their peers more easily than from adults.

Children Unable to Form Stable Object Relationships

All children discussed so far were capable of forming object relationships, which we have postulated as indispensable for therapy or education. Some children have no difficulties in this area; others need time, patience, and gratifications of some sort in order to establish relationships. The *children who seem to be unable to establish a relationship with anybody* are the ones who puzzle and bewilder us. They are called autistic, psychotic, schizophrenic, atypical prepsychotic, or preschizophrenic, depending upon the terminology used by the diagnostician. What they have in common is their inability to form a genuine object relation and their retardation in ego development.

I have already discussed the necessity of putting these children into a total treatment situation which is environmental, whether they remain at home or whether they are institutionalized.

My own experience with such cases is limited to supervision of institutional personnel, i.e., house staff and therapists. The role of house staff who function as parent substitutes is of primary importance.[3] In supervising such cases I have found it to be most important that the person or persons working with the children be more than interested in them; they are then apt to detect even the smallest sign of response. If the child likes to be held, he should be held; if he shies away from physical contact, he should be allowed to keep his distance. If he likes to be fed, he should be fed by hand, from the plate of the mother or mother substitute, or with a bottle; if he just wants to eat, he should have food, but let it be provided by a person. Physical contact, everyday routines of washing, dressing, toileting, eating, constitute the chief means of establishing some sort of relationship. Taking care of a child during an illness sometimes offers an opportunity to make contact with a heretofore unapproachable child. Regressions to all levels will occur and have to be allowed in order to establish a relationship on whatever libidinal level the child may be. When a child so spoiled becomes dependent on a person—and usually it is just one person—then we have succeeded in establishing a relation-

---

[3] Since in this particular institution, Ryther Child Center, Seattle, Washington, social workers function within the institution, children who show any interest in "having a social worker" are assigned to one—actually the child chooses the worker. Often the children do so in order to have a period during which they can have an adult all to themselves without having to share him with other children. The worker is completely informed about everything that goes on in the child's life and can talk or not talk about it at his discretion. He is an extension of house staff. When he makes observations which enhance understanding, he shares them with the house staff so that they can be used. Interviews with therapists who know less than the house staff are useless, in my opinion; on the other hand, whatever one can learn about the child can be of value if all people concerned share the information. Interviews with the children in the institution are limited to a maximum of an hour a day. They are set up in a flexible manner. Sometimes children wander in and out a few times a day for a few minutes, just to make sure that the therapist is there. Or they stay during their allotted hour, anywhere from ten minutes to the full time. If the child does not want a therapist, he remains entirely in the hands of the house staff.

ship. From here on we can start to reeducate him, though not as quickly as other children can be educated. There will be many relapses when the educator will need to give in and retreat, allowing the child to revert to old habits. These children seem to be extremely sensitive and withdraw, become panicky, or have temper tantrums at the slightest provocation. It is essential to understand what causes these relapses and outbursts. They need to be explained to the child, clarified in terms of reality in both deeds and words. But deeds come first; only after security has been gained through deeds can words be added—later, perhaps words alone will suffice.

The effectiveness of such measures depends, in my opinion, on the age of the child. My own impression is that children under five can still be reached through therapeutic efforts of this kind. However, I am skeptical about their effectiveness with older children. I know that in this matter I am in disagreement with many therapists. I hope I am wrong.

In children who are unable to form relationships, as with young children generally, behavior disorders occur side by side with inabilities to function in other areas. Although it would seem from a theoretical point of view that first things should come first, and therefore a meaningful relationship should be established first, this is not so in practice. Emotional contact eventually leading to object relationship can sometimes be established through setting controls for uncontrolled behavior, at other times by undoing inhibitions. Clarification in order to correct false impressions can be used; interpretation of symbols may be effective if done in terms of actual experiences. Children of this sort offer a chaotic picture in their development; therefore therapy may appear chaotic too. In attempting to reach the child wherever he is—and that may mean at a great many different places at once—the therapist cannot proceed systematically but has to adjust constantly to the ever-changing situation.

SUMMARY AND CONCLUSIONS

I shall attempt to correlate the techniques described above with the stages of development as we know them. I hope to show why certain difficulties of the child require certain techniques in order to achieve the aim of therapy, namely, "restoration of function and initiation of the capacity for growth and maturation" (Sylvester, 1945a).

The infant is born helpless and entirely dependent on his environment. If he does not receive any care at all, he dies; if his needs are met only inadequately, he becomes sick. During the first three to four months the infant reacts to any disturbance with physiological reactions such as colic, vomiting, skin rashes, or eczema (Spitz, 1951). Perhaps crying, too, should be regarded to some extent as a physiological reaction.

The consequences of physical disturbances, neglect, and separations during infancy have been discussed in the papers on *Psychosexual Development* and in the *Problem of Separation and the Feeling of Identity*.

Children who have been sick a great deal during their first months, whether from organic causes or neglect, are apt to retain an inclination toward physical illness when they are emotionally upset. Children who have been changed from parents to one or more foster homes frequently suffer from persistent colds, running noses, earaches, sore throats, or upset stomachs. They are not necessarily severely sick, but they are hardly ever well. When they receive adequate care for a period of several years by the same person and remain in the same foster home, they may get well. They have learned by experience that people will take care of them when they get sick; therefore they use illness for self-protection. When care is given without illness, illness becomes superfluous.

Physical illness may later on also become the fixation point for hysterical symptomatology. According to Freud

(1923)," psychophysiology has fully discussed the manner in which the body attains its special position among other objects in the world of perception. Pain seems also to play a part in the process, and the way in which we gain new knowledge of our organs during painful illnesses is perhaps a prototype of the way by which in general we arrive at the idea of our own body" (p. 31). Knowledge of the body which is imposed upon the child in a painful and traumatic way leads to fixation, which, like other fixations, has a tendency toward repetition—in this case, repetition of illness.

Hoffer's (1950) studies show how the infant learns to know his own body. Spitz shows how the infant ventures into contact with his environment through the medium of the person who takes care of him. The two processes, recognition of his own body and attachment to a person, can be regarded as the beginning of ego development. When ego development is entirely lacking, we are faced with the picture of catatonic-like behavior and apathy, as described and shown in moving pictures by Spitz, or of marasmus, as described by Ribble (1943). Scratching, violent sucking of fingers to the point of deformity, and hair pulling are disturbances which respond favorably to intensified personal contact, suggesting that these symptoms are manifestations of the need for human contact.

Just as there are all gradations between good baby care and complete physical neglect leading to death, there are all degrees between "lacking human relationship" and satisfactory "mothering." A mother who is severely emotionally disturbed is unable to give her baby the kind of "mothering" he needs. Such children are not as disturbed as the ones described by Spitz, who are retarded in all their functions; they may be prominently disturbed in some functions, less in others. They too suck or masturbate continuously, sit quietly for hours, or move about continuously; frequently they either do not talk or talk with a queer voice, repeating words without sense. They hardly respond to their names or to any directions or demands. These children too have a propensity for illness.

During the second half of the first year the healthy baby becomes more and more active. He gradually learns to use his body until he finally learns to control it. Every kind of activity is necessary to develop his muscles and his muscular control (Buxbaum, 1947, 1949b). We can distinguish three different stages in the development of the child's activities: first, the experimental stage in which he discovers a new activity and tries it out; second, that of practicing, during which the child learns through innumerable repetitions; and third, the stage when the activity is at his disposal and he can call upon it when he needs it. The paper *Activity and Aggression* discusses these stages in detail.

During the process of learning, until the child has achieved control over his vital activities and his body, his relationship to people is of greatest importance, particularly at what stage in the development of a certain activity the interference from outside sets in.

It seems that activity in the experimental stage can be suppressed to such a degree that it is difficult to revive it. Interference in the practicing stage seems to bring out strong aggressive feelings. Children who are extremely aggressive and hyperactive are frequently children who have been severely physically restricted in this period; sometimes illness which confines their movements may have the same effect. The person who takes care of the child must interfere with his activity in some way all the time; he prevents, encourages, helps, punishes, praises, detracts and deflects the child's interests from undesirable to desirable activities, promotes and restrains in any number of ways. Sooner or later education interferes with all needs and impulses of the child. Very early in life the child learns to eat different things at certain times. Eventually modes of eating are introduced. Sleeping becomes regulated; sleeping habits become established. The child is taught to postpone the fulfillment of needs, whether he wants to have food or wants to urinate, wants to run, to have mother do something for him, or wants to hit another person.

Similar to interference with activities, interference with functions and impulses may bring about disturbance of functions and impulses. The child may react by giving up a function or by increasing the forbidden function. Children who are forbidden to touch dirt or to masturbate may not be able to hold things, or they may continue to masturbate excessively, play with feces and other forbidden objects. Children who were punished for soiling may become constipated or insist upon defecating only into their diapers or on the floor. Food may become an issue between mother and child. Forbidden aggression may result in the child's complete helplessness toward other children or in fierce and continual fighting. If speech is disturbed during the early learning period, stuttering may result. Conflicts with the interfering person are unavoidable, although they may vary in degree. Disturbances of functions and impulses in this period are necessarily connected with disturbances of relationship with the interfering person, that is, the educator.

When a child is disturbed in his functions as a result of educational interference, whether he reacts with hyperfunctioning or hypofunctioning, therapy needs to be directed toward reinstatement of normal functions. If educational efforts were at fault, educational efforts must be dropped and the child must be allowed to regress to an uneducated state. If our conclusion is correct, the normal function will be resumed at such a point. When it is sufficiently secure again, re-education may set in. The educator must be part of this program, because the child becomes confused if educator and therapist disagree. The mother must uphold the therapist, repeat what he does and says, or perhaps execute the therapy herself. The therapist cannot work with the child against the mother.

Children who through education are disturbed in their

functions are always unbalanced with regard to their aggressions. They may be overly aggressive or inhibited. Their therapy will necessarily also affect their aggressions. Aggressive feelings are aroused when activity is inhibited; release of aggression may have as a by-product an ability to function. Increased ability to function, although connected with aggression, may then result in the diminishing of aggression to a normal degree.

If the disturbances are quite severe—as in long-lasting inability to eat, sleep, defecate—and the mother is unable to cooperate, the child may have to be removed from her in order to allow for more favorable conditions for therapy.

The dangers in producing disturbances of functions through too many or premature educational demands must be weighed against the dangers of too few and delayed educational demands—the eternal Scylla and Charybdis of education.

The child must learn to control his impulses and to postpone fulfillment of his wishes. In order to be able to do so, he must develop a degree of tolerance to anxiety and frustration. These are the conditions necessary for achieving mastery of functions and the ability to learn. The parents have a decisive role in helping their children to achieve these goals, as I have shown in the paper on *The Parents' Role in the Etiology of Learning Disturbances*. Therapy of the parents alone or in conjunction with the child may be necessary in order to bring this about. Lack of education which results in "primary behavior disorder" before the oedipal period cannot be treated only therapeutically but must also be treated educationally.

One part of a child's learning is directed toward achieving control over his own body; another part, toward achieving mastery of the world around him. Both can be learned by imitating people in his environment. It is most successfully achieved as a result of friendly relationship; learning is best done in the "conflict-free sphere" (Hartmann, 1939).

Imitation is, however, in many instances closely related to mastery, as in actively repeating passive experiences, whether they are pleasant or unpleasant; e.g., being fed is turned into feeding somebody else, but also being spanked is turned into spanking somebody else.

The child starts imitating very early in life—e.g. in the "smiling response" (Spitz and Wolf, 1946), and continues to do so throughout his life to some degree. He may learn to do things, he may also acquire habits and behavior; some of these imitations are changing and temporary, others become integrated into the permanent identifications and become part of the child's character.

Traumatic experiences bring forth compulsive repetition in an attempt to master them. This is not promoting learning but disturbing it, by fixating interest so that further development is blocked. Young children are often more easily frightened than older children because they are unable to act in an unpleasant situation and feel helpless; sometimes they are not afraid because they do not comprehend the danger. They are more likely to misunderstand what they see or hear. In order to remove an impediment caused by trauma, direct therapy with the child is necessary. Understanding what the child is compulsively repeating, either in everyday activities and behavior, or in dramatic play, will be the basis upon which clarification and reassurance can be given.

This technique is, however, not specific for any age group: its use is indicated whenever traumatic experiences are the cause for disturbance. What varies is the way in which the patient communicates his experience to the therapist; children usually communicate more through play than through language.

As long as functioning, activities, and behavior are predominantly controlled from the outside, i.e., by parents or parent substitutes, changes are dependent on them. Parental approval, disapproval, and example, have direct bearing upon the child; parental cooperation is indispensable in the therapy with young children.

The oedipal phase is based upon the child's previous development. The infant who is disturbed is also disturbed in his masturbatory activities: he may not masturbate at all or do so excessively. Parents may interfere with this activity as they do with all others, and consequently may disturb the young child's relation to his body in the particular area of his genitals. Cleanliness education, particularly with all its taboos, is carried over by parents, and therefore also by the child, into the genital area. Fears of body injuries become concentrated upon the genitals and contain in condensed form various previous experiences. As in all other functions and activities, the relationship with parents or parent substitutes is of prime importance in the development of genital feelings and activities, which reach their climax in oedipal fantasies.

With the oedipal phase and the development of the superego, what was previously imitated will now become internalized; i.e., it will become a permanent constituent—what we call identifications. Defenses are being built against the dangers threatening from within. Anna Freud (1936) distinguishes three dangers against which the child has to defend himself. Each of them can be the cause for disturbance. They are dangers threatening from the outside world, from the superego, and from the strength of the instincts.

The more independently of environment the child functions, acts and behaves, the more his treatment resembles that of an adult, in which the therapist is chiefly concerned with conflicts from within. The less threatening the parents are in reality, the less the therapist needs to work with them directly; their help becomes of secondary importance in the treatment of the child's neurosis.

The dividing line in therapy is the oedipal phase, regardless of age. With children who did not reach the oedipal phase, techniques used with younger children must be employed with modifications. In attempting to present different phases of development one always is reminded that development is fluctuating, that there are no sharp distinctions. Old forms conitnue into and mix with new ones. Development does not proceed to the same extent in all areas. When a child is disturbed in one area, he may still progress in others. The disturbances in one area, however, can block progress in other areas as well. If this is the case, it is to be considered pathological or at least pathogenic (A. Freud, 1946a). When there is no progress, it is rarely true that there is just a standstill. In most cases there is not only a partial regression to previous levels of satisfaction but also a loss of already attained functions.

The strategy of therapy consists of first finding the weak spot and then giving help where help is most needed. By and large there are four main areas of disturbance in development: (1) in physiological reactions, (2) in object relations, (3) in functioning (body control and activities), (4) in (too strong or too weak) ego defenses. The principal variations in technique of therapy are contingent upon the presence or absence of one or the other of these factors.

PSYCHOTHERAPY AND PSYCHOANALYSIS IN THE TREATMENT OF CHILDREN

There are people who "believe in" psychotherapy, but not in psychoanalysis, and vice versa. When asked about the difference, they will say either that they do not believe in diving into and ploughing up the unconscious, or that unless you uncover the unconscious, nothing can be done. We should like to explain that it is not a matter of believing or not believing in one thing or the other, because neither psychotherapy nor psychoanalysis are religions. They are techniques based upon knowledge and experience. The choice of the method which should be employed in the individual case should be made only by the expert, just as the therapy in an organic case can be prescribed efficiently only by the physician. A great number of people erroneously consider themselves able to judge which psychological method is appropriate to a particular case. If they happen to choose the wrong one, the results can be disastrous.

The physician who is consulted on a case will examine the patient, determine the cause of the illness, and will then prescribe the treatment. If his diagnosis and the prescribed

This paper was published originally in *The Nervous Child*, 5:115-126, 1946.

treatment are correct, the patient's condition will show improvement. Without discovering the cause of the disturbance, he will not be able to prescribe the effective therapy. The procedure in cases of psychological disturbance must be based upon a similar premise. It is necessary to discover the cause of the disturbance in order to deal with it. In this respect, both psychotherapy and psychoanalysis have the same aim. The difference is in technique.

Freud discovered the importance of childhood as a determinant of adult neurosis. He has proved that the psychoneurosis of the adult is based upon the psychoneurosis of the child. All children go through periods during which they are anxious, whining, aggressive, stubborn, withdrawn, or show any one of the numerous manifestations of unhappiness or so-called naughtiness. We consider these phases just as natural for a child as an occasional cold, sore throat or other minor illness.

When minor physical illnesses recur with increasing frequency, parents will wonder whether a more serious condition is responsible and they will consult a pediatrician. Parents are not always equally cautious when they are faced with recurrent behavior problems or undesirable habits in their children. They attack the habit, using praise, rewards, threats, or punishment, rather than seek out its cause. This approach is natural enough but has one drawback. Sometimes the method appears to work—i.e., the immediate manifestations of disturbance disappear. When the disturbance has its origin in a traumatic experience, however, such methods will be to no avail. Unless the traumatic experience is resolved, it will have a permanent effect on the child's emotional development.

Traumatically determined behavior disorders are peculiar in that they may or may not manifest themselves immediately. The longer the incubation period, the more difficult it will be to discover the connection between the two. Moreover, because the disturbance disappears does not mean it has ceased to exist. It will reappear, sooner or later, perhaps in another guise. Its change of form adds to the difficulty of discovering its true significance.

Finally, the longer the parents delay in seeking help, the harder it will be for the therapist to effect a cure. Passage of time not only clouds the connection between traumatic experience and behavior disorder, it permits the disorder to grow, to spread throughout other areas and to impair emotional development.

Anna Freud (1945) has attempted to find indications for the therapeutic use of child analysis "not so much in the neurotic manifestations themselves, as in the bearing of these manifestations on the maturation process within the individual child" (p. 92). She admits, however, that "we are only slowly learning to distinguish the various characteristics that mark a neurotic disturbance as either transitory or as permanent" (p. 93). Clinically then, the degree and extent of emotional damage will determine the form of therapy most appropriate to the case.

Analysis is the instrument we use only when we see that the child's future development is in danger or that his emotional development is already impaired. Psychotherapy is indicated in cases of recent disturbances which temporarily impair further normal development. It aims to prevent transitory symptoms from becoming permanent by engaging the understanding and cooperation of the parents and by helping the child himself to regain control over his actions and reestablish his relations with reality.

I have chosen to demonstrate the differences in technique by presenting a series of cases which show varying reactions to one traumatic experience—the birth of a younger sibling.

CASE 1

Paul's mother consulted me in order to find out how to handle her three-year-old boy's jealousy toward his baby brother. She reported that Paul had looked forward to the baby's arrival, for which he had been prepared. Judging from Paul's friendly relationships with other children, his parents assumed that he was expecting a playmate. Although they warned him that the baby would not be able to play with him at first because it would be too small, he obviously could not absorb this idea. On seeing the baby he first appeared disappointed, then uninterested. The lack of interest changed to anger when he saw his mother taking care of the baby. He tried to hit the baby when his mother held him on her lap, and threw things into his crib, including a pair of scissors which he knew was dangerous. Finally, Paul suggested to his mother, "Let's send him back to the hospital. We don't want him here any more."

I explained to the mother that Paul's reactions were an expression of his jealousy and perfectly normal inasmuch as, up to the time of the baby's arrival, he had received her undivided attention. I advised her to explain to Paul in words as well as in actions, that he need not worry about losing her attention and love; however, she must also tell him that the baby was here to stay and that he must not hurt him. The knowledge that mother would not allow him to hurt the baby contributed to Paul's own feeling of security. Had she allowed him to hurt the baby, he would have doubted whether she would protect him from being hurt. Paul gradually learned to control his jealousy, and it diminished in intensity. His mother's understanding made it possible for him to express his feelings without incurring her hostility and anger. Gradually, through identification with her, he learned to accept the baby. It will depend, of course, on the future handling of the relationship whether, Paul will be able to continue to accept his rival, as further causes for jealousy arise.

CASE 2

The following case represents a somewhat more complicated situation. It was, however, as the previous one, handled through consultation with the mother.

Margaret was three years old when her little brother was born. Her reaction to his arrival was similar to Paul's, disappointment, anger, and jealousy. One day when she saw him being changed, he urinated and made quite a spray. She watched with big eyes and squealed, "Look what he is doing!" A few nights later the little girl, who had been dry at night for several months, wet the bed and continued to do so for several nights.

Margaret had to deal with one more problem than Paul did: she was a girl, and the baby was a boy. She recognized the difference in anatomy; it seemed to her that the boy had a toy in his penis which one could use to have some fun with. She wanted to have that toy, just as she sometimes wanted to have toys belonging to children in the park. Sometimes her mother or father gave her something similar to a toy seen in the park if she seemed to want it very badly. This was different. She felt dimly that she could not get this toy, could not even ask for it. Only in her fantasies and dreams could she imagine being that baby brother herself and urinating just as he did.

Margaret's way out of her dilemma was to identify with the baby brother. This, too, is a very common reaction to the birth of a baby sibling. Yet it was slightly more difficult to help the child overcome her reaction. She not only needed just as much reassurance as Paul did, but also some understanding of her special problem. Margaret's mother saw the connection between the bed-wetting and Margaret's observation and ensuing envy and was able to help her get over it. Had she not, the bed-wetting might have persisted until it became a serious problem.

In both these cases the children reacted strongly to the

arrival of a sibling. Paul showed openly aggressive behavior; Margaret even developed a symptom. Yet both children surmounted their difficulties easily with the help of their mothers who were aware of the connection between cause and effect.

CASE 3

Joan was six years old, well-behaved and intelligent. She had a brother two years younger. Her parents came to see me because she stammered slightly. At the age of five, she had a tonsillectomy which was, according to the parents, a frightening experience for her. The child, who always had been a fussy eater, refused to take any food after the operation. The nurse apparently became frantic about this after a few days and took the child on her lap, held her arms, and forced the food down her throat. From then on, Joan ate better. She also gave up sucking her thumb. By the time Joan started school, the nurse had left. Joan's slight stammering attracted the attention of the teacher who, in turn, drew the parents' attention to it. In the conversation with me they also mentioned that Joan slept very lightly, getting up several times during the night to go to the bathroom.

When Joan came to see me she was told that I would help her to get over her stammering, about which she was very self-conscious. During the first session she chose to draw pictures. One of them was of a bird in a cage, the next one was a cage without the bird. I asked where the bird was. She answered, "He is gone, he flew away!" Did he come back? "No, maybe he fell down and was dead." Did you have a bird? "Yes, but he didn't fly away, he just died.—I have a brother, do you know that?"

It was not difficult to guess that she wished her brother would fly away or die—or somehow disappear. I responded by saying, "I know; your parents told me. I suppose he is quite a nuisance sometimes." My suggestion opened a flood of complaints which continued for several sessions. Some of her complaints were the usual ones children of her age and situation express: her brother teased her, he took things away from her; he was very naughty, but if she wanted to punish him she was not allowed to because he was "younger." If she was naughty, she was punished because she was "old enough" and also because "girls are not supposed to be naughty." When he whistled, that was all right. When she whistled, people said, "it is not nice for a girl to whistle." Before she had her tonsils out, she whistled all the time. Now she did not whistle anymore. I wondered why. Did she ever hear that little verse: "Whistling girls and crowing hens . . . ?" She laughed and said she had. I wondered whether she thought they took her tonsils out because she whistled. She looked at me, a little puzzled, and thoughtfully put her thumb in her mouth. I added, maybe she thought it was because she sucked her thumb. Self-consciously, she took her thumb out of her mouth. I assured her she could whistle as much as she liked and she could be naughty if she wanted to; it was quite all right. If she wished, she could suck her thumb, too. Did she want me to tell this to her parents? She did.

I was glad to get her permission to speak with her parents, because I wanted to insure their cooperation and understanding. It was important that they allow these "bad habits" because Joan felt that her parents were responsible for her strong feeling that her habits were bad. We—the parents and I—had to work in harmony or else the child would be torn by conflict.

Since Joan felt her brother was preferred because he, being a boy, was subject to fewer restrictions than she, I intended to show her that she could have the same privileges and that there were many areas in which she could compete with him successfully. It turned out that many of Joan's complaints were justified. There was a marked difference in the parents' treatment of the two children. The boy had many behavior difficulties for which the parents made allowances. They constantly pointed out to Joan that brother was a boy and therefore did all those naughty things, but that she was their "own sweet little girl who never gave them any trouble." It was obvious that if Joan wanted to be loved she had to repress all naughtiness, resentment, and aggression.

The parents told Joan, at my request, that she could suck her thumb and whistle as much as she pleased; that they would love her even if she was naughty. Joan was somewhat doubtful and reminded them that they had warned her not to suck her thumb. The parents assured her that they did not know she would miss it so much and that they really didn't mind. The parents also were advised to treat the children more equably. This resulted in greater restriction for the brother and greater tolerance for Joan.

During the following weeks Joan sucked her thumb a great deal; she also fell back into her old eating habits. She whistled tentatively in order to see what or whether anything would happen. She became self-assertive and stood up to her brother—and she stopped stammering.

Joan resumed the "bad habits" in which she had indulged before the tonsillectomy; she wanted to find out whether it was true that she would not be punished for them as her parents and I had promised. After a short while, she stopped sucking her thumb, did not whistle as much, ate well, but continued to be rather aggressive and to assert herself against her brother. Her relationship with other children improved; she became a favorite with them. Everything seemed to be going well, except for her sleeping, which was worse. The parents reported that she apparently kept herself from sleeping by going to the bathroom every ten to fifteen minutes. As a result, she was so tired the next day that she could not attend school. She stayed home, slept part of the morning, then stayed in bed masturbating for a long time. It seemed that this new symptom held two components—one of them pleasurable, the other painful. It was pleasant to stay at home and be spoiled and taken care of, especially pleasant because her brother was in nursery school; it was unpleasant not to be able to sleep. However, as long as the two components balanced each other, it was not to be expected that Joan would be willing to give up her symptoms.

I asked her parents either to send Joan to school, or if they kept her at home, not to make it too pleasant for her. The pleasure of being sick had to be curtailed. The result of this rather unsympathetic treatment was that Joan complained to me about not being able to sleep because she had to go to the bathroom so often. I pointed out to her that she did not have to go so often during the day—what made her go so much at night? She thought that otherwise she would wet the bed. I did not see why she should; but if she did she need not worry about it. She then said that her brother had wet his bed for a long time; that it still happened frequently, and that she thought it was dirty and smelled bad. We discussed her not wanting to be as dirty and naughty as he was —but she said, wistfully, that she wished she could wear pants all the time.

Shortly afterward, Joan got up, one night, half-asleep and urinated on the floor, standing up in front of her bed. Then she woke up completely and called her mother. She was very upset, but her mother comforted her, changed her, and Joan went to sleep again. The following day I discussed the incident with her and wondered whether she had thought that she was a boy who could urinate standing up. She confirmed this by telling me that she had often tried to urinate standing up in the bathroom. Joan was jealous of her brother because he was allowed to do all kinds of things she was not supposed to do and among these, it seemed, was urinating while standing up. She wanted to know why he had a penis, and why she didn't.

I explained the sex difference to her, assuring her that all girls looked as she did, and all boys looked like her brother.

She heaved a big sigh and said, "I am glad you told me." I wondered whether she had thought otherwise. Did she think it had something to do with the operation? The reason for my asking this question was that we already knew that Joan considered the operation a punishment for bad behavior. She did not answer immediately, but after a while said, "When I was at the hospital and did not go to the bathroom, the nurse put something in me which made me go." The mother confirmed that Joan had not urinated for a long time after the tonsillectomy and had to be catheterized.

Now we understood that Joan thought that during the anesthesia, while she did not know what was going on, somebody had removed her penis. Therefore, she imagined herself unable to urinate. In her fantasy, this was the punishment for masturbating, while the removal of the tonsils was the punishment for sucking her thumb. I asked her whether she thought that the doctors did something "there" because she had touched it. She confirmed this by saying, "I never do, my nurse said I'd get sick." Again I had to get the mother's cooperation so that she would confirm my assurance that all little girls did "that," they did not get sick from it, and it was not naughty. She reacted as she had to the explanation that she could suck her thumb and whistle—by testing. She masturbated in an exhibitionistic way for a few days. This was interpreted as another attempt to compete with her brother who masturbated openly a great deal. In this way, her competition with him was brought into consciousness. Her sleep was no longer disturbed; she no longer had to get up at night. It was just a matter of education to tell her that it was not a good idea to masturbate in public, but that she could do it when she was alone. If she wanted to, she could wear pants—many girls did—but of course they were not as pretty as girls' dresses. It was pointed out to her that her parents did not approve of her brother's misbehavior; that there were many things that he could learn from her. Joan, who was an intelligent, creative child, found an acceptable and satisfying outlet for her exhibitionism in school, where she had plenty of opportunity to excel, not only in writing and playacting, but also in bossing the children around playfully, which they accepted with good grace.

Joan's neurotic symptom, the stammering, was brought about by the tonsillectomy in connection with the punishing attitude of her nurse. One of her mouth activities, speech, was disturbed, because something, namely the tonsils, were cut out as a punishment for all the naughty things that she had done with her mouth as well, as a punishment for all the bad things that she wanted to say, especially about her brother and about her parents' partiality for him. It was her ability to express her aggression in words, which largely brought about the cure of the stammering. The stammering had made the parents apprehensive about Joan's disturbance, while the sleeplessness had gone unobserved, although it was just as important and more harmful to the child's well-being. The latter was another expression of her suppressed jealousy towards her brother, and, at the same time, an expression of her conflict with regard to her wish to be a boy.

Joan's strong oral fixation was evidenced by her thumb-sucking, whistling, poor eating. After the "punishment" in the form of an operation (castration) the old symptoms disappeared and were replaced by stammering, another disturbance in the oral sphere. Chronologically, the disturbances in the oral sphere were the oldest. Later, sleeplessness was added which, as the analysis shows, was based upon the same conflict—i.e., her rivalry toward her brother—but centered on the genital region.

Looking back on Joan's first interview, we can see that her problem was clearly defined in the two drawings she made. She drew one cage with a bird in it, another without it. The identification between the brother and the bird was directly apparent through her association bird-brother. We understood her hostility toward him, and her death wishes. At the same time, the bird as a sex-symbol indicated that her own sex organ had disappeared like the bird. It was her punishment for wishing her brother dead and for masturbating. It would not have helped Joan, had we attempted to interpret this to her at that point. We had to wait until she herself was ready to explain her ideas, not in the symbolic language of the unconscious, but in the conscious language of her experiences. Because the traumatic experience was not very far removed in time, it was possible to uncover it comparatively quickly. Her symptom dissolved and her normal behavior was restored. The treatment took about five months; that is, about sixty sessions. The experiences which had led to Joan's neurosis were near enough to consciousness to enable her to express them in words with only a little help.

Joan's disturbance was essentially the same as Peggy's. She was jealous of her younger brother and wanted to be a boy. The tonsillectomy had the effect of repressing all her aggression, especially toward her brother; as a result, stammering developed and her sleeping disturbance increased. The therapy consisted of making her aggression conscious, of changing her environment in such a way that her jealousy toward her brother was less justified in reality, and of allowing her to express her aggression in words and action.

CASE 4

The case of Ben, cited in the preceding paper (p. 111) differs from the others presented here in that his neurosis was expressed in his aggressive behavior rather than in temporary symptoms. The traumatic cause was deeply repressed. During his analysis, he developed the same reactions toward me as he had at home. He transferred his feelings toward his mother to me. It was necessary to allow him to do so without threat of punishment but, at the same time, it was necessary to restrain him to some extent, lest his guilt feelings and fear mount too high and make it impossible to feel at ease with me. Although my friendly attitude was essential to the treatment, it was effective only in conjunction with the ensuing understanding which I conveyed to him to the fullest extent.

The parents' attitude was affectionate and understanding. I advised them to restrain his aggressions more firmly in order to prevent further accumulation of guilt feelings. The more restrictive attitude at home forced his reactions out into the open in the permissive atmosphere of the analytic hour, where they could be studied and understood objectively.

We have described the reactions of four children to the birth of a sibling and the treatment offered each. The reactions vary from normal behavior (Paul), to temporary neurotic symptoms (Margaret), to neurotic symptom (Joan) to neurotic behavior (Ben).

Although we call Paul's reaction normal, it was necessary for his mother to understand it as such. Only then was she able to accept his hostility toward the baby and at the same time protect the baby from him. Had she not handled the situation wisely, Paul might have developed a neurosis.

Margaret's temporary enuresis nocturna was an expression of her envious identification with her baby brother. Her reaction was more complicated than Paul's, but not dangerous because it was recognized and treated promptly. Had it been ignored or treated repressively it might well have become a neurosis. Both Margaret's and Paul's situations could be handled with a comparatively small amount of guidance work with the mother.

Joan's disturbance went further and was of longer standing. Her normal functions—speech and sleep—were affected. Although it took some time to help her to reveal and recognize the cause, it was near enough to consciousness for her to be able to express it in words.

Such, however, was not the case with Ben. His relations

with people were disturbed, but for a long time neither he nor anybody else knew why. The disturbing trauma was repressed so that he had no way to express his feelings except in actions. It was the task of therapy to help him put his feelings into words and gradually trace them back to their origin.

Joan's disturbance cannot be treated by guidance work only, though it is an important part of the therapy. She herself must show us the connections between cause and effect which she has made in her imagination, misunderstanding the operation as punishment for forbidden actions and thoughts. The way to help her is essentially the same as that used in helping Ben, through analysis. We must understand what has happened in the child's mind, must restore the memory of what happened in reality and remove the distortions and terrifying fantasies. Sometimes the way to this understanding is a long one; sometimes we are able to understand and to make the child understand in a short time.

Whether we use psychotherapy or analysis, we shall not have accomplished our objective unless the source and the mechanisms of the disturbance are brought to the child's consciousness and his normal functions are restored.

II. Clinical Case Illustrations

EXHIBITIONISTIC ONANISM IN A TEN-YEAR-OLD BOY

Poldi came to me at the age of ten—a well-proportioned boy, large and very strong for his age, with no evidence of glandular disturbance or other physical abnormality—but his face was frequently distorted by tic-like, twitching movements: blinking, wrinkling of the nose and jerking of the mouth. In moments of excitement his facial movements increased, grew more exaggerated and he would hop from one foot to the other, at the same time opening and closing his hands convulsively and bringing his arms together, first in front and then in back. Since this condition could be induced by the least excitement, Poldi was in almost constant motor agitation.

Added to this extraordinary condition were other symptoms which had caused Poldi's parents to seek medical assistance. He was tormented by constant anxiety which made it impossible for him to be alone, even for a short time. Moreover, he was unable to keep himself occupied, either when he was by himself or with anyone else. He masturbated excessively in an exhibitionistic manner and for this reason had already been excluded from kindergarten and school.

He was especially clumsy with his hands and his vocabu-

This paper was published originally in *The Psychoanalytic Quarterly*, 4:161-189, 1935.

lary and manner of expressing himself by no means corresponded to his age level. Arithmetic was particularly difficult for him; he could add and subtract only with the help of
his fingers and even then he made mistakes; simple multipli-
cation tables which he could memorize came more easily,
but it was impossible for him to solve any written problem.

Poldi was subjected to a thorough physical and neurologi-
cal examination. No organic basis for his illness was found,
although this possibility was not excluded. The report of the
Children's Hospital after a six-week period of observation
when Poldi was six years old, did not exclude the possibility
of a cerebral defect. The results of another private examination, combined with the Rorschach Test, given at the age
of twelve while Poldi was in analysis, pointed to an earlier
encephalitis. This seemed to be confirmed by the mother's
statement that Poldi's convulsive movements began when
he was two, immediately after a febrile illness of unknown
origin which had lasted several days.

In spite of the suspicion that the symptoms might be determined by a combination of psychological and organic
factors, I undertook an analysis and reported it in Anna
Freud's Seminar on the Technique of Child Analysis. It was
worth seeing whether Poldi's symptoms were accessible to
psychological influence, and, if so, to what extent; for if his
anxiety was neurotic, or at least augmented by neurosis, it
might be diminished or dispelled by analysis, and if there
was a connection between his anxiety and his motor agitation, the latter might also be influenced by the treatment.
Another question to be considered was whether his over-
whelming anxiety inhibited him to such an extent that his
intelligence appeared even more limited than it really was.
Though the prospect of finding psychic determinants for his
convulsive movements was very tempting, I had little hope
of succeeding. The treatment outcome justified this negative
expectation.

In Poldi's case it was impossible to use the customary methods of child analysis for a child of his age, because of his limited intelligence and the great secondary gain obtained from his illness.

The first task in analysis is to give the patient insight into his illness, if this is absent at the beginning of treatment. He must understand that the disadvantages arising from his illness are greater than the advantages it affords him in relation to his environment. With the help of this insight it is possible to ask him to cooperate in the work of removing the unconscious resistances which cling to the primary gain, the substitute satisfaction implicit in the symptom. Appeals are made to his reason, to his wish to become a healthy and happy person, to his ego. Even in adult analysis, it is necessary to repeatedly call upon and strengthen the patient's insight or will to cooperate since it disappears partially or entirely when resistance is strong. In child analysis the therapeutic alliance is much more difficult to achieve and to maintain. The child who comes for treatment of his own accord is the exception; he is usually tricked or forced into coming. Consciously, he suffers much less from his illness than does his environment. A more or less lengthy period of preparation is necessary to enable a child to gain insight into his illness, and this does not necessarily occur simultaneously with his wish for recovery.[1] Only when the child calls upon us to help free him from his anxieties, his foolishness, naughtiness, or whatever he may call his sickness, is he ready to be analyzed with the technique of adult analysis. He then begins to substitute verbal communication for acting out. (This development has its parallel in adult analysis: with each new phase the adult patient must be made aware of his typical actions both outside of the analysis and within the analytic hour, so that he may regard his own behavior objectively and be ready to analyze it.) These phases of active cooperation are interrupted by phases of resistance in which

[1] Cf. Anna Freud's (1926) "Introduction to the Technique of the Analysis of Children."

the child returns to his earlier forms of communication, play, and action. However, once the wish for recovery and the desire to cooperate have been mobilized, it is relatively easy to evoke them again; their disappearance is simply one of the many forms of resistance.

Poldi's moments of insight came very seldom. Appeals to his limited intelligence would be futile. The secondary gain from his illness was so great that he did not want to surrender it. He used his illness to force his mother to remain with him and to ensure her continued care, for he wanted to remain a child and was willing to renounce everything if only she would continue to look after him. He was afraid of being forsaken by his mother and left alone to starve. Moreover, his illness served as a protection against the demands of school where he was regarded as ill and treated accordingly. Protected by his mother, he could indulge his pleasurable fantasies which he, like any patient, was reluctant to exchange for a generally unpleasant reality.

Poldi did not talk, he only wanted to play. His play and actions during the hour were the material which had to be used. Correct interpretations usually elicited aggression with concomitant changes in play and modes of activity.

Poldi's analysis contained all the difficulties usually encountered in child analysis but to a greater degree. This quantitative factor necessitated a change in technique, which on closer inspection also proved to be only quantitative. The number of interpretations had to be increased, and often were not based on facts and memories, but were more or less educated guesses. An attempt was made to interpret first the material which seemed closest to consciousness, and to proceed from the surface to the depths of the unconscious.

Poldi's mother—because her occupation before marriage had brought her into contact with the educated middle class —aspired to marry into and be accepted by this class. She married a blue collar worker however, and never freed herself from the thought that she had married beneath her. She developed a strong sexual aversion to her husband; on frequent occasions he forced her to have intercourse with him. Poldi slept in his parents' bedroom and was therefore witness to these scenes.

The mother placed all her hopes in her only child: he was to compensate for her unhappy life and unsatisfactory marriage. As long as Poldi was small and a normal, healthy baby, everything went smoothly enough, but when he became ill her disappointment began to grow. Due to her own aversion to sex, she was especially intolerant of his excessive and unconcealed masturbation. I asked if she had ever threatened Poldi with cutting off his penis or something of the kind. As parents usually do, she said she hadn't. However, on one occasion, she declared with much affect, "You know, doctor, sometimes when I see him doing it I would like to cut everything off!" It is certain that she had threatened the child with castration more than once. The father stated that she had often beaten Poldi furiously because of his restless activity, which she could hardly endure. Perhaps his restlessness irritated her because she realized unconsciously that it was a masturbatory equivalent.

Outside circumstances hindered the father in his struggle for advancement. His wife's reproaches for earning so little and never getting anywhere only intensified his sense of defeat. He, too, had hoped that his son would reach the goal he himself had been unable to attain, and therefore could not forgive the child for his limited intelligence and poor scholastic record. He studied with his son, which was torture for both of them; and according to the mother, he often beat Poldi for his stupidity. Each parent would only admit the other beat the child, and each accused the other of "whipping him silly." They both reported that on a teacher's advice the beatings had been stopped, except "now and then." Poldi's neurotic fears were also a source of the deepest narcissistic mortification to his father, who was ashamed of having such a cowardly, unmanly son. The father's harsh brutality succeeded in making Poldi so afraid that he hid his masturbation and anxious restlessness from him and would even go on errands downstairs in the dark for his father, something which otherwise he could never be induced to do.

When Poldi came to analysis he was completely intimidated and unable to say a word. For several days he sat in one corner of the room and looked at pictures while I sat in the other corner and apparently paid no attention to him. At first he was so filled with anxiety that he only turned the pages of the books hastily without looking at the pictures. When I saw he had become so used to me that he began to be really interested in the pictures, I asked him what this or that picture portrayed. In reply, he read me the title of the picture in a whisper. It took considerably more time before I thought it wise to leave my place in the corner and move closer to him. It was six weeks before he began to examine the room and its contents. When he finally discovered some toys, he chose two paper dolls and we began to play theater with them. The first play had the following content: Poldi's man met my man, pushed him and provoked a quarrel, which ended in a brawl. Poldi's doll then killed mine, but my doll had to come to life again and kill his; this mutual death-dealing lasted until Poldi declared that my doll was not allowed to come to life again. In this way he left the field a victor.

The fundamental form of the play was repeated subsequently; only the details varied. The scene was often played in the cemetery where Poldi killed and resurrected ghosts until they lost the desire to be resurrected. Around *Krampus*[2] time his enemy took the form of the Devil, but Poldi was unafraid, and even challenged the devil to battle and put him to flight. The mother reported that when Poldi was four years old his father, disguised as Krampus, had greatly

[2] Krampus day is a holy day when Santa Claus rewards the good children and Krampus, the Devil, punishes the bad ones. People appear in disguises and frighten the children.

frightened him, and every evening since then Poldi had been anxiously alert when he thought he heard his father's step in the hallway. In another fantasy, Poldi began the fight in the toilet and pursued his foe through the sewers to the Danube, where the pursued was discovered to be the devil. There, since Poldi won a bet as to which of them was the better fisherman, the devil burst asunder, "stinking and shrieking." In reality, one of Poldi's greatest pleasures was to fish in the Danube with his father. According to the mother, Poldi was the better fisherman of the two.

On the basis of this material, it was possible to interpret to Poldi that his aggression was directed toward his father. The father beat him, forced him to study, scolded him; he had reason enough to fear and hate him. Since this fear was increased by fear of his father's revenge (for wanting to kill his father he could be struck dead by him), he could express his aggression only in fantasy. I interpreted his death wish to him in the negative form: "You do not want to kill anyone because then you would be afraid that you would be killed yourself." This was the first and only interpretation he had received from me so far, and it was given only once. The mother confided that Poldi was so enraged by my interpretation that he wanted to stop coming to analysis. He told her that the analyst had "tried to talk me into things that weren't true at all." I told him what his mother had said to me and asked him to tell me himself anything he had against me, but could not induce him to do so. Finally, after much persuasion and repeated assurances that I would not be angry and would not punish him, he wrote the following: "You often talk to me like an old fishwife. You're a Buxbaum[3] that is shit on. You can go to the devil, you damned old witch."

The first part of this abusive tirade contained his conscious grievance. The second part showed the anal direction of his aggression, which came more and more to the fore as time

[3] "Buxbaum" is the German word for box-tree as well as a proper name.

went on. The anal abuse later proved to be ambivalent, for it contained also a declaration of love in anal terms. This foreshadowed the deeper significance of the struggle with the masculine antagonist which Poldi was always acting out. It revealed clearly his hostility toward his father, and indicated that the struggle was also a representation of his sadistic conception of coitus, due to witnessing parental intercourse, which was frequently accompanied by quarreling and fighting. Whether the role he played in fantasy in connection with these scenes was the masculine, the feminine, or both, was not yet apparent. (This deeper significance of his abusive complaint and his play was not interpreted to him.)

After this initial expression of his aggression, Poldi became more and more daring, at first only insofar as the analyst was concerned. He outdid himself in employing anal terms and in passing flatus. Gradually, he dared to give utterance to his aggression in a modified form at home, too, toward his mother, although he still restrained himself toward his father. To be sure, he had sufficient grounds for fearing the latter, who beat him at the least sign of recalcitrance. The mother had much more insight in this respect; it was possible to make her see that Poldi must have an opportunity to recognize that his fears were not justified. When I was finally forced to accept the fact that my arguments made no impression on the father, that he did not want to change his attitude of instilling fear in his son, I resorted to threatening to break off the treatment if Poldi were beaten again. This threat procured the desired result. The father abandoned corporal punishment but showed himself ingenious at devising other forms. However, the constant source of Poldi's greatest fear was removed and he could now express his criticism of his father somewhat more freely, in his father's as well as the analyst's presence.

The discontinuance of the beatings in itself certainly helped to diminish Poldi's objective fear, but just as important was the partial release of his aggression, which could now be turned toward the outer world. It was already evident from one of his plays which we called "Playing Circus," that his inhibited aggression was directed toward himself. As a clown or acrobat in the games, he performed all sorts of wonderful feats. His favorite trick was to jump down from the desk, table or back of a chair and throw himself full length on the couch, at times really hurting himself. The deeper meaning of the circus game became apparent only later, but the inclination to injure himself was clear enough at this time, though it was not interpreted. The interpretation that he did not dare express his hate and anger for fear of punishment was the only one that had been offered.

His fear diminished considerably when he was able to express his aggression in word and deed. He railed against his analyst, his mother, his father and his teacher. He tried to destroy all my things, which I interpreted to him as aggression toward me, whereupon he aimed his aggressive attacks directly against me. It was not easy to induce him to express his aggression in words instead of actions.

Poldi began to go out alone and played football for hours at a time with other boys—another abreaction of his aggression. To be sure, when it grew dark he became anxious and returned home to his mother. It is to be noted that the frightening scenes between his parents occurred at night, and that these scenes aggravated his anxiety. It was some time before I could speak of this special anxiety in the analysis. In the meantime, his mother was glad to be free of him for a few hours a day, and the fact that he was coming to analysis unaccompanied represented a new achievement. This was the more desirable since it was the only way in which the treatment could have been continued; the mother could no longer have found the time to bring him and wait for him. This phase, in which the most important factor was the emerging of his aggression directed largely against his father, lasted approximately two months. Then, with a new game, a new phase of the analysis began.

One day he came to his hour with two sticks, one large and one small, and, singing softly, began to play something for me on the "violin." He sang intermittently and without words. Encouraged by my invitation, he sang louder, and after two or three days the whole hour was taken up with this violin playing. The music consisted of a few measures from popular songs, operettas, operas, and classical music. The tunes were interrupted by inarticulate sounds, snorts, grunts, deep groans, very high tones like those of mating birds, flute-like notes and shrieks. The longer he played, the oftener these sounds occurred; finally the tunes disappeared and the whole performance was devoted to these sounds. He became intensely excited sexually, grew red in the face, and made unmistakable coituslike movements. My endeavors to turn this wordless game, in which he evidently depicted an act of intercourse, into a game with words were for a long time in vain, until I realized that he must have learned the melodies from the radio. Then I pretended to be listening in. I turned the knobs of a fictitious radio and said I did not hear well, whereupon some words became intelligible; after a few more attempts to get better transmission my "radio" spoke clearly in words. The violin play now changed into a dramatic play, but the climax of inarticulate sounds and coituslike movements persisted. Poldi's way of acting was unusual. Just as his violin play consisted of fragments of melodies, so his theater play consisted of scraps of speech, idiomatic phrases, and exclamations which appeared entirely unconnected. One had to try to understand his performance as one tries to understand the apparently senseless, disconnected parts of a dream. Gradually, I became an indispensable partner in this game. On one occasion he wrote me a letter asking me to come to his concert: "Dear Titterl: I invite you to come to the Raimund Theatre to see The Spendthrift. It begins in the evening at 8 o'clock and ends at 10:30. Please come tonight at 8. Admission 1.50 S; balcony 2.20 S.[4] I'm going home at 2 o'clock—don't tell anybody."

He had given me the name "Titterl" on account of its similarity to my name, Edith, Ditta. Moreover, it sounds like the vulgar expression for breast "*Tutterl.*" His invitation meant "We will play together from eight at night until two in the morning and that will be a secret." "Play" is here to be understood in the sexual sense of the word. Since, among other roles, I also took the part of a secretary, I succeeded in writing down some of his plays. I had to leave out a great deal since I could not always understand him; he saw to it that I also wrote down the music of his melodies. One of these plays is herein given as an example. The plays were in dialect which I have translated as far as possible.

POLISH BLOOD

Scene I

Ho, hoho, makulasch, Gee, look at the old people—the old fools *(Kracher).*[5] Let's get a move on and a glass of beer and a li'l glass of wine. How nice you are, everybody ought to feel grand!

Here we come again! Here we've been waiting, here comes the old woman, I didn't think of that. Are you drunk? I'm not. What are you singing then? My old Viennese *Gstanzeln.*[6] You can't do that.

Scene II

Get out of that sack! Who's got the *Gstanzeln?* Now I have stamped with more whistling. Now I'm going back to my *Gstanzeln.* The monster is here, isn't it!?

[4] Austrian schillings; usual moving picture theater prices at the time.

[5] *Kracher* may also mean old fools, in the sense of old men who run after young girls.

[6] *Gstanzeln* are a sort of Limerick, popular in the Austrian countryside, consisting of verse and chorus. The choruses are improvised and usually satirize a special person or occasion.

Scene III

No, cross that out. Something's whistling. Hello, you Kölner boy.[7] Who's screaming here? I want my li'l glass of wine. But I'd better wait 'cause I haven't earned it yet. Somebody's certainly making a fool of you. Here are the old fools, let's see what they do at night.

Intermission

Scene IV

What does the Possa do? The Trr! ch, rr, ch [he pretended to sleep and snored]. Ch . . . [inarticulate sounds]. The old fools. [More inarticulate sounds; he then spat, slobbered and made coitus-like movements.] Here we are—we old people! Rrr! Come in!

This play, by itself, would have remained completely unintelligible if there had not been other plays with similar phrases and scene sequences which suggested that the typical combination must be the most significant one. It was already evident that the violin play was a masturbation equivalent, in which he depicted one of the scenes he had overheard. Similarly, in the theater game he acted out what he had heard and seen, which excited him and made him wish to join in the play himself. The old people, the *"alten Kracherleut,"* in this play are the old people who made scenes *(Krachmachen),*[8] that is, noise *(Krach),* which may just as well refer to the sounds attendant upon intercouse as to the quarrels *(Krach),* which, according to the mother, often preceded intercourse. Moreover, it is known that children often imagine intercourse to be a fight. "Let's see what they do at night," refers to the night scene described immediately after the intermission.

At first it was not clear with which of the two parents Poldi

[7] In the Viennese dialect *Kellner,* the word for waiter, is given the same pronunciation as Kölner.

[8] *Krach* may mean scenes, noise, or quarrel.

identified himself, which role he wanted to play. In another play, The Csardas Princess, he played the Baron's part in the first act and the bride's part in the second act, which he then modified with the remark, "No, it has to be a man—well, then, a slave!" He tried to reject the feminine role. However the passive-masochistic wish was there: the new figure with which he identified himself was a man, to be sure, but a man beaten and in chains. Not until the third act did he find his way back to masculinity, when he chose the part of the Prince and concealed his former passivity to a certain extent by overemphasizing the masculinity of the role. He wavered before making the choice, but finally rejected the feminine role because of his fear of threatened castration. Here it is well to remember his first play in the therapy, the two quarreling men of whom now the one, now the other was the victor. Because of Poldi's fear of being destroyed, his doll (in this game, himself) had to win in the end. The theme is identical in both instances.

Another repetition in connection with the reproduction of the sexual intercourse scene, was the occurrence of eating and drinking. The meaning of this became clear when I told him at Easter that I was going away for a few days and he asked me if "only women" were going with me. In answer to my counterquestion whether he did not want me to have men companions, he attempted to poke the violin bow under my skirt. Thus he showed me that he wanted to do with me what he imagined my men traveling companions were going to do, which was the same thing that his father did with his mother. After I told him this he tried to pull up my skirt and look underneath it. I refused to let him do this but promised to tell him what he wanted to know. Thereupon, he drew a picture of a doctor putting a mirror into a woman's mouth and asked: "How far down can it go?" Apparently he had the idea that his father not only put something into his mother below but also into her mouth; here was the same combination of genital and oral conceptions which appeared in his plays, where eating and drinking always played an important part. This stereotyped combination could have been a displacement based on an oral fixation but it was equally possible that in his drawings and play-acting he was reproducing something he had actually seen. The suspicion that he had seen his parents practice fellatio was confirmed by his mother. However, this does not preclude the existence of a previous oral fixation. The mirror, which he explained was a dentist's mirror, was a penis symbol, expressing a condensation of genital wishes and voyeurism. Just as the dentist inserts the mirror to see into the woman's mouth, Poldi desired to put his penis into a woman's genital. Since looking at women's genitalia and having intercourse were forbidden to him, he drew this sketch containing the motif of looking, along with the depiction of the scene which he had observed. The analyst satisfied a part of his wish by giving him the desired description of the female genitalia in word and diagram.

In the second phase of his analysis, which also lasted approximately two months, Poldi had played the masculine role for the most part and had anxiously rejected the feminine role. Now, however, there was a change. For some time, according to several patients, he had masturbated, quite openly, in the waiting room. One day he came into my study with his trousers open and was unable to play theater as usual. Instead, he exhibited his penis—challenging me to do with him in reality what he had heretofore play acted during his sessions. However, he was afraid I might be angry at his indecency, as his mother and father would have been. Although I confined my interpretation to mentioning only this fear, he did not appear the next day. When he came again, I repeated the interpretation that he was afraid I might be angry. Now, just as at the beginning of the violin game, he started to play and sing without words. When, as before, the "radio" was regulated in order to induce him to speak, he suddenly stiffened, turned pale, and sprang up with the cry, "I am a monster!" He flew at me aggressively and "wanted to kill" me. He then repeatedly threw his knife so that the point stuck in the floor and at each thrust he named a part of my body which he pretended to have hit: arm, leg, stomach, head, finally "arse"; at this point he stopped and said with great satisfaction, "Now you're all cut to pieces anyway!" When I asked him why he was so angry with me, he said, "Because you insulted me." A little later in the same hour he played circus with especial ferocity and with the unmistakable intent of injuring himself; at the same time he screamed: "I am a monster, I am a cripple!" He responded to my interpretation that he was now doing to himself what he had previously wanted to do to me, with such a savage attack that he had to be put out of the room, thus confirming the interpretation in his usual manner.

The next day he played "Police"; he was the criminal and demanded that I, the policeman, put him in prison, beat and "massacre" him. When I refused, he begged me "at least to tickle him." Had I again refused, he would have become as aggressive as on the preceding day, but I prevented this by offering an interpretation. These two successive hours demonstrate clearly the nucleus of his neurosis.

Poldi's exhibitionism, one of the symptoms which brought him to analysis, had first appeared in the transference situation in the violin and theater games. Later, he turned directly to genital exhibitionism. On the basis of the previous material, his exhibitionism can be understood as an attempt at seduction, as a transference to the analyst of what he was constantly doing at home to his mother. Even though he had, by his standards, approached me most carefully, he had been rejected—"insulted," as he stated in the following hour. His rage with me was bound up with his sexual wishes; he wanted to destroy me, genitally. In fantasy, he thrust a knife into my "arse"—his expression for the female genitalia—just as his father thrust his penis into his mother. He called himself a "monster." In the play quoted, he said the same thing in the second scene prior to the scene depicting coitus. It may be that the mother had called the father that in one of their quarrels when she had been forced to have intercourse; perhaps she had said it to the child, too, when he masturbated. Poldi thought of himself and his father as "monsters," when either of them had sexually aggressive intentions.

Poldi's aggression, once expressed, turned against himself; he wanted to destroy himself, as he had wanted to destroy the analyst, by making himself a cripple. "I am a monster, a cripple," meant that he must become a cripple because he was a monster.

The next hour showed that his fear of castration also included the wish to be castrated. The policeman, representing the father and the analyst, in the transference situation, should punish him for his sexual crimes and satisfy him with the punishment, by tickling. The castration should serve at the same time as evidence of love; being castrated, he wanted to be loved by his father. This is the second component of his exhibitionism: if his mother does not love him, he wants to excite his father by exhibitionism to castrate him and to make love with him as a woman. His masturbation contained the same two components; on the one hand, it was the expression of his aggression against his mother and, on the other hand, the expression of his wish to destroy his penis through masturbation in order that his father might love him. Both wishes came to the surface in the following days. The mother reported that he had been genitally aggressive toward her. When I spoke with him about this, he repeated the behavior with me. Rejected, he played circus—that is, he felt an urge to injure himself; after playing circus he wanted to do what the analyst was doing at the moment, either knitting or sewing. This succession of genital aggression, self-castration and identification with the analyst (his mother in the transference) was repeated for some time, apparently unaffected by interpretations. Finally, I forbade the sexual aggression against me by telling him that he could not get rid of his anxiety in that way. His answer to this was that he preferred to keep his anxiety and to continue in his ways. I then added that I did not like his behavior and found it unpleasant. The next day he began his hour with the statement, "I have been discharged." Since I had refused him as a sexual partner, he gave up the violin play, his means of courting and seduction. There was no point to it any longer; as violinist, he had been discharged and sent away. With this the period of sexual aggression came to an end.

As a result of this final rejection, Poldi renounced the masculine role completely, and from then on wanted only to be like me, to sit in my chair and at my writing-desk, to possess my things. He attempted to achieve this by increasing the activities which had self-injury as their goal. Finally, one day when he was playing circus, he succeeded in really wounding himself. He was frightened beyond measure, could not be pacified, and cried until he fell asleep from exhaustion. Another day, he brought several drawings which, with his explanations, made clear the meaning of the circus game: one portrayed a child in a crib with slats "watching his parents play" in their bed; another showed a child standing on the edge of a bed, a second child falling on someone, and a nurse standing nearby holding up a threatening finger. Poldi said that in the hospital throwing one's self down had been one of the favorite games but the nurses had always forbidden it. It is apparent that throwing himself down had several determinants. He threw himself upon someone—as his father did upon his mother. The nurse threatened an injury as punishment and then, whether in identification with her or in order to escape her punishment, he threw himself down, thus both punishing and hurting himself as well as attempting to hide his erection.

This was one of the few times Poldi was willing to allow me to help him. Evidently he wanted to protect himself from his unconscious urge to castrate himself; for this reason he also brought conscious memories as material. The circus, like the violin game, after being interpreted, disappeared from the analysis, and his anxiety again diminished.

Inasmuch as summer was approaching and Poldi was to go to a children's home in the country for his health, it was necessary that his exhibitionism be restricted. After repeating previous interpretations of his sexual aggression toward his mother and his fear and wish to be castrated by his father, I advised him not to masturbate in front of others but only when he was alone. As a good-by present I gave him a railroad schedule, something he had wanted for a long time. Only when he returned from his vacation did I understand its meaning. Poldi was able to control his exhibitionism during his stay at camp. My interpretations were a contributing factor, as well as his being separated from his mother, who had been watching whether he masturbated until I forbade her to do so. Being allowed to masturbate in secret he was brought back to a situation which was really pleasurable for him; he had a secret with me—and a fantasy in common with me which centered in the timetable.

When we took up the treatment again after a ten weeks' interruption, Poldi behaved exactly as he had at the beginning of the analysis. He repeated in the course of six weeks all the phases of the treatment of the year before, beginning with silence and ending with exhibitionism. A single repetition of an interpretation formerly given, sometimes only a hint of it, sufficed to drive him on to the next phase. During these weeks several supplementary details were added. The blowing out of a fuse during his hour gave occasion for a fantasy which contained his fear of the dark: children, whom he called "night bogeys," were naughty, were stabbed by the father for their naughtiness, but came to life again. This being stabbed and coming to life again resembles his first fantasy in the analysis, in which two men kill each other and come to life again. The fight, previously between a man and a ghost in a cemetery, now takes place between a child and his father, that is, between his father and himself. He himself is the "night bogey," the spook is punished for stealing about at night, listening and watching to see what his parents are doing. At the same time, in his identification with the mother, he experiences being stabbed by the father—a construction which we already made from the monster-cripple scene. Other supplementary details supplied further proof that he had observed fellatio—for instance, he would kiss a doll on the genital area or try to put his legs on my shoulders.

New material, in part belonging to the period before vacation, also emerged. It appeared in a new fantasy connected with the train schedule, in a new symptom—a compulsion to steal—and in the recurrence of his exhibitionism.

The first time Poldi asked for a train schedule had been prior to the Easter holidays, when I was going away on a trip. This wish appeared to be in some way related to his desire to go away with the analyst. After he received the timetable, the mother reported that he played with it constantly. Again, a theater play brought the explanation for his fantasied trips: after a quarrel, in which the mother asked the father for money, both parents took a trip to Hamburg; there the father killed everybody who wanted to keep him from carrying out something which was not clear to Poldi. It is not difficult to recognize in this fantasy the same elements that were present in the former plays, i.e., to identify the quarrel between the parents with the *Krach:* the journey to *Ham*burg is the journey to the city in which one gets *Ham* —food (in the Viennese child's vernacular). The struggle with the people who want to stop the father is the quarrel between the father and the child who wishes to prevent the parents from having intercourse.

The journey is new element in the fantasy, revealing the connection with the ardent play with the train schedule which had evidently taken the place of the violin game. The fantasy contains the genital-oral combination again in the name Hamburg—the primal scene is apparent in it. The symbolic significance of traveling on a train is another welcome confirmation of this. The quarrel over money was a reproduction of episodes at home; but the fact that from among the many causes for quarrels at home he picked this particular one showed that he wanted to express something more, though it was some time before this something became clear.

In the course of the repetition of the phases from the pre-vacation time, the theme of seeing and being seen recurred. That the theme persisted in spite of the fact that the former interpretation was repeated gave proof that it had not yet been completely explained, that several important determinants for its comprehension were still lacking. As before, he now wanted to look into everything, to open all cupboards, drawers and purses; after I told him that he wanted to see what I looked like inside he reacted, as before, by attempting to look under my skirt. When I prevented this and talked instead about the female genitalia it became apparent that he was convinced that both his mother and I had a "tail," a penis—even though he knew that other women had none. An explanation had no effect as he did not believe it. He wanted to make sure for himself. His continued exhibitionism was a challenge to the analyst to show her genital, too. The interpretation that he did not want to believe that women had no penis, because he was afraid that if this were true he could also lose his, was obviously not the right one.

As his exhibitionism increased, his stealing came increasingly to the fore. According to his mother he had never stolen before. He had begun to steal money from her just before the vacation; in his analytic hour he had often begged to be allowed to take a book or game away with him and had often carried off something in spite of my refusal. Now, however, he stole more and more during his hour. There was nothing I owned which he did not want to take away from me; he was extremely clever at appropriating articles and often could not be prevented. At the climax of his exhibitionism, however, he made no attempt to hide his thievery—he stole quite openly, put the stolen object in the opening in his trousers. In this way he showed what and why he had to steal.

The forbidding of his exhibitionism and his stealing forced him to substitute talk and play for acting out. To be sure, attempts had been made repeatedly to bring this about but always without success. It seemed necessary for the child to perceive the relationship between the two symptoms before he could substitute verbal communication for obscure compulsive activity. He complained at the time that he was unable to do what the other children did because his mother did not give him what he needed, skating boots, a football, etc. When I offered to give him a football he refused it, saying he did not want one. He showed that he did not need these playthings—that something else was missing. When he again attempted to steal books and money from me and was forbidden, he insisted that he had "a right to them" and that he would take anything away from me that he wanted. In answer to the question why he thought he had a right to my things he said, "because you took something away from me too!"

Finally, he explained his stealing in his usual manner, in a bit of play-acting which was a continuation of the trip-to-Hamburg game. He asked for and was given money; he increased his demands and was given all he wanted. He took the money to a restaurant, bought and ate "stinking sausages," danced with a woman, and then went with her to Hamburg where he killed all the people who got in his way. During the play he said, "You've got to pull all your hairs out separately and then stick them in again; then you've got it."

In this sentence which had no logical connection with the play, Poldi explained the play as well as his stealing. He believed, as already noted, that women also have a penis;

he probably believed it to be hidden under the pubic hair. The money, books and games which he wanted to take from me were symbols for the penis which he really wanted but did not receive; his thefts from his mother may be interpreted similarly. Money is, however, also the means by which one can buy things for oneself—again the longed-for penis in the form of a "stinking sausage." Poldi had the habit of smelling his hands whenever he had touched his penis. "Stinking sausages" are also bad, spoiled sausages. Poldi's mother had episodes of nervous morning vomiting. It may be that he had connected his mother's vomiting with the fellatio he had observed the night before, and thought that she vomited because she had had his father's "stinking sausage" in her mouth. Perhaps he had the idea that this act represented a threat to his father's penis.

There is nothing, to be sure, in Poldi's attitude toward his father to point to the fact that Poldi believed that his father had lost his penis, or had been castrated by his mother. In his eyes his father was much too powerful to let anything like that happen to him. Only the struggle between the two men acted out at the beginning of the treatment, one component of which was recognized to be a reproduction of the act of intercourse, seems in its varying outcome to admit the possibility that the father, too, might succumb. The contest with the ridiculous devil who bursts asunder "stinking and shrieking" also points to the fact that the father-devil can be overcome. Then the fellatio would be mother's revenge on father: she eats away his penis, the weapon with which he vanquishes her.

In his fantasies Poldi repeated with his mother what his father did. He feared, however, that what was only a threat for his father, with which the latter could successfully cope, had really happened to him, Poldi. His mother had taken his large penis away from him so that he now possessed only a small, inadequate one. Perhaps this assumption was supported by the comparison which he had had the opportunity to make between the erect penis before coitus and the small one afterward. Furthermore, this was the fantasied consummation of his mother's castration threat. She had stolen his penis from him. What she had stolen from him he had a "right" to steal back, then he "had it," could dance with her and go away to Hamburg with her, and be a man like his father.

After this interpretation, his exhibitionism came to an end. A little later, and after repeated interpretation, the stealing also stopped. A talk about babies, "about whom you couldn't tell whether it was going to be a girl or a boy until after three or four months," led to memories from his early childhood. He told me how he used to eat noodles with his hands; I interpreted to him that he thought this was the reason he had become a boy, that one got a penis from eating, just as the mother had one because she had eaten his.

After a time Poldi sought further information from me to supplement the interpretation; he wanted to know how I (meaning his mother) was formed. He still suspected that a penis must be hidden somewhere: "between the breasts— or perhaps it goes from the navel into the stomach—or sticks in the hole." He showed by these reflections that he feared that his penis would be bitten off or lost in a vagina. When told that these ideas were false and given the true anatomy of this part of the body, he was satisfied and never returned to the subject.

Poldi's fear of losing his penis through the vagina was much less intense and therefore easier to dispel than his fear of its being eaten away. The source of his anxiety was probably connected with his oral fixation. Perhaps (the motif did not appear in the analysis) he thought his mother wanted revenge because he had bitten her breast and drunk from it. Certainly the breast was an object of great interest to him; he often fondled his mother's breast and had nicknamed me "Titterl" which, to him, meant breast. From its beginning to the complete interpretation and disappearance of symptoms, this phase of the treatment lasted approximately six months.

In the final phase of the treatment Poldi developed fantasies which showed his rivalry with his father. The following example may be cited. Poldi and I built a house with a high tower; we expected an attack from a "wild Indian." Since Poldi thought that the Indian would tear the tower down as soon as he saw it, he demolished it himself, thereby depicting self-castration through masturbation. Other games showed his concern that he might have injured his penis by masturbating; at the same time, masturbation was his method of reassuring himself that his penis was still intact. Finally, one day when Poldi saw his father naked, he asked him if his own penis would ever grow to be so large. This direct question is to be understood as another question, namely, whether his father would have any objection if his penis should grow so large. It showed that Poldi had, to a great extent, overcome his fear of the castrating father and that, in spite of the presence of opposing tendencies, the masculine role predominated.

This sudden advance to the genital phase is to be ascribed partly to the treatment and partly to onset of puberty. But, above all, improvement could be noted, since Poldi showed by this question not only that he had overcome his fear, but also that he could adapt to reality. Although he had previously denied reality and had lost himself in fantasies wherein he played the part of a grown man, he now postponed the fulfilment of this wish for the future; he accepted the fact that he was still a small boy and therefore had a smaller penis than his father.

At this time the treatment was broken off. Poldi had given up his exhibitionism and stealing; his anxiety had considerably diminished, so that neither he nor his mother was greatly disturbed by it; he continued to masturbate, but no more than was normal. The mother was so well satisfied with his condition that she saw no reason for continuing the treatment. We cannot say with certainty whether the remaining symptoms, ticlike and spasmodic movements, as well as the remnant of his anxiety, would also have yielded to further treatment. Neither can we know to what extent his unanalyzed, oral fixation on his mother and the anal-passive fixation on his father may disturb his later development.

The first obvious diminution of anxiety appeared when Poldi was able to express his aggression, raising the question of the connection between the two.

Although Poldi was wild and aggressive in his games and fantasies, he was in reality afraid of the successfully vanquished figures of his fantasies; and when his games came too close to reality he was frightened. He therefore never allowed himself to be defeated. Only in the final phase of his analysis, when his rivalry with his father had lost much of its anxiety, did he tell me to play as well as I could, as he did not want "to be handed anything on a silver platter."

Because in fantasy he hated and persecuted his father as a rival, he feared his father's revenge in reality. A part of this fear was objective, for Poldi had often experienced his father's anger in the form of punishment. This part of his fear had to be removed by the punishing father himself— the father had to show him that he had nothing to fear. With the discontinuance of the beatings, it became possible to penetrate to the neurotic sources of his anxiety.

In the circus game Poldi punished himself: (1) to escape his father's punishment, (2) in identification with his punishing father, (3) in identification with his mother who was punished by his father as he was, and (4) to win his father's love through his identification with his mother.

The less Poldi was able to express his aggression, the more he hated his father. His fantasy of the revenge to be expected from his father mounted in proportion to his hate. The more dreadful the form he imagined his father's revenge would take, the greater his fear of his father became, the greater also his urge to self-injury whereby he inflicted on himself the punishment he imagined was his due. The aggression which had formerly been directed against his father was now turned in on himself; that is, his anxiety was his fear of his aggression directed against himself. When his aggression was reduced, his anxiety likewise diminished.

On the other hand, it was observed that Poldi reacted to the rejection of his sexual aggression by renouncing the active-masculine role and that, after having castrated himself symbolically, he took over the antithetical passive-feminine role, in his identification with the analyst transferred from his mother. That which he could not have, he now wanted to be. At this time his fear in reality increased. He was afraid that his castration wishes, the wish to give himself as a woman, to a man (his father), might be realized. His fear protected him from the castration which he desired.

Poldi's exhibitionism was at first expressed in anal terms, and so was his aggression. The anal material which Poldi brought is to be understood from two points of view; he tried me out with something which was forbidden, to be sure, but something which was associated with less danger for him than his genital aggression and exhibitionism for which he feared the punishment of castration. At the same time, however, he revealed material deriving from a deeper libido and fixation level: but this level also is subdivided, the anal-passive underlying the anal-active. The concealment of his passive strivings by active strivings was typical of all the phases of the treatment; his overemphasized aggression was intended to conceal his passivity and protect him from it.

Thus his genital aggression represented his wish to stab the woman (the "monster" scene) and, insofar as it was directed against the father, his wish to kill and castrate his father. His masochistic wish was that his father would castrate him. Since he suspected his mother too of having a penis he wanted to take it away from her, for had she not taken his away from him?

The taking away is effected not only genitally but, as we have seen, for the most part orally. He wants to eat and drink, to practice fellatio, that is, to bite off the penis and to have the same thing done to him (the kissing of the doll's genital area, and the attempt to put his legs on my shoulders). Aggression was expressed on all libidinal levels.

The hope that Poldi's intellectual functioning would be improved with treatment did not come to pass. He continued his play on words and sounds and seemed at times to use it like a secret language. His ability to express himself verbally remained on a low level. His tics and compulsive movements continued, although with the reduction of his excitement and his anxiety, they were less frequent. Altogether these symptoms point to the presence of a coexistent organic disturbance quite distinct from his neurosis.

HAIR PULLING AND FETISHISM

Hair pulling as a symptom occurs in both children and adults. Very little has been written about it in psychoanalytic or psychiatric literature. Romm's paper, "Some Dynamics in Fetishism" (1949), touches on the problem. In contrast, quite a number of psychoanalytic papers deal with the problem of fetishism: among them, following Freud, those by Phyllis Greenacre. Freud's theory (1927a) that the fetishist reacts to seeing the mother's genitals and to observing her apparent castration at a time of masturbatory arousal is basic to psychoanalytic thinking on the subject. Greenacre deals with the problem of fetishism in two papers, "Certain Relationships Between Fetishism and the Faulty Development of Body Image" (1953), and "Further Considerations Regarding Fetishism" (1955a). She described fetishism as a disturbance which appears

> . . . clinically as an unusually severe castration fear [that] comes essentially from disturbances of pregenitality which render the child structurally unsound and insecure to meet genital-oedipal problems and especially to meet the normal castration threats of this period. In those cases which I saw these threats were already overwhelming, having appeared before the full oedipal development in unusually severe

This paper was published originally in *The Psychoanalytic Study of the Child*, 15:243-260, 1960.

actual traumata of a specifically castrative type—threats not merely by seeing the mother's genital and observing her apparent castration at the time of special masturbatory arousal, as was first postulated by Freud [1927a], but much more than this by witnessing or experiencing bloody mutilating attacks in the form of operations (on the self or others), childbirth, abortions, or accidents [1955a, p. 187].

She thinks that the child is particularly vulnerable when he is exposed to such experiences between the first and second year. This conception of fetishism seems to me to be incomplete. It is common knowledge that all children go through a phase in which they are particularly attached to one object or another—a stuffed animal, teddy bear, blanket or pillow, etc.—and I think that fetishism, like other disturbances, must go back to a fixation point in the pregenital phase of libidinal development as Greenacre describes, but also to the period when children have intense feelings about such objects.

Several authors have studied the significance of early possessions. Wulff (1946) wrote a paper on "Fetishism and Object Choice in Early Childhood," in which he in turn reports extensively on previous papers written by Freud, Sterba, and Friedjung. Stevenson published a paper on the "First Treasured Possession," a study of the role played by especially loved objects and toys in the lives of children (1954). Her paper was of course based on Winnicott's study of "Transitional Objects and Transitional Phenomena" (1953) in which he significantly distinguishes between the pathological forms of fetishism and the early infantile love of things. He says:

There is a wide variation to be found in a sequence of events which starts with the newborn infant's fist-mouth activities, and that leads eventually on to an attachment to a teddy, a doll or soft toy, or to a hard toy. It is clear that something is important here other than oral excitement and satisfaction, although this may be the basis of everything else . . . I am staking a claim for an intermediate state between a baby's inability and growing ability to recognize and accept reality [p. 89].

Winnicott is dealing with the progress which the baby makes in handling truly "not me" objects. He says,

To some extent these objects may stand for the breast. . . . The first possession is used in conjunction with special techniques derived from very early infancy, auto-erotic activities, which can include or exist apart from the more direct auto-erotic activities. [In some cases] there is no transitional object except the mother herself [or in other cases], an infant may be so disturbed in emotional development that the transition state cannot be enjoyed, or the sequence of objects used is broken. The sequence may nevertheless be maintained in a hidden way [pp. 90, 91].

Winnicott, referring in a paragraph to Wulff's paper, protests the use of the word "fetish" for these beloved objects of children, the first possessions, and says that Wulff "has taken back to infancy something that belongs in ordinary theory to the sexual perversions." Further on he says,

. . . yet I do consider that transitional phenomena are healthy and universal. Moreover, if we extend the use of the word fetish to cover normal phenomena we shall perhaps be losing some of the value of the term. I would prefer to retain the word fetish to describe the object that is employed on account of a *delusion* of a maternal phallus [p. 96].

This is in agreement with Freud's paper on "Fetishism" (1927a).

During the past years I have treated two girls whose chief symptom was hair pulling. The symptom appeared to be related to the transitional object in Winnicott's definition and to a form of fetishism which bears out Freud's and

Greenacre's formulations. Both children pulled their hair out in patches and used it to tickle the area around their mouths, lips, and noses, while they also sucked on one of their fingers. From time to time they swallowed the hair.

Among the transitional objects which Winnicott enumerates is wool. He says, "In common experience one of the following activities occurs, complicating an auto-erotic experience such as thumb sucking. [Point three.] The baby starts from early months to pluck wool and to collect it, to use it for the caressing part of the activity; less commonly the wool is swallowed, even causing trouble" (p. 90). My patients used their own hair for exactly this activity.

CASE 1

I saw Beryl, age six, for two years, three times a week in analysis and the mother about once every two weeks. Beryl was the eldest of three daughters. The mother was Catholic, the father Jewish. The mother had married him for his money and for the security which she hoped to get. She was a pretty woman, meticulously and expensively dressed, and vain to a ridiculous point. She wanted to be the belle of the ball, wanted to go to parties and to give parties, but she could never do it. She did not like her husband's Jewish friends and was ashamed to be with him in Gentile company. The parents were having severe marital difficulties when Beryl was brought to treatment. The mother had been her own father's favorite and companion. Although there were sons in the family, he treated her like a boy, having her accompany him on hunting and fishing trips. She very much wished to present him with a grandson and was disappointed when the first child and the following ones were girls. However, Beryl seemed to have been well taken care of and was described as a happy baby.

Her next younger sister, Mary, was born when Beryl was eighteen months old. According to the mother's report, Beryl was very jealous of the baby and attacked her by pulling her hair. She was slapped for it repeatedly, and finally stopped, but, according to the mother, started pulling her own hair.

When I met Beryl she was a whining, painfully shy child, small for her age, and constantly had her thumb in her mouth. The mother admitted that she was so disgusted with Beryl's appearance that she could hardly stand to wash her hair or help her take care of herself. Beryl in turn was so ashamed of the way she looked that she always appeared with a stocking cap which hid her head completely, and which she refused to take off, either with me or in the schoolroom. Beryl represented herself and her family problems in her doll play. She brushed and combed a long-haired doll incessantly and was a loving mother, while she told me and showed me how her mother grimaced when the latter brushed Beryl's hair. Beryl was forever playing "going to parties" with her dolls. They competed with each other; yet taking the other one's boy friend away brought disaster and loss of beauty and life upon the culprit.

Beryl mothered her youngest sister very much the way she treated her dolls when she was well disposed toward them. But she was still jealous of Mary. Beryl adored her curly-haired mother, loved to kiss and hug her, but her mother was repelled by Beryl both because she was a girl and because she resembled her father. She could scarcely tolerate the child's demonstrativeness, much less respond in kind. At the same time, guilt made it hard for her to set limits for Beryl. She endured Beryl's caresses without returning them, as she did with her husband.

After about six months of treatment, I gave Beryl a sleepy doll as a Christmas present. She immediately started to take it to bed with her and became inseparable from it. She pulled the doll's hair out instead of her own (which was fine). Still, when either the mother or I left her for a few days, she again pulled out her own hair.

In the second half of the first year of treatment, Beryl adopted a new form of acting out which clarified the nature of her fantasies and made it possible for me to offer an interpretation. With great ostentation, she moved her hand from her genitals and her anus to her mouth. She chose candy that was either red or black and put it in her lap or sat on it before eating it. When we played Old Maid, one of her favorite games, she hid the cards behind her, sat on them, took them out, kissed them, and then showed me her behind; obviously she was eating "dirty stuff" and whatever she was eating was supposed to have contact with her body orifices. The peak of the dirt orgy was reached one day when she made a mess of red paint powder which was slightly mixed with water, and squirted it through her fingers. I finally stopped her and, while cleaning up, I talked with her.

Knowing that the children had access to their parents' bathroom and bedroom at all times, I asked, "Did you ever see mommy's hair between her legs?" Her contemptuous answer was, "Who didn't see that!" I continued: "Did you see daddy too, and his penis?" Again she replied, "Who wouldn't know that!" I proceeded, "Sometimes I wonder whether you pull your hair because you don't like hair down there." She answered, "That has nothing to do with it!" Such a distinct "no" can be a confirmation rather than a contradiction, but one cannot be sure. I continued, "Do you know what Kotex is?" She answered, "Yes." "Do you know what it is for?" The answer was, "You don't need to know." This answer was obviously a quotation. She did want to know and probably had asked about it, but apparently mother's frankness in showing herself had ended here. When I insisted, she said, grimacing and with great affect, "It was in the wastebasket all bloody." I talked about menstruation and wondered whether she had seen blood between her mother's legs in the bathtub or perhaps in the toilet. Again I received the answer, "You don't need to know." However, the next day she showed me a very small cut in her finger and said, "It was a deep cut. It bled terribly."

Some time later the mother reported to me that she had overheard Beryl talking about sex with some of her school friends. Beryl had listened to them, then told them the straight facts, saying, "I know all about it. Dr. B. told me." So far the mother had been cooperative, reported well, and understood what was going on. She agreed that the bathroom doors should be closed from then on. However, when we came to talk about Beryl's obvious masturbation, the mother was shocked. She had completely repressed any observation of it. I told her that if she could not accept Beryl, her genitals, her sexual feelings, and her masturbating, I did not see how Beryl would be able to give up her hair pulling. The mother then admitted that she preferred that Beryl pull her hair rather than masturbate. At this point I suggested she have analysis herself.

Only months later, after she had acted on my suggestion, did the mother overcome her disgust with Beryl's appearance and accept her as a girl. She could shampoo Beryl's hair without grimacing and Beryl in turn allowed the mother to take her to a skin doctor who would help her hair to grow. Mother and daughter treated this as a secret between the two of them. Mother's administrations, putting lotions on her head, brushing and combing her hair, were, from the dermatologist's point of view, psychotherapy rather than medical treatment. Beryl could now allow her hair to grow. Feeling accepted by her mother, she could like herself and her appearance. Of course, this was not a straight up-hill development—there were many relapses, particularly when the family planned to leave the city, which meant leaving me. However, Beryl's conscious desire to have her hair grow continued. When she did pull, she was afraid of losing her hair again and she cried bitterly, asking for help. Pulling her hair at this point was a sign of her conflict between wanting to go with her family and her desire to stay with me.

The father had always played an important role for Beryl. She was his favorite; he accepted her with or without hair. So long as Beryl had been afraid to compete with her mother for his attention, she had either ignored him or, in identification with her mother, had treated him with contempt.

In the course of her treatment, she became fiercely loyal to him, belligerently defended his or anybody else's Jewishness, and criticized her mother's attitude toward him. Her shy, girlish demeanor changed to that of a tomboy. He played ball with her and enjoyed playing rough. When we talked about her wanting to be a boy, she said in her usual negative form of affirmation, "No, who'd want to have one of those silly things dangling between one's legs!" When she had overcome her fear of mother's jealousy and felt more accepted by her and accepting of her, she became flirtatious with her father, who was a little too pleased about it. However, eventually they both got on a more even keel. Beryl turned her attention to boys and even developed crushes on them, to her parents' amusement and delight.

When we terminated treatment, I gave her a diary as a birthday present, and a stuffed poodle as a good-bye present. She had told me that she wanted a stuffed poodle as a replacement for a real dog which the family had had and which had been more the mother's pet than anybody else's. She explained to me that it would be too big and stiff to have in bed with her, but "I could have it standing in front of my bed to watch me, if I should pull my hair."

A few weeks after she had left, she wrote to me: "Thank you for the diary and the dog [although she had thanked me before]. I have written in the diary ever since I got it. I sleep with my dog almost every night. I keep the key on my chain which you gave me," (I had given her a chain and locket as a Christmas present the second year). Apparently, the dog and diary became a substitute for me, or, as one might say, the intermediary objects. She finally replaced her hair with other objects and thus developed a relationship to a "transitional object." It is significant that all these objects were presents which I had given her. I heard from her a year later. She was doing all right and felt happy.

CASE 2

Ann, my other little patient, was three years and two months old when she came into treatment. She was extremely shy and anxious and refused to stay alone with me. My contact with her was entirely through the mother who remained in the room. For two months, I saw Ann and the mother together once a week, and saw the mother alone once a week.

The pertinent points of the history were these: Ann was an only child who was very welcome, since the marriage had been childless for ten years. The marriage was peculiar in that the parents seemed to be very much in love with each other but unable to live together. The husband, who came from a wealthy family, refused to take any money from his family, and they were always on the brink of financial disaster. They moved innumerable times. He would move first, leaving her behind until he called her to join him, but he would soon move on again. During the time of my contact with the family, he was prospecting. Of course, wherever he did prospect was hardly a suitable place for a family to live. His letters, some of which I read, were beautifully written, affectionate, and to the point. I saw the man only once, on one of the rare occasions when he was in Seattle. He was highly intelligent, observing and sensitive, yet, he struck me as a lone wolf rather than a family man. The mother was a good-looking woman, not striking but pleasing, well dressed, with very little makeup. She was devoted to her daughter and in conflict with her husband because of the child. For the first ten years of the marriage there had been no question about her following him around. However, since she had had the child, she desperately wanted to settle down in one place. Although she spoke of divorce, she did not want it. Her own parents had been divorced when she was a child. When her father, who was a drunkard, finally left the family, her mother had said, "Good riddance." She expressed admiration for her mother, but I do not know what their relationship was like. In our weekly conferences this material was discussed, and she expressed a good deal of feeling with regard to her husband.

It was clear that Ann was disturbed when father and mother disagreed and quarreled. Ann, who was a bottle-baby, seemed to develop well until she was about eighteen or nineteen months old. According to the mother's statement, the baby stopped drinking from the bottle at nineteen months. "She gave up the bottle voluntarily." She started walking at twelve months. At around eighteen months when, according to the mother, she started to pull out her hair, she also woke up crying at night. This crying lasted for about six months. The mother said, "She started pulling her hair some time after she was eighteen months old. I don't remember just when it started. At that time we had moved twice in four months, and my husband was in the hospital for minor surgery." As I learned later, this surgery had been an operation for the removal of a tumor on a testicle and of hemorrhoids. During his convalescence and probably before he went to the hospital, the father took to locking the bathroom door. Ann had been accustomed to going into the bathroom with father or mother, but during this period he left her standing outside the door, wide-eyed, listening, while he moaned and cried out in pain. It was at this time that she gave up the bottle, cried at night, and started pulling her hair. During the same period her grandfather, to whom she was very attached, lived in the house. He became sick and incontinent and finally died. Mother thought that Ann pulled her hair more when Ann's father was away. She reported that at that time Ann was so upset about having her hair washed that she vomited; therefore, for the last few weeks the mother had desisted from washing her hair.

My first contact with Ann was around Eastertime. We had a party for the three of us, plus a few dolls. I had some Easter eggs as well as some feathery chickens. Ann took one of the chickens, quickly pulled out its feathers, and then fondled it, and would not let it go. I also had a whistle which blows out and has a little feather bush at the end. When I showed Ann how to blow it, she whispered, frightened, "Don't," and I apologized and threw it into the wastebasket. After a while she went to the wastebasket, took the whistle out, and learned how to use it. The things which we used during this hour were considered presents, so she went home with Easter eggs, a chicken without feathers, a whistle with feathers, and a doll baby-bottle we had used for feeding the babies. Throughout, Ann spoke very little to me. She wanted to write a letter to daddy, which she dictated to me. We also made some Easter eggs out of paper, colored them, and enclosed them in the letter to him. After the hour the mother telephoned to let me know that Ann had talked constantly about me and had wanted to play our games again; the mother had to play my role or Ann's, while Ann played either me or herself. They repeated the hour with me over and over again with reversed roles. Ann also sucked on the baby bottle herself occasionally, but did not show any wish to have a bottle herself, although the mother offered one to her. Her playing with the chicken without feathers and with the whistle prompted me to let her have something with hair which she could pull out instead of her own hair.

The mother had made a habit of sleeping with Ann when her husband was not at home. Upon my suggestion, mother put Ann to sleep in her own bed, but at the same time allowed her to take some toy to bed with her. The mother provided a woolly thing, I think it was a kitten. Once when Ann was in my office we talked again about her father, where he was, and what he was doing. Ann had quite often said to her mother, "Do you want me to go away?" which the mother interpreted, according to the books, as a sign of insecurity. While Ann was playing with a small doll, she made the doll take a long walk all over the room, all over the tables, finally getting to the mother and walking up and down her body. For me it was a demonstration of the symbolism of the mother's body as the world and the earth on which we walk. When she asked, "Do you want me to go away?" she might have added, "like my daddy." The wish to be like her father was promoted by the mother's intensified attachment to Ann in the absence of the husband and by letting Ann sleep with her. Ann's reaction to unpleasant experiences was to do to herself what she did not want to have done to her. For example, after having had a fight at nursery school, she played out the whole fight with her mother, showing her how that naughty girl had beaten her up, but also how strong the girl was and how Ann admired her and wanted to be like her. The question, "Do you want me to go away?" indicated that she preferred going away herself to having father go away from her. The mother was able to understand this mechanism in Ann very well.

About four weeks after the beginning of my contact with Ann, the mother wrote me the following note:

I had a conversation with Ann that may or may not be important; I take a bath with her because she slips on the mat and is afraid to get into the tub by herself. I was washing my genitals and glanced at Ann who was looking at me with rather a frightened expression. I said, "Honey, does this hair on my body worry you?" She said, "Yes." I said, "It's nothing to worry about, dear. When people grow up they grow some hair on their bodies. Is that the reason you pull the hair on your head?" She said, "Yes." I said, "Because you don't want it to grow?" She said, "No, sometimes I just feel like pulling and sometimes when I'm hungry, it tastes good."

At my instigation, the mother repeated the conversation in one of our joint sessions, and we talked about it some more, wondering why Ann did not like hair and whether it was because she thought it was dirty. We talked about masturbation and about the difference between men and women. Obviously Ann differentiated between pulling her hair out in order to prevent it from growing so that she would look like mommy, and the other expression which she used, "just pulling her hair." I assumed that her interest in and horror at the genital region was connected with having seen father's genital and having heard his moaning and groaning behind the locked bathroom door when he was in pain. We also talked about this: that daddy had had something hurting on his penis but that mother knew, and Ann did too, that he still had his penis and he was all right now. Mother, however, as well as Ann and I, never did have a penis. A few days after this explanation, Ann said to her mother, "Give me a shampoo." The mother was pleased but said to Ann, "I'll give you one if you give me one first." Ann was only too happy to oblige and, as the mother said, "She was very careful not to get soap into my eyes, and did a good job." Then she allowed the mother to give her a shampoo. For the first time in weeks, she submitted without crying.

When Ann had overcome her anxiety at having her hair washed, the father came home, praised her for her attempts to stop pulling her hair, told her how much he loved her, and suggested that she see a skin specialist who would help her to have her hair grow faster so that she could be as pretty as mommy. Ann went to the doctor very happily.

My contact with Ann was, on the whole, a friendly one. We played whatever she wanted, we fed the ducks at the lake nearby, we fixed food and generally had a good time. At the same time, my talks with her mother continued and contained whatever interpretations I wanted to give the mother and the child regarding her behavior at home. This is a technique which I find helpful in the treatment of young children (Buxbaum, 1946). Ann now was willing, for the first time, to stay alone in nursery school.

The contact was interrupted after eight weeks when I went on a prolonged vacation. I had suggested to the mother that she return after my vacation; however, she did not do so for a number of reasons, the most important one being that she left town to join her husband. I received a letter from her in August in which she said:

> Ann stopped pulling her hair two months ago. She said to me, "Mommy, I don't want to pull my hair anymore. I want it to grow"—and it is growing. She is taking great pride in it, doesn't mind her weekly shampoos, loves the water at the beach and turns the lawn sprinkler on her head when the children are playing with it. She is playing with four little girls on the block and is very popular with them. She is even minding pretty well, wets the bed occasionally at night when she has had too much liquids but never wets at nap time, seldom takes a toy to bed and she sleeps well. She is overcoming her shyness very well; she visits almost everybody on the block.

DISCUSSION

The therapeutic process in these two cases shows some similarities and some differences. Both girls resolved a conflict with regard to identification with mother when the misunderstood experience regarding the genitals was clarified. Such clarifications in children's cases have the same effect that interpretations have with adults. I discussed the importance of such clarifications in other papers (1946, 1954). Both girls accepted an intermediary object (instead of their own hair) in the transition to object relations.

The chief difference between the two cases lies in the children's relationship to their families, particularly to their mothers. Ann's relation to her mother was essentially a good one. Her neurosis was really a traumatic neurosis. Beryl's relation to her mother was poor; the relationship she established with me became a corrective experience, allowing the clarification and resolution of the traumatic experience. However, her response to the traumatic experience was only one part of Beryl's neurosis. In addition, the internalization of her conflicts had already led to a neurotic character disturbance, which was treatable only by psychoanalysis.

Both girls had occasion to see their parents' genitals repeatedly at an early age. Ann saw her father's injured genitals, Beryl saw her mother's bleeding genitals which she misunderstood as being injured. In both children eighteen months was the crucial age. I assume that the hair-pulling syndrome was caused by these traumata, because in both cases the hair pulling stopped after the experience had been discussed and the misconception clarified. These traumata are very similar to those which Greenacre and Freud described as leading to fetishism. The children continued with their autoerotic activities of sucking and stroking and, in addition, used hair pulled from their own heads.

Ann's relationship to her mother was fundamentally a satisfactory one—she trusted her mother, felt safe only when she was with her, and wanted to be like her mother with the exception of having her genitals. She regarded pubic hair as dirty, and did not want mother to have any. Perhaps she wanted to pull it out, but instead she pulled out her own hair. She refused to have her hair shampooed, and did not want mother to wash her own hair in the genital area. She did not want mother to touch this dirty part—as she had been forbidden to masturbate. Father's injured genitals supported the idea of punishment in the genital area. Pulling her hair was a form of self-castration, but also a way in which she tried to prevent herself from becoming like mother. She did not want to have the genitals of either mother or father. When the mother intuitively allowed Ann to wash mother's hair, she gave Ann permission to touch and wash her hair instead of pulling her hair; to Ann, this meant that mother symbolically allowed her to touch the mother's genital region as well as her own. She also gave her some thing to pull which Ann accepted temporarily as a part of the mother as well as of herself. The kitten became her sleeping companion instead of the mother. She pulled its hair, sucked it, and masturbated by putting it between her legs.

This good mother allowed Ann to use *her* as an inter-mediate object (to use Winnicott's expression), alternately with an inanimate object—a true intermediary object—which Ann accepted from her and in her stead. With the help of this intermediary object furnished by the mother, Ann could finally give up her ambivalent relation to a part of her own body, namely, her hair, as a representative of her ambivalent relation to mother. Her attachment to the intermediate, inanimate object was only short-lived and led to true object relationships. She began to like other people as well as her mother.

Beryls' relationship to her mother was not as satisfactory. Her mother was, to use Winnicott's term, a "not good enough mother." To call her "rejecting" would be to ignore her concern and the efforts she made on Beryl's behalf. But her narcissism, her incapacity for forming genuine relation-ships, caused Beryl to despair of winning her love and, sub-sequently, of identifying with her. Beryl, like Ann, did not want to be like her mother in the genital area, that is, bleed-ing and maimed. She was aware of mother's disgust at her genital area and of her disapproval of her masturbation. When Mother overcame her disgust she could wash Beryl's hair in a "good enough" way. As with Ann, this was received as a symbol of mother's accepting Beryl's genitals as good.

During her treatment, Beryl soon accepted gifts from me as intermediary objects. She did not accept similar objects for this purpose from her mother or anybody else. She slept with the sleepy doll whose hair she pulled, kept the locket around her neck, fondled it and never parted with it.

The stuffed poodle and the diary became substitutes for me when she left treatment. These objects became important and were alternate recipients of her aggression. When her hair pulling stopped, her relation to the intermediary objects remained important. It seems that she could accept the intermediary object from me rather than from mother because I accepted her, whereas her mother did not. The diary and the poodle also represented me; they stood for a benevolent superego figure, which "reminded her" not to pull her hair and allowed her to pet herself. Berta Bornstein (1936) has described the roles of these bedtime toys as representations of the child's id and superego. The intermediary object, the poodle dog, was removed from the child's body and was at the same time invested with the qualities of the superego. Beryl apparently could not yet entirely dispense with a visible reminder of the superego. A photograph, a picture, or symbol of an idol might serve the same function. Beryl used the intermediary object as an aid in the formation of her superego.

Winnicott (1953) says that children treat intermediate objects very roughly but, so long as they are interested in them, do not destroy them completely. Beryl pulled her sister's hair before she pulled her own. She apparently displaced the aggression meant for her sister onto herself. Ann, too, turned her aggression onto herself. Both girls accepted a gift offered with the explicit understanding that they could pull its hair.

Hair pulling cannot be described only in terms of aggression turned against the self. Ann pulled the chicken's feathers very gently; Beryl sometimes slowly and carefully pulled one hair. Beryl pulled her hair more when she felt deserted and unloved; Ann, too, pulled her hair when she was upset. We are reminded of the expression "to tear one's hair" as a sign of despair and mourning. In this respect, hair pulling resembles a form of masturbation to which the child resorts in periods of anxiety and loneliness, attempting to hold on to himself when people fail him; he reminds himself that he exists by making himself feel. These children were careful not to hurt themselves badly while pulling their hair; moreover, by using their hair to pet themselves, the slight pain was immediately connected with tenderness toward themselves. This amalgamation of painful and pleasant sensations is where masochism starts. The use of an intermediary object allowed the children to deflect these feelings from themselves. It may then be that, in these cases, the masochistic tendency was, at least for the time being, not pursued.

Apparently, intermediary objects, as well as parts of the child's own body in this role, became carriers of the positive relationship of the mother to the child and recipients of the child's feelings for the mother, positive as well as negative. The children express positive feelings for the mother by eating their hair.

Ann says, "I feel like pulling and it tastes good."

Beryl ate black and red candy with which she touched her genitals or her anus, kissed the Old Maid on which she sat—all of which indicates what hair means to her. It is good tasting, sweet—like mother's body, but also like her own excretions. She also ate mucus from her nose, saying, "It tastes good." It seems to me that eating serves both to destroy and to preserve. What is dirty about the mother's body or their own should be destroyed by eating. What is sweet of the mother's body or their own should be preserved by eating. Hair is both dirty and sweet.

What these two children did with their hair, other children do by eating mucus, fecal matter, skin, or nails.[1] Such behavior is a normal phenomenon in all children before the barrier of disgust as a reaction formation has been established. It seems, however, that eating one's own sweet dirt is also a sign of the incomplete separation from the mother.

[1] It is usual for animals to clean themselves by eating their own dirt.

The child uses a part of his own body—symbolizing a part of the mother's body—as intermediary object.

However, the edibility of hair as well as of other parts of the body is only one aspect of the satisfaction which the children derive from it. The other lies in the manipulation and the tactile and skin sensation. It is particularly this quality which becomes transferred onto the intermediary object. Stroking, petting, fondling of the hair is the satisfaction which the children seek. Beryl could give up her hair pulling when mother stroked her by shampooing and brushing her hair. Ann, on the other hand, gave it up when she was allowed to stroke her mother's hair.

Apparently the mutual, active and passive skin contact is of as great importance as the oral contact. Escalona and Leitch (1954), as well as Spitz (1959), have called attention to this fact. Experiments with young monkeys removed from their mothers have shown that skin contacts are extremely important for their development and well being. They develop adequately if they are given a terrycloth figure, which is soft but without lactation, while they become disturbed if left with a wire figure which furnishes them milk (Harlow, 1959).

Mittelmann (1955) stated that children become aware of the distinction of what belongs to their body and what does not during the toddler stage, which he thinks is the crucial age for the development of fetishism. The crucial time in my patients was eighteen months—which would agree with Mittelmann's findings.

I think that inanimate objects are libidinally cathected as a reaction to the child's leaving his mother, i.e., putting distance between her and himself. An example is Linus in "Peanuts," who drags his blanket along like a string, holding, touching, sucking it, and reassuring himself all is not lost. The toddler age is also the age in which cleanliness education takes place. The skin contact with the mother at times becomes unpleasant and occurs less frequently. Both my patients associated dirt and the genital area. In their therapy both children became free to pet and stroke themselves in other areas of their body, but also, with the help of an intermediary object, to adopt a friendly, physical contact with people.

The traumatic experience disturbed the children in a phase in which tactile and skin sensations are of great importance. Consequently their ability to adapt themselves was impaired, and they remained fixed at the level of libidinal development and of object relations which they had reached at the time of the traumatic experience. When traumatic experience was brought into consciousness the children relinquished using their hair as the means with which to fulfill their need for tactile and skin sensations. They proceeded to accept "other than me" objects for this purpose. The intermediate object facilitated the transition from the undifferentiated (self and mother) to "other than self" objects. The mother became a separate entity for the child; the child moved in the direction of greater independence and formed relationships with other people besides the mother. Both children then were able to derive pleasure from touching themselves as well as from touching others; I would like to say that they were able to "feel themselves," because I think such "feelings" of one's body are precursors of feelings, i.e., emotions of his own which the child develops for himself as well as for others. They were able to continue in their libidinal development, to separate themselves from their mothers, and to reach out for other relationships; Beryl made a plunge into the oedipal relationship as if she had to catch up with a development which had been long overdue. As long as tactile contacts were disturbed, the ambivalent differentiated relationship to the mother's body and to the child's own body existed, and the genital feelings as well as object relations were disturbed.

THE ROLE OF DETECTIVE
STORIES IN THE ANALYSIS OF A
TWELVE-YEAR-OLD BOY

Detective stories are a recognized part of our literature, although the basis of their appeal is not equally recognized. Some adults, it is true, consider them unsuitable for children and try to place a ban on them, but with little success. The child will simply resort to subterfuge to satisfy his need.

When a child's habit or misbehavior proves impervious to reasoning and advice, we may attribute to it an unconscious significance. In an article, "The Popular Adventure Story," Hans Zulliger (1933) analyzed one of these adventure stories and disclosed its unconscious meaning for a boy whose favorite story it was. He found that by reading adventure stories, the boy was able to ward off his anxiety. I should like to report on a similar case.

Charles, a large, handsome boy with an open countenance but reserved manner, began analysis at the age of twelve. His paternal uncle brought him to me because of severe anxiety and difficulties in learning. Charles, his mother, and a sister about two years older lived with his uncle. His father had died two years previously. The mother suffered

This paper was published originally in *The Psychoanalytic Quarterly*, 10:373-381, 1941, under the title, "The Role of Detective Stories in a Child Analysis."

from epileptic attacks which usually occurred at night. The uncle said that, although Charles shared a bedroom with his mother, he took no notice of the attacks but slept right through them.

In the first session, Charles told of his fear that a man might leap upon him from the darkness and choke or crush him. He was afraid to open his eyes lest someone might be looking at him. In the second session, it transpired that Charles' difficulty in learning did not originate from a lack of intelligence but from a compulsion to read detective stories. He had them with him always, at home and at school, and read them instead of studying. When he tried to study he could think only about the stories. When he finished one, he seized upon the next with which he was always provided. He behaved like an addict who is afraid of going to pieces without his accustomed drug. They were cheap stories of the most sensational type, forbidden to public sale but nevertheless always obtainable by those who wanted them.

Charles' hero was the detective, invincible, generous, farseeing and clever. Naturally he had chosen the detective as his ego ideal and wanted to be like him. Furthermore, he was fascinated by the different ways a person could be done to death. He enjoyed the shudders that the horrors described gave him and recalled the cruel things which children do to animals. But even animals are not defenseless. He recounted a fearful tale of a teamster who had blinded both his horses and kicked them in the belly. One day they forced him against a wall and crushed him. Since Charles' starting point was the detective stories with their human actors, I was curious to know whom the unhappy and abused, yet dangerously vindictive, animals represented.

The next session provided the answer. Charles complained bitterly about his sister who teased him. She was the uncle's favorite. When he and his sister quarreled, she kicked him. He was therefore the tortured horse and she the cruel driver.

He would like to have taken revenge upon her as the horse had upon the driver. He defended himself from her by interposing a chair, "So that I would not hurt her." It was remarkable how often she was hurt by the chair through her own clumsiness!

Since I knew of Charles' fear of being choked and crushed, I could assume that he identified himself with the victim or victims-to-be of the detective stories. His hostility toward his sister was the first hint that he might also be the murderer. In addition to an identification with the detective which he readily admitted, he played the murderer and victim as well.

As a token of his confidence, he next brought me a detective story. It dealt with ghosts in which Charles, of course, did not believe. But spiritualism was another matter; as for hypnotism, that was dangerous. One could get sick and even die from it. He was afraid that a man might be looking at him in the dark; that was why he kept his eyes shut. The man might hypnotize him and during hypnosis forbid him to call for help and then throttle him.

In the following session he remembered that, when he was about seven, he had suffered from breathlessness and a fear of choking to death. In preparation for a tonsillectomy when he was five, his mother had told him it would not hurt, and he had not been afraid. He was angry at her for misleading him. He thought next of the death of his father who died when Charles was ten. His description of the death was rather strange and later proved to be not quite accurate. According to his version, the father "put out his tongue and fell over." He concluded the hour with an account of "something odd." He used to live on a farm where there were hogs. When the hogs had been "cut underneath," they were not allowed to lie down. He had kept them moving and had ridden on their backs.

Charles, it developed had looked upon the tonsillectomy as a castration such as had been performed upon the hogs,

and had suffered severe pain and fear of death, especially
as he had been unable to cry out or resist because of the
anaesthetic which had rendered him helpless. He suspected
that his father had been rendered defenseless in a similar
way and then killed.

The father's death and his fear of castration were directly
related in Charles' mind. He had spoken of his father in
immediate association to the ghost whom he feared to see
gazing at him. Later he recalled his father saying to him during a confidential talk, "But surely you don't do *that,* do
you?" This prohibition of masturbation had caused Charles
to hate his father and wish him dead. Charles added, "Shortly
after, father died." Charles felt vaguely that his hatred and
death wishes had killed his father. Fear of the ghost was,
moreover, a fear of being discovered masturbating and of
punishment in the form of castration, as well as fear of death
in revenge for his father's death. In keeping his eyes tightly
closed, Charles' feigning not to see was shutting out the
fearsome vision of his father's ghost. The description of his
father as "falling over" suggested the probability that the
mother's epileptic attacks had a greater part in his anxiety
than was apparent.

The characters in his detective stories embodied the various roles which Charles himself played in fantasy. The victim who was taken prisoner, put in chains and drugged or
poisoned was himself in the grip of the anaesthetic. Helpless
and in great danger, like the hogs before castration, or his
father before death, he was about to face his unknown persecutor. In Charles' fantasy, this individual was as mysterious
and unknown as the villain of the stories. Every person in
the story, even the detective himself, might be the murderer,
and was under suspicion. Similarly, Charles was suspicious
of his mother, uncle, doctor, nurse.

Following the painful memories disclosed in these sessions, there was a period of resistance. He continued to bring
me detective stories, and recommended one in particular,

which had relevance to the acuteness of his fear of being choked. A period of intensified anxiety followed, and one day he stayed home, suffering from an "attack of breathlessness." He acceded to my request to come to the session despite his attack and told me that after accompanying a friend home, he had to go through dark and gloomy streets to return to his own house. Fearing a man might jump out from a doorway and throttle him, he had run all the way home.

Very cautiously Charles started to complain about his uncle who was strict with him and refused him permission to do everything he enjoyed doing. He confiscated the detective stories which Charles was forced to read in secret. This was not true; the uncle had given his full permission. He complained above all that his uncle preferred his sister and sided with her when they quarreled. He also told of the uncle's taking part in his play, giving him presents and otherwise indulging him to a great extent, probably more than his father would have done.

A detective story with a menacing claw on the cover elicited associations to the various ways of killing animals. He described the great pleasure he experienced in watching the slaughter of bulls, hogs, and chickens. He had never killed an animal himself from fear of its rage before it was mortally wounded.

During the Christmas holiday, in a game of "Indians," Charles's uncle was bound by the other children. Charles did not assist in tying him up, only "gave them the rope." At the time he had reveled in fantasies of gagging the fettered man, rendering him defenseless and cutting off his genitals. He added, "If you can't help yourself, you get wild with rage— so wild that you could kill anyone who is holding you." Held against his will, anaesthetized, and having his tonsils cut out, Charles had been "wild with rage," and wanted to retaliate. It had been his father then. After his father's death the rage was transferred to his uncle, for the uncle was in control now. In fantasy, the boy held his uncle responsible both for the operation and for his father's death. In his fear of attack on the street, he was afraid that a man would throttle and kill him. What the uncle had done once he might do again. In addition, Charles feared unconsciously the revenge of his uncle and of his father's ghost for his own rage and hatred towards them. Hatred was uppermost in his every thought and feeling about them. The uncle was still more dangerous than the father because he had taken the father's place as Charles had wished to do. He felt powerless to act against him, just as he did not dare to kill animals.

The detective story provided a medium through which Charles could commit murder as well as be the victim. He acted this out with a flashlight which he had received on Christmas. He played at flashing the light in his own eyes. He was both detective and criminal; he must watch himself to save himself from his own murderous impulses.

In the period which followed, Charles' sadistic fantasies were directed chiefly toward one of his schoolmates. From the description given, this boy was suffering from chorea. He thrashed about with his arms, grimaced and made meaningless movements, especially when he was angry. Charles justified his harassment of the boy on the grounds that he had stolen his fountain pen and had cheated and lied to him. One day he reported that he had stuffed his muffler into the boy's mouth to gag him, and then bound him with a belt. He brought muffler and belt and a large pocket knife, suggesting that he would have liked to play the same game with me.

I pointed out to him the resemblance between the epileptic mother and the choreic classmate. The boy's spitting was comparable to her foaming at the mouth, the muffler to the handkerchief thrust into her mouth to prevent biting the tongue. He had, moreover, transferred to me his attitude toward the mother. Up to this time there had been no mention of his mother's attacks. At the beginning of the analysis she had been in a sanitarium for another ailment. The allu-

sion to her illness had been general and omitted any refer-
ence to the convulsions which were not occurring at that
time. Now that she was home his associations revealed that
he was familiar with the onset and the course of her attacks.
He became much preoccupied with the subject, and I therefore felt justified in discussing it with him.

In the following session he gave a detailed account of another attack his mother had had. Hearing his mother's rapid
breathing, he thought, "Oh, gee, it's beginning again!" Then
she fell out of bed. (In the first session he had reported sleeping well except "when the covers fall off.") By the time he
was thoroughly awake, his mother was unconscious, foaming
at the mouth, her body twitching. It so terrified him that he
covered himself and pretended to sleep. He added that he
was not afraid of his mother, but he had been afraid of a
beggar whom he had seen in an epileptic attack, afraid that
the beggar would fall on him or leap at him, carrying him to
the ground when he fell. He had dreamed that he was running through a forest, chased by someone and he fell into
a pit.

His fear of falling included a fear of catching or of inherit-
ing his mother's sickness. But chiefly the fear of falling was
the feeling of persecution by the father-uncle-surgeon, and
by his mother who had deceived him about the operation,
had held him, "threw herself on me," as he said, so that he
could not defend himself. Describing his impression of the
anaesthesia, he had said, "Women [his mother and the nurse]
overpowered me." The charges he made against the schoolmate of lying, deceiving and stealing from him—of these, he
directly accused his mother.

In the game of "Indians" he had not taken an active part
but only provided the ropes to bind his uncle. In his acting
out with the schoolmate, he did gag and fetter the boy,
which he had not dared do to his uncle. The choreic boy and
the epileptic beggar were in his fantasy both males afflicted
with his mother's dangerous "falling sickness." Thus we see

that Charles' "persecutor" was a combination of his mother and the uncle who was also the displaced father. If this persecutor should attack him, Charles, like his mother, would fall down, and be castrated, become a woman. Charles would prefer to overthrow the man. In terms of his detective stories, he would have preferred to be the murderer rather than the victim. His play with the flashlight confirms this interpretation.

The measures taken to relieve the mother during an attack all represented violence to Charles. According to the fantasies acted out with his classmate, the handkerchief put into her mouth was a form of restraint. When the doctor came, he gave her an injection which, according to Charles, "paralyzed" her, and he did something else which Charles could not explain.

In the next session Charles spoke of some moving pictures he had seen on the capture of Andreas Hofer (a freedom fighter in the Napoleonic wars), of a fight between a boa and a crocodile in which the crocodile's back had been broken, of a gorilla's attack on a man. He recounted the horrors which occur in such struggles, of being made deaf and blind and speechless, of losing arms and legs, and of breaking one's nose. To be protected against these atrocities, one must be stronger than the uncle who, in Charles' fantasy, was the strongest of all because he had done away with his father and substituted himself.

From his associations, one could reconstruct what strongly suggested memories of a primal scene revived by the mother's nocturnal convulsions, a primal scene to which he had been a frightened and passive witness. In his unconscious fantasy, his father's participation had resulted in his father's death. As a detective or a witness he must try to protect the persecuted mother, and at the same time protect himself from her and the uncle. He must be able to overcome his uncle as he, in Charles' fantasy, had overcome his mother and father. He read detective stories to find out how to protect himself from this danger. He was distressed by those stories which turned out badly because they failed their purpose of allaying his anxiety; rather, they increased it.

After the relationship between the fear of the persecutor and the illness of his mother had been established, Charles' urgent need to read detective stories ceased except in periods of great resistance or increased anxiety. He became outspokenly dissatisfied with them and finally rejected them as stupid and foolish—always the same and always untrue.

The analysis of the detective stories covered a period of six months out of a two-year analysis, and was divided into three phases. In the first, Charles identified with the victim, the manifest content of his fear. In the second, he was the criminal, his aggression directed toward his sister, his mother and his uncle who also represented his father. He feared the vengeance of his victims and the consequence of his aggressive wishes which would entail castration as a punishment. But the figure which caused him greater anxiety was the epileptic: mother, beggar and classmate. Here it was plain that his aggression was a defense against his own passive wishes to be overcome and castrated. On a deeper level, his passive homosexual fear protected him from his instinctual drives, both aggressive and passive, which would result in his castration. Aggression would be punished by castration and passivity entailed castration as its condition.

Identification with the detective served the same function as the fear. It protected the victim and hindered the criminal from carrying out his evil designs. Therefore, the identification with the detective temporarily did away with the need to fear. This identification, in contrast to his identification with the victim and the criminal, is not easily recognizable in the analytic material except that in all its phases Charles was consciously identified with the detective. This was the only role acceptable to his ego. The analysis disclosed which forbidden instinctual desires the detective had been installed to combat, and the impulse gratifications he had to prevent.

While the detective served in defense against the instincts, the criminal and the victim were in the service of wish fulfillment. This two-sidedness reminds us of the structure of the neurotic symptom which likewise serves as instinct defense and instinct gratification. In addition, it serves the function of allaying anxiety. Since reading detective stories fulfilled these conditions, it was a symptom and as such was clung to compulsively.

The analysis of Charles' compulsion to read detective stories agree with Zulliger's analysis in that here, too, the stories are a form of defense against fear.

A CONTRIBUTION TO THE
PSYCHOANALYTIC KNOWLEDGE
OF THE LATENCY PERIOD

———•·•———

Psychoanalytic and psychiatric literature have described
and explored at great length the period of early childhood
which ends with the latency period. Prepuberty and puberty,
which follow the latency period, have also received a great
deal of attention. The latency period seems to be the step-
child of our literature. Anna Freud (1946a) says that it is
characterized by a definite decrease in neurotic manifestations. Maybe this is one of the reasons why we do not hear
much about it. Little children are brought to therapy mostly
because their parents are anxious and disturbed about them;
adolescents come to therapy because their disturbances are
obvious, because they ask for help, or because their parents
feel baffled and helpless in dealing with them. During the
latency period, the child's trouble is, in the majority of cases,
not disturbing enough to the family to call their attention to
it so that therapists have relatively little opportunity of dealing with this age group. Luckily for the children, there is
one group which is very much interested in them—the educators, some of whom are psychoanalytically oriented (Al-

This paper was published originally in *The American Journal of Orthopsychiatry*, 21:182-198, 1951.

pert, 1941; Finley, 1943). They find children of this age challenging and good material for the achievement of educational goals.

According to Helene Deutsch (1944), "during the latency period the child's interest in sexual matters largely subsides, but does not disappear altogether. All the . . . drives in this period of weakened sexual urges can be used for the unhampered development of the ego. Training and education strengthen the ego in its struggle for liberation from instinctual forces and further its adaptation to reality and its socialization" (Vol. 1: p. 2). Anna Freud (1946a) attributes the decrease in infantile neurosis to the dying down of the infantile wishes. The decrease in infantile neurosis makes the children of this age group less interesting for psychoanalytic exploration while at the same time the strengthening of the ego seems to recommend them for educational procedures. This division of interests looks very simple and logical; but as is usual with oversimplifications, it is incorrect.

Obviously, during the latency period ego development is prominent, or is expected to be prominent, while the instinctual drives are supposed to take a less significant position. Anna Freud speaks about two important indicators for infantile neurosis: the disturbance of libidinal development and the disturbance of ego development. She thinks that as long as ego development of the latency child is progressing and fluid, education should take the leading role; when ego development seems to be disturbed, therapy is indicated.

What is this so-called ego development? Helen Ross (1943) describes it as follows

. . . we assume that reaction formation patterns are well on their way to crystallization. The battle of conformity to the environment versus the child's own wishes has passed its initial stages and the drives have capitulated to a great degree. Exhibitionistic tendencies have given way to modesty; messiness to cleanliness; uncontrolled aggression and cruelty to sympathy and a feeling for one's fellows; unbridled curiosity to sublimated investigative pursuits; greediness to cooperation and willingness to share. We could enumerate all the virtues we wish a child to attain. We cannot expect that they have all been achieved to their optimum strength, nor can we expect that lapses will not occur. According to the degree of satisfaction reached in the early years, according to the adequacy of the superego, i.e., of the character training of the early years, is the child equipped with ego-strength. This equipment varies widely as we know. As the ego gathers strength under the abeyance of the drives, the child becomes free to turn his attention to the larger world around him" (p. 502).

Ego development thus is identified with the growing strength of the ego. In Anna Freud's (1946a) words,

The term ego strength is not meant to denote an absolute quantity of ego forces which are, in themselves, not measurable. It refers to the relative efficiency of the ego with regard to the contents of the id (the instincts) and the forces of the environment with which the ego has to deal. . . . It is only the final frustration of the oedipus wishes, with the consequent fading out of the early libido organisations, which changes the situation decisively in favor of ego strength [p. 84].

Part of the ego strength at this point comes from the identifications with the parent figures, which are used in the formation of the superego.

The passing of the Oedipus complex and the resulting diminution of sexual feelings mark the onset of the latency period. Fenichel (1945) sums up as follows:

Freud was of the opinion that the occurrence of the period of latency is a characteristic of the human species. The early blossoming of infantile sexuality is, as it were, 'doomed to destruction' by nature, and this fact is a biological precondition for repression and thus for neuroses. Other authors have pointed out that since among some primitive tribes a latency period never appears, cultural restrictions must be responsible for the renunciation of sexual wishes. However, there is no clear-cut contradiction between 'biologically' and 'socially' determined phenomena. Biological changes may be brought about by former external influences. It may be that the latency period is a result of external influences that have been in effect long enough to have left permanent traces; perhaps at this point we are watching external influences becoming biological [p. 62].

According to the different authors, the latency period is distinguished by the development of the ego—its increasing strength—accompanied by a recession of instinctual drives and a consolidation of the superego—the heir to the decline of the oedipus complex (Freud, 1924). Its prominent defense mechanisms are reaction formations. The child of this period normally makes great strides in his recognition and adaptation to reality and society; his ability to sublimate is increased.

The problems which I would like to discuss in connection with the latency period are these: What causes the recession of the oedipal feelings? Do they always recede or fade out? How does the ego grow in strength? What defense mechanisms develop or are prominent in this period? Which ones are normal? Which ones pathologic or pathogenic? The presentation of the case of a boy who was in analysis with me for two and one half years will serve as a starting point. The presenting symptom was stuttering. I shall, however, omit any discussion of stuttering as such, except where it is part of the character neurosis.

CASE PRESENTATION

Jimmy, age eight, came into treatment because of severe stuttering. He was an obese boy who moved quickly, darting around. He was always in a hurry to do something, and yet at the same time succeeded in being slow and looked morose most of the time. His speech was explosive; his words tumbled over one another until he could not bring out the next word and came to a stop; he went through agonies and distortions until the ban was broken and the torrent of words proceeded. His obesity was partly a family feature—both his parents were obese—but he also came by it through excessive eating. He ate enormously and was very messy. Occasionally Jimmy complained of headaches. He was not an attractive child. He was puzzled and annoyed that I did not suggest he get speech training, as were his parents. He was eager to get over his stuttering; he was in a hurry about that to.

His parents were orthodox Jews. His mother was a warm, gentle person who lived in awe of her husband, a teacher at the Hebrew School. Out of respect for his wisdom, she did not interfere with his way of handling the children although she did not really agree with it. The father was a mass of defenses. He had been unhappy as a child, but brought up his children as he had been brought up; his parents had been right—it was all to the good. He had never questioned their authority and he neither expected nor tolerated any criticism from his children. He was in agreement with his parents as well as with his God—he was right. It was against his conviction that the boy was brought into treatment; the boy's stuttering, however, interfered with his plans to have him become a rabbi. A rabbi must not stutter! He knew vaguely that he was taking a chance that the treatment might further estrange the boy, but he decided to let him come anyway.

There were three children in the family: a girl three years older than Jimmy and a little girl of one. The older daughter compliantly followed in her parents' footsteps. The baby was everybody's pet and could do no wrong. Jimmy, who according to Jewish custom, as the only son, should have had an important place in the family, was demoted from his position on account of his stuttering. He was not satisfactory as a son—he was a disgrace.

The demands made upon the children were extreme, partly because of religious and cultural factors. Of course, the religious and dietary laws had to be observed. The boy went to public school for half a day and to Hebrew school the other half. Since he had homework from both schools, his evenings were taken up with studying. There was no time for play or for friends. From the beginning, treatment plans interfered with his education since it was necessary to make a choice between going to both schools and coming to see me three times a week. The parents agreed to his absenting himself from Hebrew school during the hours he needed to spend with me, planning to alternate this schedule with the public school for the second half of the school year.

Although I considered this heavy schedule one of the difficulties in the environment which eventually would have to be modified, I did not think it wise to bring the matter up before treatment was well under way, inasmuch as treatment was largely dependent upon the cooperation of the parents. The parents were suspicious of me as a therapist because I belonged to a different cultural group, one toward whom they felt antagonistic. They felt defensive about their methods of education, expecting that I would consider them responsible for their child's difficulties. I decided that I had a better chance of making any demands with regard to changes of education or schedule if I could base them on material obtained from the patient. I also wanted to wait until the parents had gained some confidence in me, or at least until they had overcome their great distrust. I had doubts as to how successful therapy would be if I had to depend entirely upon the ability of the child to make use of it. It was essential to secure the parents' cooperation.

When Jimmy first came he was eager to "get to work on my stuttering." He wanted to know what he should do. I explained that I didn't think there was anything wrong with his ability to speak, but there were things in his mind which interfered with his saying what he wanted to say—maybe

some naughty thoughts which he did not like or perhaps
contradictory thoughts or feelings. He might not even know
what they were. I added, "We'll find out together in time;
but we could really do lots of things—play, make things,
whatever you like to do—and talk too."

This offer to play threw Jimmy into a conflict. He knew
he had come to work on his stuttering. His parents were
paying for it. They would ask him what he had learned, and
what would he tell them? He was unable to accept this
license to play; he had to do "some work." From the material at hand he chose "to make things"—first to make "useful" things like notebooks, scrapbooks for school, and pencil
cases. While we worked on them, he told me what he had
done during the day, and about his studies at school. I
gathered that his days were spent at working, working; he
was never at play. There were not even any toys at home—
except for the baby. He did not complain, just stated facts.
I told him I would explain to his parents that we would play
here, and would make sure that we could do whatever we
wanted. I asked him to tell his parents that I wanted to see
them and gave him the choice of being present or not when
they came. He decided to be present. When they came,
Jimmy took over the interview after my explanation that we
needed to be allowed to play. He opened all the cupboards
and drawers and showed them the toys and materials, with
an air of proud possessor. His parents' attitude was one of
condescending tolerance, although they did not express it in
words. They had no use and no understanding for this "kid
stuff." Apparently it was necessary for Jimmy to get approval
from his parents before he could proceed to play. Even then,
he had to camouflage. He still "made" things, but now they
were toys, presents for his little sister—the only one in the
family who was entitled to waste her time playing—but he
kept them in my office and never gave them to her. Finally
he accepted the fact that he could make and have some
toys himself and that he wanted to play too.

It was about eight to ten months before Jimmy was able to play without feeling guilty. His parents went along with this development in an obedient, dutiful, and unconvinced way. However, they made some significant concessions: they allowed Jimmy to drop the Hebrew school and had him tutored instead; the following year they allowed him to go to a private progressive Jewish school where Hebrew was taught as a second language. Some of the external pressure was thus relieved, and he was given the opportunity and encouragement to play on the playingfield, which gave him an acceptable outlet for pent-up aggressions.

It may sound peculiar to hear someone say that she worked for a period of eight to ten months getting a child to play. For Jimmy, playing was not only forbidden from the outside; he had internalized this prohibition. He was unhappy that he had to do so much work, but he could not get away from it. He hated his father for the demands which he imposed upon him, but did not dare defy him openly. If he secretly did something of which he thought his father would disapprove, he was even more afraid that God would know it anyway. In his opinion God and his father were allies, and the two of them together were overpowering. "They are too much for me to fight," he sometimes told me in a discouraged way.

He could allow himself to draw and paint, because, as two of his school subjects, they could be considered "work." He drew some pictures which he said were about some of the things that frightened him in his dreams, and about which he thought before he went to sleep. He had had a dream about a big fire on an island. All the people on the island burned to death; he was the only one who stayed alive, but then the people who were burned came back as ghosts and haunted him. This dream was connected with the memory of a house on fire when he was about five years old; he was in nursery school at the time and saw the fire when he returned. Since that time Jimmy had been afraid that while he was gone a fire, flood, bombing, or earthquake would destroy his parents' house and everybody would die except himself, since he was not there. He continued to have these fantasies when he was on his way to see me. Sometimes he arrived at my office pale from a splitting headache. These fantasies of destruction would then appear as the cause for the headache, the headache as the punishment for them. The fantasies in turn were his revenge for his feelings of anger and frustration which he suffered through somebody at home.

I learned by and by that the island about which he dreamed and fantasied had a name: it was the Island of Eno. I understood it as the place where everything was condemned with the forbidding "no." It was home where everything he liked to do was not allowed. The island was governed by a president, a cruel man. Jimmy was his son, the vice-president. The vice-president sought to find out his father's secret which would give him the power that his father had. In reality, Jimmy loved to rummage through his father's desk and steal his papers and pencils, but he never could get to his important papers because they were locked up. Finally, the island burned up, through no fault of the son, who then inherited the father's power. (Only through the father's death could the son win over the father. No wonder he was afraid of his revenge, particularly since the father was in such close alliance with God.) When the ghosts returned, some of them were on the son's side; others, under the leadership of the ghost father, were against him. There was a war between the two armies of ghosts. It was a war of a peculiar kind: the thin ghosts ate up the fat ghosts. It was like the story of the seven thin cows eating up the seven fat cows in the famous dream of Joseph. This led to Jimmy's voracious eating. He ate to destroy the ghosts! This is the way he fought his fat parents in reality. He ate sloppily, voraciously, in enormous quantities—but only the food which he was permitted to eat, although he sometimes wanted to eat something that was not allowed. Also, he had watched his little sister drinking at the mother's breast, but biting it too. He was worried that she might hurt his mother and really eat her. The ghosts eating ghosts were himself and his sister eating mother. Whenever he was depressed, he sought out his little sister and played with her; sometimes he induced her to be naughty. She was his "ally" while at the same time he attempted to move her out of her favored position by getting her into trouble. He loved his little sister, but he was also intensely jealous of her. In many of his destructive fantasies he debated which of his family he would save, and invariably he decided to save his baby sister's life—the one of whom he was most jealous and whom he loved the most.

This fantasy, which goes back to the burning house when he was five, contains his oedipal feelings: the son takes the father's place; the masturbation—the fire of his body that keeps him awake—and the expression of his wishes toward his mother on an oral level. The regression to the oral level lessens his castration anxiety; by becoming a baby like his sister—sucking at the mother's breast—he is free of restrictions and prohibitions as she is. However, since his fantasies are oral-destructive, he is again haunted by his fear of retaliation. His castration anxiety catches up with him; the disguise into the baby, the regression to the oral level were in vain. Jimmy had to work through his fantasies in order to free himself from his fears. Playing was for him the symbol of everything his parents disapproved of: his oedipal wishes and his aggressive, destructive fantasies against them.

One of the difficulties against which we had to work was that not only the patient, but also his father believed in the magic of thoughts. At one point I said that it was all right to think about forbidden things as long as one did not do them. Jimmy told me very seriously that was not so; one must not even think these thoughts—his father said it was just as bad as doing them. I asked his permission to discuss the question with his father. I felt it was necessary to get the father's cooperation at this juncture to avoid subjecting Jimmy to an unbearable conflict. As on many other occasions, his father argued with me but finally agreed to tell the patient he could think whatever thoughts he wanted. These included thoughts about God, something that the father may have sensed but did not mention.

The permission granted was crucial in this case, making possible for Jimmy to express his hostile thoughts against his father, to use forbidden language, swear words, dirty words, even to express his blasphemous thoughts. We called talking in the hours with me "thinking out loud," in this way utilizing his father's permission for the analytic treatment. Since no retaliation from Heaven or any other place followed, Jimmy felt vastly relieved. It was only now, by getting Jimmy to express the forbidden, interfering thoughts as well as the conscious ones, that we could attack the stuttering. Once, when he wanted to tell me something that had happened in school, he stuttered very badly, interrupted himself, and said—his usual formula at that time—"Now, let me figure this out: I think it is bad that I think it is good that I think the children make fun of my father." What had happened was that Jimmy's father, as a substitute teacher, had taken over the school class which Jimmy attended and the children raised hell with him, to Jimmy's secret delight, for which he felt very guilty. The way he expressed it was a tongue-breaker in itself. Jimmy could now tell me, since he was less afraid of his father's magic powers, that he was afraid to stop stuttering lest he then would have to become a rabbi, which he did not want to be. We discussed his fear of his father and I assured him that his father would not really force him to do something he did not want to do. It was essential to his recovery to eliminate this secondary gain.

Jimmy's need for haste resulted in his making a shambles of everything he touched; he got splashes of paint on his pictures, tore threads, broke the wood. If I tried to help him, it only made matters worse. He wanted to do things alone. He told me that his older sister, his mother, his father —everybody—did things for him and in doing so they took things away from him. We compared his determination to do things alone to his hurried speech, which at times made him stumble over his words. He said, "Do you suppose I am afraid she [the older sister] might take my words away?" He told me that whenever he tried to say something, she quickly said it for him. This anxiety that she might "take it away from him" by helping him in words or actions was an expression of his castration anxiety. She already had "taken away" his place in the family; she was the accepted one who was given authority by his parents to scold and reprimand him. He hated her much as he hated his father, with whom she identified. He frequently attacked her—which he did not dare do to his father.

Jimmy repeatedly had occasion to watch ritual killing of chickens and also was present at a ritual circumcision. He was taken to all these occasions by his father, whom he identified with the men who killed the chickens and performed the circumcisions. He wanted "to do it himself!" he said, obviously instead of having it done to him. He wanted to castrate—"do it himself"—but could not do it; he did not want "to be helped," which meant to be castrated. When his anxiety about doing things for himself diminished, his relationship to his father and sister improved. At my request the parents restrained his sister's authority toward Jimmy, which helped him to separate her from them in his thinking.

Jimmy remained in the progressive school, where he performed satisfactorily, and made friends. After two years of treatment, I reduced his hours and asked his parents to send him to a speech specialist with whom he made good progress. I continued to see him once a week for a few more months. He loved to take part in school plays. He played with toys like any other boy. After I had given him a train, his parents, aroused to a feeling of competition, gave him one too. His father took him on a trip to Israel. The last I heard, he wanted to farm in Israel where his father owned some land. This was a sign of the father's reconciliation with his son, a sign of Jimmy's compromise with his father. He did not want to become a rabbi; but he also did not want, or rather was unable, to detach himself completely from his powerful father who was in alliance with God. The idea of farming his father's land in Israel was pleasing his father and pleasing God, and yet he could safely give up his speech defect since the father did not insist he become a rabbi.

In the treatment, Jimmy used me as an ally, one who apparently was nearly as powerful as his father since I could influence his father. Whenever I saw his parents, Jimmy and I agreed ahead of time on what I would say. He used me as his emissary. As his fears diminished we experimented. When he wanted to get his parents to give him permission for something, he attempted to speak for himself with the understanding that I would come to his rescue if he needed me. Sometimes, when he was too afraid, he let me arrange things for him. Toward the end of treatment, there was something he wanted to discuss but found rather difficult. I offered my help, but he turned me down, saying, "You know, I won't have your help very much longer. I have to do it myself." When we parted, he wanted to make sure that he could call on me in an "emergency."

Reviewing the structure of Jimmy's disturbance and the changes which occurred in treatment we might say this:

Jimmy's stuttering was the result of contradictory strivings in his feelings and thoughts. While he attempted consciously to say the permitted and expected words, he preconsciously rebelled against the demands imposed upon him. He did not want to learn to speak in such a way that he might be able to become a rabbi, although he obediently went to the prescribed schools and obediently said his prayers. He did not dare rebel openly against the father "who was in alliance with God." His speech unconsciously expressed his rebellious thoughts against his father and God; his explosive sounds contained fragments of foul and blasphemous language. Equally, his stuttering was connected with his jealousy of and hostility toward his older sister, both of which contained sexual undertones.

The mouth movements, which accompanied his stuttering as auxiliary gestures, revealed his desire to devour—which was brought out in his fantasies—while his phallic aggression and castration fear were symbolized in conspicuous movements with his tongue. The stuttering is the expression of conscious, preconscious and unconscious thoughts and feelings, compressed into words which, in their distortion, contain a thought and its contradiction. They are structured like compulsive symptoms. Sometimes the contradiction is expressed through auxiliary movements, which make it possible for him to keep his words undistorted.

His thinking shows the same mechanisms. He ponders and deliberates painfully. He is afraid to think for fear that God and his father will know his thoughts; he is afraid of their magic as well as of his own. Yet he is not a child who stops thinking; he thinks a great deal, debates with himself as well as with others. In the areas which contain his conflicts he thinks in circles. But even here he can do something about it. He cheats himself, hoping to cheat God and father too. When he cannot allow himself to play for the fun of it, he does something under the heading of "work" or "present," knowing full well that he only pretends to work and that he really enjoys himself. He can bribe or circumvent his conscience. He can accept treatment under the condition that his father approve of it. His father's acceptance was, throughout treatment, a pretense and Jimmy knew it. Yet he could bribe his conscience and appease his fears by taking his father's word for it. All he needed was "the magic word."

When he doubted that his father would approve of his discussions with me on family and religious matters, he would console himself by saying, "After all, he sends me here so he must know it's all right." But he never repeated our discussions at home. In his way of arguing, he was like his father—clever, shrewd, and logical. He identified with and competed with his father in ways of thinking and debating, although his thoughts frequently contradicted him. Here again, as in speech, obedience and rebellion are combined in one process.

His feelings were expressed in fantasies of destruction and fear of retaliation. He wished to take his father's power for himself. He also wanted to take his father's penis, but he was afraid of his retaliation and of losing his own. He identified his father with the man who circumcised and killed—Jimmy wanted to "do it himself" and was afraid that his father (sister) "might take it away" from him. He masturbated while he fantasied. The competition with his father's power in his fantasies was brought out; the competition concerning the size of the penis was acted out—in masturbating so that the penis would be bigger; he remarked to me with admiration about the size of his father's penis. Love and hatred were combined; he destroyed and saved in the same fantasy. In constructing objects he destroyed them while he did them; while he went to his little sister out of loneliness and craving for love, he drove her away from him by teasing her to tears, saving her from his own destructive tendencies.

In speech, thinking, feeling, and actions, Jimmy's outstanding characteristic was his ambivalence, against which he fought with varying success. He held his ambivalence in check through reaction formations, obsessive thoughts, compulsive actions. In all of them the repressed impulses broke through the defenses which were put up against them.

Treatment consisted of untangling these contradictory thoughts and feelings. His anxiety—fear of death and castration—had to be reduced so that he could accept his aggressive and hostile thoughts and feelings. The school provided sufficient opportunity to express aggression on the playing field in open competition with other boys. When the disturbance was removed in the area of speech and thinking processes, Jimmy showed a general widening of his range of interests, which had heretofore been restricted through outside and inside prohibitions.

The role which Jimmy's relationship to me played in this treatment was a very important one. He related to me easily on a superficial level. But on a deeper level he suspected that I might seduce him to follow his forbidden impulses and thereby bring him into conflict and danger. One might say that he saw me as the representative of all the ungodly, evil thoughts he fought against in himself. By my proving to him that I accepted his parents—the living representatives of his superego—and that they accepted me as a mediator, his fear of me gradually diminished. He made use of me as "an ally" in his fight against his anxieties, his destructive tendencies, and in reality used me as a mouthpiece with his parents. I served as an alter ego, as a sounding board on which he could test his fantasies and thoughts without danger and look at them objectively. He also used me as reconaissance to see what would happen if I expressed his wishes to his parents.

Jimmy's use of me as mediator and mouthpiece included transference elements. His mother sometimes attempted to help him, to interfere on his behalf with his father. He loved her, but she was weak, under his father's domination and therefore not much help or protection. He did not expect anything from her or from me. My prestige rose considerably when I returned to him with positive results. When he saw I could cope with his father, he decided I was as powerful as his father was. I was promoted to a superego figure—with a slight slant toward Superman. He made comparisons between his father and me, telling me that his father, also, "talked" to people and helped them with their problems. Speech and words were used by both of us; his father's words had magic power, he thought; he was inclined to believe the same of mine. This was a rather ticklish situation. If I became as powerful as his father, I might become as dangerous, too. By telling Jimmy about my conversations with his father and allowing Jimmy to tell me what to say, I deflated myself and his father simultaneously. I showed Jimmy how to "work" me and his father; I reduced the "magical powers" of both of us and Jimmy learned how to do it himself—by taking over discussions with his father himself. With this process I was again reduced to the friend and ally whom one could call in an emergency. His ego gained strength and his superego became less threatening both in him and in the image of his father.

Jimmy's reaction formations, his obsessive thinking and compulsive activity were the defense mechanisms with which he repressed, more or less successfully, his hostility and aggression. Castration anxiety colored his fantasies. But even at the time when his neurosis was disturbing him greatly, Jimmy was highly intellectual, able to learn well, productive in art and crafts, and highly imaginative. All these abilities were used in the service of his neurosis and were disturbed because of that. His efficiency increased with his recovery but all along one was convinced of existing abilities which were disturbed in functioning. This is in keeping with the inhibiting, repressing influence which his superego exercised over his ego. As soon as superego pressure was diminished, the ego became better able to function. With Jimmy, as well as with other children in the latency period, I know comparatively little about his actual masturbation. It is a subject which could be touched upon and which I could refer to from the material; I could in this way elicit contradiction and stand corrected. But it was not discussed in the sense one might discuss it with a young child before latency or an older one in puberty, although the accompanying fantasies were extensively analyzed.

Another area in which interpretation is missing in Jimmy's case is the area of his anality. He was sloppy, at times dirty; his parents complained about it. Also, anal material disturbed his speech. During treatment Jimmy was given freedom in smearing with paint, clay and glue, which he turned into controlled, sublimated activity. No material from the past was revealed in this area. Both of these shortcomings are frequent in the analyses of latency children. It seems that they resist analysis in those areas in which defensive measures—in Jimmy's case repression of oedipal material and reaction formations—are already in operation.

DISCUSSION

In reviewing cases of children between the ages of eight and nine whom I have treated in analysis, I find a majority of them like Jimmy, with prominent obsessive-compulsive trends. M. Klein (1932) describes a number of cases which show prominent obsessive-compulsive trends. It is of particular interest that one of these children, "Inge," whom Klein describes as a "normal" child on whom she made a prophylactic analysis, also shows obsessive-compulsive trends characterized as "clinging to reality," as "an effect of repression of phantasies." Klein finds this attitude characteristic for the latency period.

There are children who in their behavior are the exact opposite of Jimmy and the type of child I have just described. They are wild, aggressive, unable to study; sometimes they steal, wet the bed, soil; other times they masturbate excessively, sometimes exhibitionistically. Their fantasies are largely destructive and aggressive. Undoubtedly in their unconscious these children and Jimmy are similar; the difference lies in their behavior. Whereas they act out their fantasies, Jimmy repressed his. Whereas Jimmy is under the domination of his parents and his superego, these children are under the domination of their id. Somehow parents and superego do not function adequately. Sometimes we find that literally or psychologically disrupted homes, alcoholic or psychotic parents are responsible for this inadequacy. Other times the responsibility of the environment is not as clear-cut and simple. Frequently we find that parents hesitate to give the children definite directions lest they damage their initiative, or inhibit or restrict them too much. They alternate between overpermissiveness and sudden outbursts of temper. Lacking any consistent direction, the children have no standards to follow. Yet this does not mean that the children have no superego. They do—as do the parents—but it is as inconsistent as their parents' and as unpredictable. These children are terrified by their fantasies of punishment which surmount anything that might happen in reality. They measure their parents' capacity for hostility by their knowledge of their own hostility. The children are constantly on the alert for an attack by the parents or by other parental figures, and react with attack in lieu of defense, thus provoking the punishment in order to be rid of the unbearable tension of anticipation. There is one thing which, in contrast to Jimmy, they do not do; they do not repress the instinctual impulses which get them into trouble. What they repress is their loneliness, their helplessness, their fear of being deserted, their cravings for the security they never had.

Several authors have dealt with this problem, explaining it as one of education rather than of neurosis: Balint (1936) and S. Bornstein (1937) both recognize the necessity to "educate the instinctual drives"; they say that the children have to learn how to tolerate tensions. S. Bornstein adds to this that children need to learn "how to tolerate anxiety." Parents who misunderstand analytical thinking are inclined to remove every difficulty and experience which might arouse anxiety, with the result that the child's ego remains weak for lack of any demands made upon it. Alpert (1941) also finds that "undue permissiveness . . . an over-corrected error of the past" was the reason for her patient's prolonged polymorphous perverted period in which he was left without adequate support for ego formation. In working with these children, whether in the home or in an institution, an educational job needs to be done. They calm down when the parents or their substitutes make definite demands, tell them what to do and what not to do, and are consistent in it. It is interesting to see how, after some time, the children start thinking about what is allowed and what is not, how they become hesitant in their actions; they look critically at others, to whom they are more ready to apply the new standards than to themselves. They grow fussy about their clothes, their beds, their belongings. Gradually their impulsivity becomes hemmed in; they enjoy each achievement in self-control: they develop some compulsive traits, sometimes even a compulsive neurosis. When this development sets in, treatment intended to reveal the unconscious or to modify the compulsions is contraindicated. While the child is attempting to set up controls, he may veer to an extreme; yet we have to wait until he finds an equilibrium between no controls and too much control.

There is another reason why interference at this point of development may be untimely. From the disturbances of adult patients we know that obsessive-compulsive mechanisms are frequently set up as defenses against the underlying chaos of psychosis. The obsessive-compulsive neurosis is in such cases the best adjustment the patient can make; the therapy is directed toward the strengthening of these defenses rather than toward their analytic solution. With children of the described background and impulsive acting out, we do not know how strong the defenses need to be in order to control instinctual drives. We therefore have to leave it to them for the time being. It seems to be necessary for these children to set up obsessive-compulsive mechanisms in order to control their instinctual drive impulses and to adapt to the demands of society and reality.

But is it correct to say only "these children"—meaning the disturbed children of this type? Isn't this true for all children? Some time ago, in discussions with progressive school-teachers of six-year-olds, I found that many of them had difficulties in getting certain students to settle down to study. They wanted the children to develop a liking for reading, writing, and arithmetic of their own accord, but the children had a wonderful time playing and were not interested. After a while, when the others were well along in their studies, these children felt left behind and "stupid"; they did not enjoy their play any more; they became whining, unhappy, or mischievous, and masturbated more than before and more than the others. The teachers decided then to change their approach. They made their demands on the children more definite, at the same time offering them more individual help. They assigned work and specified that it had to be done within a certain time. All but the children with deeply rooted difficulties responded well. They started to work; they regained their self-esteem and became more outgoing; their masturbatory activities diminished.

This experience demonstrates the importance of establishing a routine and making demands on children. The resulting work habits, compulsive in appearance, are built upon some measure of repression of masturbatory activity and aggression. S. Bornstein (1937) made similar observations, and emphasizes that the educator needs to be able to "set frustrations" and to "make demands," of the children in order to force them to make an effort. Similarly, Alpert (1941) finds "too much instinctual gratification" a hindrance in achievement and sublimation.

Whoever has had anything to do with normal children in the latency period knows how many rules they establish in their games. From hopscotch to cops and robbers or cowboys and war games—everything goes by rules; of course, the rules are broken as frequently as they are made, but then new rules are set up. Collection hobbies turn up at this age which involve barter trade and legitimate cheating, both taking the place of the illegitimate, recently abandoned stealing. In all these self-made rules, the control of aggression takes an important place. Possessions are highly valued; nothing is thrown out—the closet and pockets are filled with "valuable and useful" junk. At the same time, the children use their intelligence in collecting knowledge and informaiton, and make substantial gains in this direction. In Kris's (1948) words, "Involvement in conflict need not necessarily act as a force which reduces ego functions. Obsessional proclivity may act as a stimulus to develop certain abilities in problem solution through thinking" (p. 632).

CONCLUSIONS

I think that oedipal feelings do not always recede or fade out, so that there are children who appear not to have a latency period. Generally, it seems that children show "an approximation to the sexual quiescence supposedly characteristic of the latency period." I have not seen any child with a complete latency of sexual feelings. In Jimmy's case as well as in others, castration anxiety was the cause of the "decline of the oedipus complex" and the partial repression of sexual feelings.

The latency period is distinguished chiefly by the growing importance of the ego. As Anna Freud (1946a) says, "While the sex drives remain latent (latency period), the ego assumes superiority, directs the actions of the child, establishes the reality principle and effects the first real adaptation to the exigencies of the outside world" (pp. 84-85). The superego becomes firmly established (Rambert, 1949; Fenichel, 1945). The ego learns to cope with sexual and aggressive drives and with the superego demands by building defenses which permit the child to function. If the defenses are too weak, the child is swamped by instinctual forces and is given to impulsive acting out; if the defenses are too rigid, the child is inhibited. The child who acts out —who follows his every impulse—is unable to wait or tolerate tension and is therefore unable to concentrate or make an effort. His learning abilities cannot be used; his relationships to people are unstable, again because he cannot tolerate tension or frustration; he is poorly adapted to society and reality. The child whose defenses are too rigid is able to apply himself, but his efficiency is limited since most of his efforts are used for keeping up his defenses; his relations to people are steady but unsatisfactory.

The defenses which we find at work in Jimmy's case are repression of sexual and aggressive impulses. The repression is reinforced by other mechanisms, particularly obsessive-compulsive ones, by reaction formation, and sublimation. While we find Jimmy's reaction formation the same as those of normal latency children, his obsessive-compulsive mechanisms are definitely pathological; his sublimations are normal as such; insofar as they serve the neurosis, however, they are disturbed and may be considered symptomatic.

Repression, reaction formations, obsessive-compulsive defenses, and sublimation are operative during latency. These defense mechanisms, though normal, are potentially pathogenic as Jimmy's case illustrates.

Whereas projective thinking may be part of normal development, particularly connected with superego formation, it seems to be more prevalent, sometimes to a pathological extent, in the children whom we described as impulsive. Jimmy used projective thinking in his ideas about his father as all-powerful, which prevented him from seeing his father as he really was. When he became able to discriminate between the real and fantasied father, his fear of his father diminished and his superego became less punitive.

Therapy during latency must be directed toward freeing the ego from the pressures of instincts; educational help in building ego defenses takes a prominent part in this process. Therapy must be directed toward freeing the ego from the pressures of the superego, by reducing the strictness and rigidity of the superego, which in turn will make the defenses more flexible. The goal of therapy is to enable the ego to function adequately within the limitations normal to this phase of development. Some repression, resulting in reduced interest in sexual matters, reaction formations and obsessive-compulsive defenses are considered necessary at this age for the development of satisfactory personal relationships and of the ability to sublimate.

THE ROLE OF A SECOND
LANGUAGE IN THE FORMATION
OF EGO AND SUPEREGO

During the analyses of four patients with bilingual backgrounds, German and English, I had occasion to observe the
way in which the ego and the superego contributed to the
acquisition and use of a second language. From these observations some conclusions can be drawn as to the role of
the second language in the formation of the ego and the
superego.

Generally, adults who learn a foreign language retain an
accent, even if they speak the language fluently and without solecisms. However, most children who are relocated
in a different country lose their native accent completely,
even though elders in their homes may still use their former
tongue or use the new language incorrectly. Yet there are
exceptions among children. Some retain an accent and, although they may be unable to speak their native language,
they never learn the new one perfectly. They are thus for-
eigners to both languages: to the old one because they cannot speak it, perhaps do not even understand it, and to the
new one because their accent sets them apart.

This paper was published originally in *The Psychoanalytic Quarterly*,
18:279-289, 1949.

During the course of their analyses, two boys, both of German parents, lost their conspicuous accents. Their pronunciation was never discussed in the analysis. Having learned English as an adult, I still retain a foreign accent, although my speech is fluent. Thus an identification with my way of talking could not have improved their speech. It is therefore the more remarkable that, despite my own faulty pronunciation, these children should have improved theirs.

Eric, aged six, was an anxious, whining, only child who clung to his mother and had no relations with other children. He was born in this country. His mother, having learned and used the language in her childhood, spoke English with a scarcely perceptible accent. His father spoke it correctly but with conspicuously poor enunciation. He preferred to speak German whenever possible. He objected to many customs in this country, looked down on American education and culture, and let his family and friends know how he felt.

A large part of Eric's analysis consisted in dramatizing his fantasies and in helping me to write them down. They were mostly Western and gangster stories, in which he was the hero who conquered the villain, represented by man or beast. In this well-known pattern he expressed his hostility toward his father. The fantasies were accompanied by a great deal of excitement. Part of the excitement was anxiety, fear of his father's retaliation; part of it was fear of losing his father's love. Some of the excitement was clearly sexual, accompanied by masturbatory movements. The fantasies were like Western movies: fights for justice, honor, a girl—any excuse to get into a good fight was acceptable. It was fighting for the sake of fighting, so often observed among children. The fighting itself represented a sexual relationship with his opponent. Obviously he had to win for fear of being forced into a submissive, passive role, which to him would have meant being a woman and being castrated.

The latter, nevertheless, was the role which he acted out:

His cry-baby behavior provoked children to taunt and bully him. He similarly provoked his father to scold and punish him. He imitated his father in many ways but the imitation was hostile, as evidenced in the course of his dramatic play: his characters so clearly became caricatures of his father that they were recognizable even to the patient. Mimicking his father's speech was part of his provocative caricaturing of him. By the hostility, he elicited his father's wrath, which gratified his desire for a love fight in which he could be the beaten woman. He clung to his mother for protection against his father's retaliatory punishment and his own desire (from guilt) to be the punished. Clinging to his mother aroused the father's jealousy, and defeated its purpose.

Working through of this conflict brought about a change in Eric's relationship with his father. They became good friends. Instead of unconsciously making fun of his father, he achieved an openly "kidding" relationship with him which they both enjoyed. His improved relationships with his playmates had long since enabled him to make friends and hold his own. He developed initiative and interest in his studies; he became an excellent student, particularly gifted in English composition. His accent disappeared, since he no longer required it for his hostile and provocative imitation of his father. His speech became indistinguishable from that of other American boys.

John, aged eight, came to this country when he was three years old. Both his parents highly disapproved of American education and culture; both spoke English correctly but with strong accents. John shared their disapproval of everything and everybody and, like Eric, had no friends. He admired his father, envied him for his ability and knowledge, and for being his mother's husband. He competed desperately with his father without success. In the course of analysis, he abandoned his father's interests, and began to play football and baseball. He knew all the teams, players, and scores and, to his parents' despair, he spent his free time in the streets with his friends. His English did not become letter-perfect but he spoke the vernacular of the neighborhood.

It was interesting to observe that when they were angry, and wished to convince me of the "silliness" and the "unreasonableness" of their elders' ideas, both boys were adept in mimicking the speech of their teachers, their relatives, and their parents. In doing so, they would deliberately exaggerate their parents' foreign accents. They became critical of their parents for being different from other children's parents; they wanted to be allowed to be like other boys. Both believed that to please their fathers they had to scorn their adopted country. That required, however, renunciation of the companionship of playmates and of interest in school. Rejection of the language was a means of excluding the influences of American culture to win the approval of their fathers. It was also part of their hostile caricaturing identifications with their fathers which served their own libidinal aims: Eric's provocative attitude was to make his father punish him, which would gratify his passive homosexual tendencies; John's hostile identification was an attack on his father in order to replace him in the mother's affections. Apparent compliance with their fathers' wishes, in both boys, was a defense against unconscious castration fear. Eric feared castration as a means of gratifying his unconscious wish to be woman; John feared retaliation for death wishes against his father. Their foreign accents, being part of their hostile identifications, disappeared as the resolution of their neurotic anxieties enabled them to express their aggression openly, and to establish less ambivalent, friendly relationships with their fathers.

Further observations were made during the analyses of two German women who emigrated in adolescence and completed their schooling in this country. Both understood German perfectly but refused to speak it. Anna maintained that she had been a singularly happy child until she moved to this country at the age of sixteen, when she became depressed. She believed that until then she had had an ideal relationship with her mother, which then became most unpleasant. Memories of her German childhood, as presented, were vague, romantic, and obviously false. As is well known, childhood memories come alive in analysis only when the verbal expressions of that period are used; it became necessary for Anna to use the German idioms of her childhood.

Her preoccupation with the penis, including compulsive looking and obsessive fantasying was extreme. In her associations, sausages played a major part. The interpretation "sausage equals penis" and discussion of her voyeuristic impulses did not relieve her symptoms. When, however, she translated the word "sausage" into German, she identified it as a sausage of a specific color and appearance. This released from repression the memory, from about the age of seven, of a man exhibiting his penis. She had thought, "What is that *Blutwurst* he has hanging there?" This memory led to another of visiting a girl who was her partner in masturbation, and with whose father she had been in love. This girl and her father were substitutes for the patient's sister and her own father. Her sexual wishes toward her own father and mutual masturbation with her own sister were uncovered—all from associations to the one word, *Blutwurst*.

She had great difficulty in using the childish terms for defecating, urinating, the genitals, as well as for endearing words used by herself and by her parents. Recollection of a secret childhood jargon, spoken with her sister, released a flood of memories concerning her forbidden infantile curiosity and a guilty sexual relationship between her older sister and herself. Her resistance to speaking German was a denial of her infantile sexuality. A new language enabled her to detach herself from the psychic traumata of her childhood. With the recovery of these memories she easily became bilingual.

The other patient, Bertha, a woman of thirty-six, had finished high school in Germany. She professed that she had deliberately abandoned the German language when she came to live in the United States because she was disappointed in love while she lived in Germany. On emigrating, she had decided: "Now I will be different. I will never again be swept away by my feelings." She resolved never to fall in love. She knew almost consciously that never to speak a word of German would make it easier for her to repress her feelings. When she realized that repressing her feelings made her life empty, she said, "I know I should talk German to you—but I don't dare. I don't know what would happen. I'd probably go to pieces!" As her anxieties decreased, she brought me her diary, written in German. It contained the story of her love—an adoration from afar of which the boy had been scarcely aware. Then she brought me some notes written in German. They were really love letters to me, in much the same mood in which the diary had been written. For her, German was the language of love. Finally she spoke German to me. She would leave sentences half-finished, or sometimes only say a word and stop, expecting me to understand. She would quote a few words from the writings of well-known German authors, assuming I would be able to finish the quotations. This proved to be the way she used to speak to her father, and "only he could understand her." We may add that she wanted only him to understand her. Like Anna, she too had had a secret language.

In the course of her analysis, she dreamed repeatedly about windows to which she could produce no associations. One day the word "window" was translated for her into the German *Fenster*. Her immediate association was *fensterln*, a word having no English equivalent. It refers to a courting custom of Austrian peasants wherein a young man draws attention to himself beneath the window of the girl of his choice. If she accepts his love, she opens the window and he climbs into her room. This custom provides occasion for much joking and teasing. However, Bertha interpreted it as rape. She had been afraid of intercourse ever since she had known about it. For she discovered it at the same time as she discovered the existence of menstruation and immediately decided that menstruation resulted from intercourse. From her reading of forbidden books, she had learned about the hymen, and decided that menstruation was not possible before the hymen was broken. When she first menstruated, she explained it with the fantasy that she actually had had intercourse. The fantasy referred to talking with her father about sex. It was intercourse in words—hence the language in which the explanation was given was the language of incestuous love, which later on became forbidden like her incestuous feelings for her father.

Richard Sterba, in a discussion of this paper, stated:

> Language expresses mental contents in a threefold way. First, it is used to express *conscious* contents which the ego wants to communicate; that is, it expresses what a person wants to say. Second it expresses *unconscious* contents in the verbal expressions of the patient which we try to interpret when we observe the sequence of thoughts, the concatenation of associations in the patient's productions, the peculiarities of *verbal* choice and slips of tongue. Third, we find that the peculiarities of *pronunciation* of language and the mannerisms of speech serve in their own way as manifestations of unconscious contents apart from the contents of the verbal expressions in their obvious and in their hidden meaning. This third meaning of speech is the deepest, very closely knit into the character structure of the personality and the most difficult to objectivate in analysis; yet it is most revealing in the analysis of character. It was mainly Wilhelm Reich (1927, 1928) who stressed the importance of directing our analytic investigation not only toward *what* the person says, but also *how* he talks in general, and in periods of resistance in particular.

In the analysis of the two boys, the accent was a mannerism taken over from the father, which expressed, by hostile identification, both submission and revolt. When they were enabled to express their hostility openly, the accent became separated from their language; it became detachable, like a symptom on its way out. As long as the meaning of the symptom was unconscious, it was part of an identification and, as such, beyond the child's control; when it became conscious, it could be used at will in the form of imitation or it could be dropped. The unconscious identification was resolved partly into conscious imitation, which is historically the forerunner of identification.

The faulty accents of children, which proved in these analyses to be symptomatic, show certain basic similarities to other speech difficulties. Sterba suggested that they be called "pathological accents." In some cases of stuttering among young children, the symptom has been found to be a suppressed impulse to say something which, in the child's experience, incurs punishment. Such stuttering has the same etiology as slips of the tongue which betray the unconscious by unintentional substitution or misuse of words. Like stuttering, the faulty accent represents a compromise between conflicting feelings.

The two women patients refused to speak their native language as if it were the key to secrets they had determined to forget—repressed memories of oedipal masturbation fantasies which conflicted with superego demands. A new language provided the ego with an additional defense in accordance with Fenichel's (1945) observation: "A person's relation to language is often predominantly governed by superego rules."

Sterba recalled a similar mechanism of repression from the writings of Ferenczi (1911): the ". . . same emergence of word and emotional content is observed in connection with one language, which, however, is divided into an ego-syntonic part and an ego-rejected lower part, which contains obscene words with all their forcefulness of infantile sexual and sensual representation."

It has been noted repeatedly that language is full of elements of magic. Nunberg (1932) calls language "a substitute for actions." He who tells a story vividly brings it to life for his audience. Young children do not differentiate clearly between their fantasies and reality; hence the telling of their fantasies may cause them to become excited or scared (Piaget, 1926). Obsessional neurotics use certain words to create magic, to make things come about or to undo them. Superstition endows words of cursing or blessing with magic power. In the same sense, verbalizing experiences in the language in which they occurred makes them become real; speaking of them in any other language renders them unreal. Language thus becomes the vehicle for reviving the past and releasing unconscious wishes and emotions into consciousness. The difficulty encountered by a patient in expressing himself is one measure of his resistance; in some instances, the pressure exerted by the superego is so strong that the patient is unable to say anything. The superego uses its power to counteract the magic of speech.

For the two women patients, speaking English meant avoiding the language which contained the keywords to their repressed fantasies and memories. The suggestion that they speak the language of childhood, now forbidden by the superego, aroused full resistance to the point of silence—with the added effect of interrupting contact with the analyst. The silence, representing a withdrawal from the outside world, has a parallel in infants' reactions to the prolonged absence of their mothers, in what Spitz (1946b) calls "anaclitic depression." Severely neglected children—and those whose attachments to adults are interrupted and infrequent, as often happens with children reared in institutions or in a succession of foster homes—are slow in learning to speak and may remain retarded in speech throughout their lives. They are anxious, insecure, inhibited children who were punished for self-expression, or suffered the pangs of hunger, cold, and loneliness. The silence of the patient in analysis is often the equivalent of the helpless, wordless, desperate silence of the young child. Although the women discussed here used a second language as a mechanism of repression, it saved them from having to resort to long periods of complete silence and was therefore valuable in their treatment. Children who for neurotic reasons, are unable to talk, are nearly always able to sing the words of songs. A second language might be compared to the singing of silent children; both free the words of the emotional charge which burdens and inhibits the use of the native tongue. With the help of the new language, the superego was circumvented, its efficacy was weakened to some extent.

Imitation and identification are the most important methods of learning; they are, however, dependent on the relationship of the child to the person it imitates. Lack of relationships can result in severe inhibition of speech or in deficiency of vocabulary, which closely resembles retarded speech and retarded intelligence. Early conflicts, however, expressed in pathologies of speech such as stuttering and the like have no bearing on the development of intelligence. Stuttering children are frequently highly intelligent. It seems that speech development is profoundly disturbed when early object relationships conducive to imitation are poor or absent. Speech is one of the ego functions impaired when the ego itself is impaired in its development. Speech in early childhood develops as an ego function concomitantly with the ego. In later years, as the superego becomes fully developed, replacing the authority of the parents, speech comes more or less under its domination and becomes, in some instances, "predominantly governed by superego rules."

Erikson (1946) makes the suggestion that "the analysis of the ego should include that of the individual's ego identity in relation to historical changes which dominated his childhood milieu. For the individual's mastery over his neurosis begins where he is put in a position to accept the historical necessity which made him what he is" (p. 395). The two women described in this paper attempted to establish an ego identity with the new group by repressing their identity with the past; the result was an amputated ego identity, a neurosis. They had to re-establish the past within the ego identity to gain mastery over the neurosis. The two boys attempted to forego current group identity to preserve the one from the past represented by their parents; they had to learn to reconcile the past with the present. Speech in all these cases was the symptom of their disturbance, expressing a conflict between two worlds, differing in time, space, and language.

III. Psychoanalysis and Education

TRANSFERENCE AND GROUP
FORMATION IN CHILDREN AND
ADOLESCENTS

———◦•◦———

Most observers take it for granted that the main purpose of the group is educational in that it makes the child sociable. The approach in this paper is different. My purpose is twofold. I would like to explore the role the group plays in the emotional development of the child. I am also concerned with the question of what needs within the child are specifically satisfied by participation in a group, needs which cannot be answered by any other relationship available to him.

Statistical observations show that children under five years of age associate in groups of two to three for periods of from ten to forty minutes. A definite change is noticed in the size and stability of groups in the age between five and seven, when four to ten children can be associated for one to three hours. After age seven, the spontaneous interest in group formation seems to come to a standstill and even decreases slightly, until pre-adolescence and adolescence, when it rises sharply. According to Thrasher (1927), 51 per cent of young people between eleven and seventeen, and according to

This paper was published originally in *The Psychoanalytic Study of the Child*, 1:351-365, 1945.

C. Bühler (1933), 67 per cent of boys and 59 per cent of girls between ten and fifteen, belong to groups.

Freud (1921), in *Group Psychology and the Analysis of the Ego*, points out that libidinal factors are at work in the formation and preservation of groups, and that the libidinal needs are satisfied through member-member relationships as well as through member-leader relationships. He implies that the group plays a role in the development of the group member's ego as well as of his superego. Freud's formula reads: "A primary group of this kind is a number of individuals who have put one and the same object in the place of their ego ideal and have consequently identified themselves with one another in their ego" (p. 116).

A number of psychoanalytic investigations have followed upon Freud's formulation. One of the first was Bernfeld (1922). Zulliger (1930) shows how common guilt feelings tie groups of children together, and how common confessions to the teacher-leader release their guilt and increase their positive response to him. Redl (1942) describes ten types of group formation, each with its own kind of leadership. He substitutes for the ill-famed expression "leader" the term "central person." The "central person" does not necessarily have to assume a leading or even an active part, but sometimes may act as a catalyst. Because he possesses certain qualities, he attracts children who have corresponding drives. Redl distinguishes three main types of groups: those in which the central person is (1) an object of identification; (2) an object of instinctual drives; and (3) an object of support for the ego of the group member.

So far it would seem that the child's emotional needs which the group satisfies could be answered equally well by some other sort of relationship. The group's function, in other words, does not seem to be specific. However, there are indications to the contrary. Thrasher (1927) describes the gang as:

. . . largely an adolescent phenomenon . . . [It] occupies a period in the life of the boy between childhood, when he is usually incorporated into a family structure, and marriage, when he is reincorporated into a family and other orderly relations of work, religion and pleasure. . . . The gang appears to be an *interstitial group, a manifestation of readjustment between childhood and maturity*" [p. 36, italics added].

Thrasher thinks that the group has a part to play in the life of adolescents which cannot be substituted by any other individual relationship. This may serve to explain their tremendous interest in joining groups. As mentioned above, there is a similar period of increased group formation between the ages of five and seven. The two peaks are significant in that they indicate that there are certain needs within the child which compel him to join the group. Public school systems of all Western countries have made use of these needs by setting the beginning of schooling at age six or seven. In turning our attention to these peaks of group development in childhood and adolescence, we hope to understand the needs which the child or adolescent seeks to satisfy in the group rather than in any other social relationships.

Observation of two- and three-year-old children in nursery schools shows that in the beginning there is little contact between them. They do not notice each other. After some time, however, Billy notices John playing with a toy that seems interesting. Billy tries to get it from John, who will either surrender the toy without showing particular feeling, yell, or fight to keep it. The other solution to the dilemma is introduced by the teacher, who shows Billy and John how to play together with the desired toy. This little group of two, or perhaps three children, is then able to play together as long as the toy holds their common interest. As soon as they feel tired, however, they will start fighting again.

A year later the group will contain three or four children, and the periods of playing together will increase to thirty or forty minutes. In moments of tension, when the children threaten each other with murder, or at least bloody noses, the teacher's presence is required. The child is under a certain strain as long as he is on his own with the others. He knows he doesn't feel altogether friendly toward them and expects no more from them. He expects the teacher to control his aggressive impulses against his playmates as well as theirs against him. She will see that nothing happens to him and that he, too, keeps the peace. In this respect, the teacher is temporarily accepted as a substitute for the mother. As the child learns to control his impulses and to defend himself, his need for supervision diminishes.

Because of his helplessness, the infant's affection is originally bestowed on the person who answers his immediate physical needs. As he gains physical independence, he can afford to widen his libidinal horizons. This process takes place so imperceptibly that we are generally not aware of it. Every skill that the child acquires—his learning to grasp and hold, to move about and walk, to feed himself, to dress—helps him become independent of the person who has previously done these things for him. The physical independence is also expressed emotionally. The feelings of the child, which were centered around the caretaking person from an instinct of self-preservation, are freed for use elsewhere and in other ways. The word "attachment" which we use in describing anaclitic relationships, preserves the original meaning of the physical adherence. It seems that the child is not detached from the umbilical cord just once. With every new development, as he withdraws further from physical unity with his mother, his libido is directed less toward the anaclitic object choice and more to the outside world.

This detachment is reinforced in the phallic phase of the child's development. According to Freud (1921):

In its first phase, which has usually come to an end by the time a child is five years old, he has found the first object for his love in one or other of his parents, and all of his sexual instincts with their demand for satisfaction have been united upon this object. The repression which then sets in compels him to renounce the greater number of these infantile sexual aims, and leaves behind a profound modification in his relation to his parents. The child still remains tied to his parents, but by instincts which must be described as being "inhibited in their aim" [zielgehemmte]. The emotions which he feels henceforward towards these objects of his love are characterized as 'affectionate.' It is well known that the earlier 'sensual' tendencies remain more or less strongly preserved in the unconscious, so that in a certain sense the whole of the original current continues to exist [p. 111].

Because the child's desire for physical affection persists he is not satisfied with the new relationship. He must reach out for other love objects and transfer part of his feelings to them. One of the objects which lends itself to his need may be the teacher. He expects the same kind of understanding from her as he has been getting from his mother. He is even more willing to accept it because he does not hold against her the grudge which he has against his mother for rejecting his libidinal demands, and for disappointing him. Following the anaclitic type of object choice, he forms a transference to the teacher.

His independence and comparative freedom from fear enable him to use his energies in exploring the world around him. He is now eager to learn. We realize that the time for the beginning of academic teaching has been chosen wisely. It would be rewarding to follow up the development of the child's interest and intelligence in connection with his growing independence from his primary objects and his predisposition to form transferences. Such, however, is not the object of this paper.

The increase in object libido manifests itself also in the

greater sociability of the children. While the two-to four-year-olds form small groups for short periods, the size of the group, as well as the period of common satisfactory activity increases after the fourth year; the children associate in groups of eight to ten, and extend their common activities to two to three hours. Independent as far as his immediate physical needs are concerned, and emotionally secure through the transference that he has formed to the teacher, the child no longer feels threatened by the other children, and can accept them more easily. His feeling for the group is far more than an unwilling resignation. He is tied to his peers through mutual identification. He gets a feeling of safety in the group which contrasts with his previous feeling of being threatened by the rivalry situation. At this stage, group formation in a dynamic sense takes place. The child's castration fear, which is derived from the Oedipus complex, lends mother's rejection additional power through the threat of the father-rival and thereby makes it insurmountable. In the attempt to master this double pressure, the child becomes more independent than he would wish to be. He reacts with the need to transfer his feelings from mother to other people, and is ready to be part of a group because it offers him something he cannot find elsewhere.

However, while we understand the child's readiness to form transferences and while we recognize that this transference is essential to his being part of the group, we have not yet answered a crucial question: How does the gratification afforded by the group differ from that gratification which could be afforded by the individual relationship of two children outside the group?

For additional clues, we must turn our attention to adolescence, the other significant period in which group relationships are formed. In adolescence the youngster's need to be part of a group is imperative; when he cannot find a group in school, he will do it elsewhere, but he is determined to find it. Adolescents are also known for the violence as well as for the inconsistency of their emotions:

> Adolescents are excessively egoistic, regarding themselves as the center of the universe and the sole object of interest, and yet at no time in later life are they capable of so much self-sacrifice and devotion. They form the most passionate love-relations, only to break them off as abruptly as they began them. *On the one hand they throw themselves enthusiastically into the life of the community and, on the other, they have an overpowering longing for solitude. They oscillate between blind submission to some self-chosen leader and defiant rebellion against any and every authority.* They are selfish and materially minded and at the same time full of lofty idealism. They are ascetic but will suddenly plunge into instinctual indulgence of the most primitive character. At times their behavior to other people is rough and inconsiderate, yet they themselves are extremely touchy. Their moods veer between light-hearted optimism and the blackest pessimism. Sometimes they will work with indefatigable enthusiasm and at other times they are sluggish and apathetic [A. Freud, 1936, p. 137; italics added].

The emotional upheaval of adolescence colors their group life. Study of this period reveals general principles as if seen through a magnifying glass.

We propose to distinguish two types of groups among adolescents. First, those with a leader whose authority is enforced by some outside agency, e.g., the state, school, church. This corresponds to what Freud classifies as an artificial group held together by external control. The other type of group is that which forms itself spontaneously around a central person (Redl, 1942). Leadership depends on approval of the group and is subject to change. The artificial group apparently gives the individual who joins it a feeling of strength. In Freud's (1921) words:

A group impresses the individual as being an unlimited power and an insurmountable peril. For the moment it replaces the whole of human society, which is the wielder of authority, whose punishments the individual fears, and for whose sake he has submitted to so many inhibitions. It is clearly perilous for him to put himself in opposition to it, and it will be safer to follow the example of those around him and perhaps even 'hunt with the pack.' In obedience to the new authority he may put his former 'conscience' out of action, and so surrender to the attraction of the increased pleasure that is certainly obtained from the removal of inhibitions [pp. 84-85].

The adolescent may feel strong, but he is not really independent. His new authorities are the leader and the group. He is a revolutionary, though not necessarily in the political sense. The adolescent is a revolutionary by emotion. He is struggling to leave home, to break away from the family and its traditions, to become independent. The leader and the group who agree with his revolutionary tendencies help him in his struggle.

But the leader no longer serves this purpose when he becomes entirely identified with the parental authorities: the adolescent then tries to break away from him.

As a student, later as a high school teacher in Austria in the Twenties, I could observe the process of breaking away from the leader in the classroom. The classes in the high school were different from the classes in the United States insofar as the group stayed together as a unit, while different teachers taught different subjects.

The student government was the result of a revolutionary movement, similar to the student revolts in this country today, and it chose its leaders independently from the administration, much to their regret.

The group of children, i.e. the class, could at times be attached to a teacher and accept him as a leader or it could be following one of its peers. In either case, it might suddenly drop the leader or turn against him. The ostensible cause was often a trifling one; yet it seemed to be the spark that caused the explosion of long-stored resentments (Buxbaum, 1936). The leader, idolized up to this point, was seen as a villain; erstwhile followers turned into enemies. They either joined another leader, or chose one among themselves and united under his leadership against the former leader. The uniting factor now was the group's hatred for him, just as it had been their love for him before. They dismissed him along with the ideas and ideals he represented.

As long as a leader is acknowledged, love for him prevails. Yet we know that he has to place all sorts of restrictions on the individuals within the group which they would ordinarily resent and hate. Where are these resentments? What has happened to them? They exist, but the group does not allow their expression. The student who criticizes the leader soon becomes an outsider and no longer belongs to the group. On the other hand, every single member of the group tends to feel rejected by the leader, is jealous of his companions and resents the fact that he is not allowed to brush them aside. These accumulated feelings find their expression when the dependence on the leader becomes more painful than rewarding—when a large number of the group suffer under the rejection of their positive feelings and demands. The teacher who is a leader understands the situation and will give the children an opportunity to tell him what their objections are and will thus be able, with them, to revise their feelings toward himself. In so doing, he is giving up his authoritative position for the time being and identifying himself with the children in their criticism against himself. He lowers himself to their level, sides with their ego rather than represents their superego.

By submitting to their criticisms he allows them to temporarily change roles with him: they are the judges of his actions as he has been of theirs. He makes it possible for them to identify with him by encouraging them to take his place for a while. By this process their identification with him becomes greater than before; their negative feelings are resolved along with part of the transference. The teacher's position in the classroom is slightly changed, but he maintains his position as a leader. The teacher who is not able to cope with the criticism and the negative feelings loses this position. The classroom group may lose their cohesiveness for a while and may attach themselves to another teacher or peer leader.

If the teacher or leader is successful in overcoming the opposition of the group, he may be sure that a similar crisis will arise again sooner or later. If the youngsters succeed in breaking away from one group they will soon join another. Joining a group and breaking away from it seems to be a standard feature of the adolescent group. The more rigid the leader is the more dramatic the break will be.

Within the artificial group subgroups constantly develop and dissolve. They may be considered as spontaneous group formations. They may be in agreement with the leader of the overall artificial group or be opposed to him and thus become instrumental in removing or replacing him. The leaders of the spontaneous subgroups usually evolve from the peers. They are accepted by the members of the group only for limited periods or for certain tasks. After that another child assumes the position of leader. The change is performed without great upheaval; in fact, any child in the group can be leader for some time. He can play both parts alternately, the part of the leader and the part of the group member. There are, of course, children who never try to take a leading part. They are mostly those who lend themselves to being bossed and who for individual reasons are unable to assume any part but that of dependence.

The repeated change between submission and opposition toward the leader, joining and leaving the group, alternating between being obedient member and active leader, shows a certain pattern. We recognize the swinging back and forth between activity and passivity. It reminds us of the repetitive character of children's dramatic play (Waelder, 1933). Children repeat actively what they have been subjected to passively before. The greater the trauma they have suffered, the longer the play which reenacts it persists (Freud, 1920). The child who had been treated by the doctor, however unpleasant the experience may have been, begins to play doctor with a doll or with another child. Similarly, the child who becomes leader in a group enjoys treating his companions as he has been treated by the former leader. The child in the doctor-play with his playmates will also accept the part of the patient. In play he will put himself into the unpleasant situation which in reality he feared and resented, without minding it too much; he even enjoys it. We should have reason to be concerned if he wanted to take the role of the patient all the time; we should then suspect him of being thoroughly masochistic. If, however, he takes both parts alternately, we consider it as a rule of the game and wonder just what he gets out of it. Apparently he is satisfied to have the situation in hand. He is putting himself into this position instead of being forced into it as he was in reality. He can break it up whenever he pleases. The same is true for the child in his position as a member of the group. Submission to the rules of the group is self-imposed to a certain extent. If he does not agree with the group he can leave it by staying out, by choosing another group, or by becoming a leader himself. Even the most rigid groups offer a chance for these possibilities through subgroups which develop within the big one. When the child chooses to be a member, he voluntarily chooses the position of submission, obedience and dependence. As a group member he repeats the dependence situation of home in the transference to the leader.

The adolescent turns against his parents in an attempt to establish a life of his own; he may run away from home or be rude and contemptuous without apparent reason.

The more attached he is the more he fights. In adolescence,

this breaking away from home is connected with the youngster's growing desire for sexual relationships, which cannot be satisfied in the family. He is left strictly alone with his desire, and has the choice of either giving it up and staying in the family or of looking for satisfaction elsewhere and leaving the family. As when he was in the phallic phase, he is being deserted by the family in his sexual needs. He tries to shift his attachment from his parents to a love object outside the family.

The leader and the members of the group present themselves as intermediaries: the child finds in them new love objects which at the same time repeat the family situation including its limitations. For the group, as in the family, overt sexual relationships are forbidden. The group of two is not compatible with the general group conditions. The couple has no need for the group, the group no room for the couple. In fact, when sexual relationships enter the group, the group dissolves. The members who find a sexual partner outside, leave a group temporarily or completely (Bernfeld, 1922; Buxbaum, 1936). Yet it seems to be easier to make the step into adult sex life from the group than from home. The child's fear of being left alone when he leaves the family proves unwarranted. He finds a new family. While in the original one it was forbidden to take the father's place, he now discovers that it is possible to take the leader's place without being in any danger of punishment. Every time he breaks away from the leader or himself takes the leader's position, he becomes more assured in his independence. When by entering upon sexual relations he takes the final step in identification with the father, he gives up his dependence. The repeated experience of breaking away from the leader and of being allowed to assume his place, makes the adolescent less afraid to do in every respect what adults do, to be fully an adult himself. The spontaneous group serves this purpose better than the authoritarian, artificial group.

We return to our question: What has the group to offer to the child? What needs within him does it meet? The two periods in which he tends to be part of a group are high-points in his sexual development: the phallic phase, and the onset of adolescence. Both times castration fear forces him into group formation.

To put it briefly, the childhood period of group formation occurs at a time in which the child is forced to give up his physical dependence on his mother. His close relationship to her has been severed gradually by his achieving independence in mobility, expression, eating and body care. He no longer needs his mother in order to survive. His relationship to her changes from an anaclitic one to one of object-libidinal character. The rejection of his sexual wishes leaves him frustrated, and drives him to transfer his feelings for her to other people. It is this readiness to form new relationships that brings him into the group. The increased need of adolescents for groups arises from similar sources. The growing sexual drive forces the adolescent to seek satisfaction which the family normally refuses to give. He therefore looks for it outside the family.

In the group the young child finds support for his new-found physical independence from mother, the adolescent finds reassurance for his moral independence from home. Both child and adolescent feel deserted, ousted from the protective atmosphere upon which they have used to rely and not yet sure enough to face the world alone. The group is a highly welcome shelter in the meantime. Fear of separation from mother and home is overcome by transferring allegiance to the group leader.

Young children constantly gain in independence through a widening range of activities. Adolescents, striving for intellectual independence, accept, together with the group and the group leader, the ideas for which they stand. While the young child grows primarily in the sphere of the ego, the adolescent's changes occur in the superego.

The adolescent's breaking away from the leader attracts the attention of the observer more than does his submission. It seems, however, that both processes are of equal importance for his development. In breaking away from the leader he repeats his attempt to break away from home. Every break results in an increase in identification with the leader, which in turn makes him more independent. On the other hand, the periods of submission give him a chance to repeat actively experiences to which he had to submit passively before. Repeating these experiences under conditions over which he has control makes them pleasant and acceptable; and the adolescent is enabled to satisfy his passive tendencies. He learns that submission as well as attempts to take the leader's place do not result in punishment and castration.

Dependence, as well as independence, are imposed upon the child by his parents. They are situations and relationships which are largely beyond his control. The group makes it possible for him to choose his place between indifference, membership, and leadership. While he is afraid to disagree with his parents for fear of losing their love, he is courageous in the group because he feels strong in the identification with his companions. He is supported in his striving for independence and accepted when he finds it more comfortable to submit. Instead of being forced to submit, he is obedient because he chooses to be. Instead of being forced into independence by the traumatic experience of rejection, he does the rejecting on his own. His preconscious knowledge that his companions share his desire to take the leader's place diminish his guilt feelings and his castration fear to the extent that he is able to actually be the leader himself. The allowed identification with the leader prepares and encourages him to give up his position as a child and to behave like an adult outside the group as well. The swinging back and forth between submission and revolt is most apparent in adolescent groups. We see the same tendencies in groups of younger children—they have plenty of opportunity to turn their passive experiences into active ones in different forms of dramatic play—but their desire to obtain final independence is not as strong as their need for protection in the group. The opportunity to submit and revolt alternately against leadership and group is one of the characteristics which in particular make the group indispensable for the adolescent.

The child and the adolescent seem to use the forcefulness of the group to surmount obstacles in daily life that they cannot tackle alone. In reality, they are using it to fight obstacles within themselves. The group helps them at the crucial point in their development, in their physical and emotional breaking away from home. It provides the necessary transition between the dependence of the child and the independence of the adult (Thrasher, 1927).

In observing groups of children we cannot help comparing them with the group formations of adults. Freud has described the libidinal factors responsible for making people in groups behave differently from individuals. He emphasized that people in groups are apt to regress to infantile levels.

Looking at people who are easily inclined to join one group after another, we are struck by the similarity in their behavior to that of adolescents. They mime the views of their group, they are devoted to the leader and unable to be critical of him or his ideas, and they cannot accept or reasonably discuss dissension with their viewpoint. When they are disappointed in their leader, they turn against him, form or join an opposing group. There are also individuals who stick to the leader or the group whatever development he or it may take. They are tied to both, and entirely helpless and hopeless without them.

We know that the neurotic lives in the shadow of his past. The group which he joins ostensibly to further a certain cause revives in him the old situation in which he found relief for his infantile anxieties. He regresses to the level at which he needed the group for consolation and reassurance. The group goal becomes secondary.

It is obvious that education plays an important part in establishing the adult's relationship to the group. The more mature a person is, the more valuable his contribution to the group will be. The degree of maturity to which education will try to develop the children will, however, greatly depend on the degree of maturity which the society, whose servant education is, will find desirable in its future citizens.

AGGRESSION AND THE FUNCTION
OF THE GROUP IN ADOLESCENCE

Ever since Freud (1901) published the *Psychopathology of Everyday Life,* we have become increasingly aware of the blurred distinctions between normality and abnormality. If we accept the premise that, clinically, the question of abnormality is raised when the individual finds himself troubled, or when society finds itself troubled by the individual, then we have every right to say that the normal adolescent is abnormal. Few will question the fact that adolescents feel disturbed and that they disturb the adults around them.

To speak generally about "the" adolescent, normal or abnormal, is as inaccurate as it is to speak about "the" delinquent, psychotic, neurotic, or normal person. However, there are a few basic rules which are universally applicable. Since Freud (1905) published his *Three Essays on Sexuality,* we have learned that each phase of development forms the basis for the following one, as the foundation of a house supports the structure of the whole. How the individual adapts depends on constitutional hereditary endowments as well as on the experiences to which his environment exposes

This paper, part of a panel on aggression, was presented at the opening of the Freud House in Frankfurt in 1964 and has since been published in German (Buxbaum, 1964b). The headlined events of the past few years make my examples of antisocial and presocial youth groups sound small and insignificant. Nevertheless, I think the instinctual forces which I describe apply to large groups as well as small.

259

him. If the environment is sufficiently propitious, it can help him to realize his potentialities and to withstand traumatic experiences. The clinician is, luckily enough, frequently amazed to see how much unpropitious environment and trauma some individuals can adapt themselves to without suffering complete destruction, and how great is their resiliency and ability to recover.

Anna Freud (1958a) summed up her paper on adolescents by saying, "(1) Adolescence is by its nature an interruption of peaceful growth, and (2) the upholding of a steady equilibrium during the adolescent process is in itself abnormal" (p. 275). According to this description, abnormality is considered a characteristic of normal adolescence *in general* and not only of an individual adolescent.

Adolescence is, above all, a period of change. The adolescent must cope not only with changes going on within himself but with very definite changes in the attitude of his environment. As he emerges from the latency period (of relative "peaceful growth"), he finds hostility where he used to find acceptance or approval. His parents, lulled by his years of "peaceful growth," are startled to find an unpredictable creature on their hands.

The suddenness of the change is symbolized in initiation rites, of which bar mitzvah and confirmation are remnants. In *Adolescence and the Conflict of Generations,* Pearson (1958) says:

> The pubertal ceremonies among primitive peoples are imposed on the initiate by the adults in order to make him consolidate his loyalty toward the taboos and customs of the adult social organization and to solidify the importance of the adult to the initiate: at the same time, of course, they allow him to take over some of this importance himself [p. 87].

Erikson (1956) calls the period during which the adolescent is suspended between childhood and adulthood a "moratorium." He describes it as a period of grace, granted to the adolescent by society, to allow him to find his identity and his capacities. Society grants the moratorium not only to the adolescents but to itself. By keeping young people economically and emotionally dependent, society attempts to preserve its *status quo*.

Society's distaste for adolescents is reflected in its ambivalence toward them. On the one hand, they treat them like children, on the other, they expect them to behave like adults. The adolescent, expressing drives adults have had to repress, reminds them of themselves and makes them acutely uncomfortable. Hence the wish that the adolescent would grow up and get over it.

The adolescent faces a number of new demands above and beyond the usual stress and strain of daily living. On the one side is the increase in instinctual, particularly sexual, demands and the desire to become independent; on the other side are society's demands that he adapt to its rules and regulations and be productive.

The adolescent's sexual urges are not satisfied because he is not sure of his own sexual role and is afraid to seek satisfaction. When he attempts to experiment, he is faced with the taboos and prohibitions of the adult world. He must not have intercourse with the other sex, he must not have homosexual relations, and he must not masturbate. The rules concerning the sexual behavior of the adolescent differ from one culture to the other, but in all societies the adolescent is restricted to some degree from satisfying his instincts. When he attempts to act independently he is reminded that he is a minor, has to go to school, is financially dependent, and that only a few poorly paid jobs are available to him. His situation is truly frustrating and he reacts to these frustrations in his own individual way. When the foundation of his personality is sound, he will be better able to tolerate these frustrations; wherever weaknesses have developed previously, anxiety, regression and aggression will come to the fore and disturb him.

Elsewhere (Buxbaum, 1947) I have described how frustration in the practicing stage of mastering a new activity produces aggression in small children. The change from frustrated activity into aggression does not always go directly from one to the other, but may take devious routes by changing the object, activity and libidinal drive, which may lead to regressions or push the child into the following developmental phase. This is what we explore in analysis of the single patient, who has trouble expressing aggression.

I have used the term "aggression" without distinguishing constructive from destructive forms. I have used it in the sense in which Freud used it in his early concept of instincts, in which he distinguished between ego-instincts (or instincts for self-preservation) and sex instincts; later on he considered instincts of self-preservation and of the preservation of the species as falling within the bounds of the eros. Aggression in this sense is a manifestation of self-preservation (life instinct). When the child feels restrained from developing his strength and ability, he feels threatened in his ability to cope with the world around him.

Optimally, the adolescent has developed all ego functions, has gone through the developmental stages. He has experimented with most aspects of adult life in play situations. He has played at working—pretending to be father, mother, teacher. Sometimes he has actually worked by doing chores of one sort or another. He has engaged in all kinds of sex play—with boys, with girls, and with himself. I don't think we can distinguish how much of what he does at this point is experimenting or practicing. With the sudden spurt in growth, strength, and instinctual demands, the adolescent wants to do more and feels blocked from every direction. Not only the "kleinen Triebe der Arterhaltung" are blocked but the "grossen Triebe," sex and aggression, as well (Lorenz, 1966). The amount of aggression caused by frustration through inner and outer forces is too great to be handled through the usual devices. The defenses do not hold; displacements into other areas, substitutions, and sublimations become insufficient. Just as the river, swollen with melting snow and torrential rains, breaks through its dams and floods the land, so the inordinately increased aggression floods the adolescent's whole system, explodes, and inundates society.

Adolescent aggression is more noticeable when it finds expression in group rather than individual activity. Adolescents, as we have seen (Buxbaum, 1945), are joiners. College and university students in all parts of the world tend to join radical movements which satisfy both their need to rebel and their need to identify with the group. We read about them in the daily newspapers: Thousands of adolescents fall upon the little town of West Yellowstone and take it apart until a group of irate citizens chases them out with poles and axes—or hundreds of adolescents crash a debutante coming-out party and smash the house—or again, actors and singers are mobbed and sometimes hurt.

The phenomenon is not a peculiarly American one. There are the Halbstarken in Germany, the Teddy Boys in England, the Teppisti in Italy, the Blousons Noirs in France. We hear of similar groups in Africa (the Tsotsies) and in Japan as well.

We may be inclined to look upon these groups, which seem to spring up out of nowhere and to disintegrate equally fast, as a phenomenon of our own disturbed time. But accounts of similar groups and their destructive activities come to us from the distant past. Kiell (1964), has compiled a collection of references to adolescence from autobiographies. I am quoting from his collection: Juvenal (60-140 A.D.) bewailed "the young hoodlums, all steamed up on wine," who started street fights in Rome for "no reasons at all" [p. 770]. Richard Wagner describes his participation without the slightest provocation in "the frantic onslaught of the undergraduates, who madly shattered furniture and crockery to bits." He recalls "with horror the intoxicating effect this unreasoning fury" had upon him. This was in Leipzig in 1830. He does not remember that enjoyment of alcoholic drinks contributed to his feelings (p. 786). Benvenuto Cellini (1500-1571) reports his successful fight with the bully and leader of a gang who ruled the town of Florence (p. 780). Maxim Gorki describes his group stealing "in sight and with the approval of parents and of the whole village—it was a way of life" (p. 792). Gorki's parents and their fellow villagers were the dissatisfied subjects of the landed lords, whom it was considered right to rob, if you could get away with it. Gorki and his contemporaries were the forerunners of a revolution, which in retrospect justified their acts; considered from the point of view of the then ruling class, the youngsters were delinquent.

The last description has something in common with a study of Fishman and Solomon (1963) which concerns itself with the student sit-in movement in the South. The authors say, "The motivation and style of student involvement in antisegregation activities are linked to (1) the emergence of a new social character based on older traits in Negro personality as well as on recent sociohistorical developments and (2) certain psychosocial aspects of late adolescence" (p. 872). The authors distinguish prosocial acting out from antisocial acting out, although they find that the dynamics—namely rebellious, impulsive acting out of aggression—are the same. Delinquent acting out is antisocial because it is opposed to the morality of the community. It is the result of the delinquent's rebellion against severe superego dictates or occurs within the framework of defective superego development. Prosocial acting out is more in agreement with an ego ideal and a self image based upon the dictates of community morality and conscience. These adolescents feel "they are doing society's work for it." This view of the sit-in movement is substantiated by a number of interviews with the students. They describe their parents as frequently being in open disagreement with these dangerous and rebellious ideas, afraid of retaliation from worldly and heavenly authorities, but secretly admiring the young to whom they cannot look in any other way than as their liberators. Both Gorki's delinquents and the sit-in movement participants show themselves as forerunners of socio-historical developments. Their aggression was and is goal-directed. This is the decisive difference from the diffuse, unchanneled aggression characteristic of the "surfers," and similar groups.

These unorganized masses, which dissolve after a short time, are unlike the adolescent gangs who meet in certain places at certain times, have leaders, and hold initiation rites of their own. Pearson (1958) describes their initiation rites in contrast to the initiation rites which are imposed by adults upon adolescents:

> The gang initiation ceremonies . . . are a rebellious method of changing the adult organization through revolution. The gang solidarity comforts the initiate in the face of his superego; the whole group shares his feelings of guilt and so lessens them. The conflict between the generations is increased by this rebellious attitude of the adolescent group [p. 87].

Aggression is an integral part of these youth groups. At times society is able to make use of it; at other times it is turned against society. The Red Guards of China are an example of a youth group which is for a period of time working with the society, and while doing so, is turned against it. Seen from the outside, it is difficult, perhaps impossible, to assert which side they are on. When there are wars or revolutions, young people take part; rarely do they assume a leading role. They feel important in taking part in the business of society, feel comfortable with their contemporaries, and can accept the leadership and discipline of adults for a while.

During the depression, the United States Government organized the C.C.C. camps (Civilian Conservation Corps) in order to create work for the young unemployed. I have been told that in some cases the young people rebelled against the authorities when they thought they were given unproductive work for lack of adequate machinery.

There is in the State of Washington a private institution on an island, Secret Harbor Farms, which takes care of adolescents, mostly schizophrenics and severe delinquents. Since the institution is on an island, the youngsters are given freedom to go where they please. They work on the farm, build houses, barns, fences, take care of the animals. The personnel consists of social workers, teachers, and maintenance people. The youngsters are not forced to work, and very often don't. However, if a certain type of work has to be finished because it is going to rain, or because the tide is coming in, or the harvest has to be gathered, they work voluntarily and willingly. Although they generally do not accept adult leadership, they do accept expert advice in technical matters. They respect the adequacy of adults in working and seek appreciation of their own workmanship. They resent being slapped on the back or being patronized.

Recently, in working with a runaway delinquent girl of 16 who was a member of a gang, I learned that she left the gang for two months in order to work. During this time, she got along well with her parents. She explained her lapse into good behavior by telling me that her parents were broke just then and she wanted to buy groceries for the family.

I have already described (Buxbaum, 1945) how the group fulfills an extremely important function for the adolescent. Skillful workers in the field have shown that gangs can become prosocial if the group as a whole is given purpose and satisfaction within the framework of society. Of course, some, and perhaps many, of the members are ready-made material for adult criminal gangs. However, they too are a strictly organized society—using the death penalty for minor infractions.

In an institution, group formation and group behavior can be studied as in a laboratory. It shows on a small scale what we can only surmise is going on in youth groups at large. The adolescents in an institution can be part of a group organized either by, with, or around an adult; the adult is usually the focal point. The group is organized on the basis of the members' identification with him, so that the adolescent's ability to relate to an adult is a precondition for joining. I have described such groups in my paper "Transference and Group Formation in Children and Adolescents" (Buxbaum, 1945).

Groups which are formed without adult leadership are difficult to observe outside institutions because they do not accept adults. Institutions offer an opportunity to observe them, although the fact that staff persons are present and the adolescents are contained within the locality of the institution serve as modifying factors.

It is interesting to observe how groups form in an institution for disturbed and delinquent adolescents—how they select, accept and reject newcomers. Their rejection of an adolescent is a surer diagnostic judgment than any test, as is their acceptance. An adolescent may be asocial by adult standards, but he may be social from the point of view of his contemporaries. Social, in this sense, is devoid of any value judgments; it is limited to the ability to form relations.

Some adolescents who do not relate to adults or to single individuals of even their own age can still be members of a group—accepting their companionship and being accepted by them. There are some who remain outside the group and are yet accepted by it. They are usually individuals who have particular interests and abilities and who are productive in such areas as painting, writing, or music. Their efforts and accomplishments are acknowledged and respected by the group.

Such acknowledgement and respect is something the adolescent needs more than any adult, because he is still not sure of his own worth. Even when adult recognition is available it is unacceptable. The struggle for independence is incompatible with the wish to be praised by the ones from whom the adolescent struggles to free himself. The group fills this role by setting up its own standards and goals. Just as they recognize and reject or eject a youngster who is unfit to be part of their group, so they also have a sense of a person's abilities and talents; where the most willing and friendly adult is unable to understand, they are able to tune in, provided the youngster himself can make himself understood.

The group provides a society for the adolescent, while he is in limbo between the world of childhood and adulthood; it gives him recognition for his abilities, be it as a member, a leader, or for a particular talent. It gives him an opportunity, sexually or otherwise, to experiment in areas adults disapprove of. As Erikson (1956) has formulated:

It is of great relevance to the young individual's identity formation that he be responded to, and be given function and status as a person whose gradual growth and transformation make sense to those who begin to make sense to him . . . such recognition provides an entirely indispensable support to the ego in the specific tasks of adolescing [p. 67].

The group can fill this need for the adolescent when the adult is unable to do so. However, although groups give the adolescent importance and a place to function, a free-floating aggression is evident all the time. Constant squabbles are intermingled with major explosions in the form of serious fighting, destructiveness, rebellion against adults, and running away. I am not referring here to individual adolescents running away from the institution, but to three or four adolescents running away together. Frequently they stay away for one or two days and nights, sometimes longer. They may loot some place, usually for food, and sleep somewhere, rather uncomfortably, then come back to the institution cold and hungry. Or they go to friends or parents or turn themselves in to the police, who in turn send them back to the institution. When a few of them leave, they usually do not stay away for long. On the island institution mentioned before, running away is only possible with the help of the one motorboat which the institution owns. When the youngsters use the boat, it has been noted that they always tie it up carefully where it can be found; while they are gone they do not act particularly destructively.

Loosely organized groups which are noted for their wildness apparently get together for a specific occasion with the more or less outspoken intention of "raising hell"—"just for the hell of it"—no other rhyme or reason. They are not organized for criminal purposes, although crimes may occur, or for any other goal-directed action. It seems that their need to do something aggressive in a group becomes a goal in itself and becomes destructive and antisocial in the absence of prosocial motivation. The unorganized, temporary groups seem to offer adolescents a short-lived release of aggression. Perhaps they could be compared to orgies, like the saturnalia or the sacrificial orgies of the Maya. A friend, who is working as a mining engineer in Alaska, told how he handles the drinking problem which is ubiquitous among his crew. Usually at the time of official holidays, but sometimes on a company-declared holiday, everyone goes on an alcoholic binge. Some drink for one day, others for a week. When they are sober again, they return for work—no questions asked. While they work, they stay sober.

I think the short-lived aggressive outbursts of youth groups are such "binges"; they make it possible for the individuals involved to adapt to society's demands again when they return to normal. However, when society as a whole is in a state of change, when its rules and morals are in a state of flux, it fails to give the adolescent the external limits which he needs to control his inner turmoil. Society fails him, as his parents might have done in their confusion in knowing right from wrong. It is at such times that youth groups find a place to act out their aggressions: at times rationalized with ideas, ideals and contained in organizations; at times unorganized, representing aggression in its destructive form, directed aaginst everybody and themselves. Goal-directed and organized groups have sublimated their aggression to some extent by the fact that it is put into the service of a goal and an organization. When it cannot be contained within the organization, it becomes destructive and destroys the group. Golding's *Lord of the Flies* demonstrates this aspect in surrealistic form. Aggression, unfused with libido, is destructive and apparently cannot be deflected in sublimated form.

PROBLEMS OF KIBBUTZ
CHILDREN

In 1965-1966 I served as a supervisor and consultant to the therapists and educators at Oranim, the Child Guidance Clinic of the Kibbutzim. The conclusions I have drawn from my experience are subject to certain limitations. As usually happens in a busy child guidance clinic, the material I dealt with represented the most pathological cases. Then too, there was the possibility of misunderstanding, owing to the language barrier. Because I do not know any Hebrew, my information is largely second-hand, received through the adults working with the children and through my contacts with other adult members of the kibbutz. When a therapist works in a setting familiar to him, he recognizes deviations from the expectable behavior of that environment. My knowledge of what is considered normal in the kibbutz society is limited.

Kibbutzim are communal agricultural settlements run on more or less socialist principles. They differ from one another according to the political position of the particular kibbutz. The national origins and socioeconomic backgrounds of the members differ widely although, for the most part, they come from Western European and American backgrounds. The Jews from Africa and Asia tend not to enter the kibbutzim.

The first kibbutz was founded in 1910, and as of 1960 there

271

were 225 kibbutzim with a population of 82,000, which was about 4 per cent of the population of Israel (before the war of 1967). The members of the kibbutz work eight to nine hours a day in the communal economy; all their needs are supplied by the community. Each couple lives in private quarters which consist of one or more rooms, depending on the economic conditions and politics of the kibbutz. The children are taken care of in children's houses during the day; whether they sleep there during the night from their first day of life or only later, depends again mostly on the political party to which the kibbutz belongs. The Child Guidance Clinic Oranim where I worked is the creation of the Education Department of the Kibbutz-Artzi (Hashomer Hatzair), which is the most radical kibbutz movement. The majority of the cases which were brought to me came from this group, although cases from the less radical groups were also discussed.

Both practical and theoretical considerations determined the physical arrangements made for education in the kibbutzim. By placing the children in separate houses in the center of the settlement, the Israelis hoped to protect them from the constant threat of Arab attacks. At the same time, with the children under the care of the metapelet [house-mother-educator] the mothers were available for work during the greater part of the day.

GOLAN'S IDEAS ON EDUCATION

Golan (1959), whose ideas were based largely on psycho-analytic concepts of development of the early 1930's, was one of the creators of the method of collective education. He has given us a comprehensive description of the psychological and pedagogical principles underlying the educational aspects of the kibbutz.

The children of the kibbutz live from birth on in children's homes near the houses of the members . . . [p. 167]. The course of their training takes them from the infant's home, where they remain until they are one and a half, to a pre-school nursery until the age of four, to a kindergarten until the age of seven, to a children's society until they are twelve, and finally, until the age of eighteen, to the youth community. In each of these homes, the same metapelet [housemother-educator] usually takes care of the child throughout his stay there with, beginning in kindergarten, the aid of a teacher [p. 170] . . . The purpose of this arrangement is to remove the early training of the child from the parents in order to avoid undesirable features of parental education. The by-products of this education have been many thousands of unfortunate people—neurotics and psychotics—who are a burden to themselves and to society. To the extent that these by-products are due to the capitalist system itself, the kibbutz movement has hoped to eliminate them by creating a new society based on justice, cooperation and equality. To the extent that they are due to factors in traditional family education, the kibbutz tries to counteract them by collective education [p. 168].

Yet, according to Golan, the kibbutz "retains the family as a social unit," and "the child grows up in intimate contact with his family," which is considered "the most important factor in the education and desirable development of children," for which "there is no real substitute."

[Kibbutz education] hopes to minimize the negative influences of the parents on the child, assuring that the parents can bestow upon their children that degree of love and attachment which will guarantee a sense of security and normal development but minimizing the effects of excessive love or of neglect and lack of love.

The development of the parent-child relationship within the traditional family structure is a hazardous matter. It is through the training of the instinctual drives—which is entirely in the hands of the parents—that the young child learns to adjust to reality. . . . Unfortunately . . . parents often fail

in the training of the instinctual drives . . . in their function
as early love-objects [pp. 168-169].

The training of instinctual drives is often a source of conflicts which are "greatly aggravated when the child is from
three to five years old, at which time the relations between
parents and child—always involving instinctual elements—
become central concerns of the child" (p. 173). Golan mentions the parents' role in hindering the child's development
toward independence by excessive care and exaggerated protection. Obviously, the training of instinctual drives com-
prises toilet training too, which is known to be accompanied
by many conflicts. The family, with its tendency to protect
its privacy, is inclined to conceal the deleterious effects of
parental education, while the kibbutz and collective educators, who function on the basis of cooperation, equality, and
mutual aid, feel responsible for the welfare of all the children and "insure an early discovery of deviations and disturbances in the development of each child and the possibility of immediate treatment" (p. 173). One of the procedures followed is parent-guidance which attempts to
change the parents' behavior toward the child by the advice of the metapelet or, in more serious cases, by consultation with specialists. The restriction of the contact between
the child and overanxious or disturbed mother allows for a
less disturbed development. It also promotes a strong bond
between the father and his children, particularly in early
years. He is not "an authoritative figure to be feared, but
an intimate friend who plays with the child." When parents
die or divorce, when they are absent or sick, the child is
cushioned against such trauma by the metapelet who, next
to the parents, "is the main additional love object" (p. 173).

It was to be expected that, due to circumstances and human conditions, not all of Golan's ideas would be imple-
mented. In 1958 Rapaport said, "The upbringing of children
in the agricultural collectives in Israel is for the social scien-

tist what an 'experiment of nature' is for the natural scientist." During my year in Oranim, I had an opportunity to observe and to compare the results with the original plan, intentions, and expectations.

EARLY TRAINING

According to plan, the babies were to be entrusted to a metapelet, who was supposed to be a professionally trained kibbutz member. She was supposed to stay with the baby from birth until he was one and a half; then another metapelet was supposed to take care of the child until he was four. The mothers, who constantly went in and out of the children's houses in the first six or eight months, later on less, were supposedly guided by the metapelet in their treatment of the child.

In fact, inasmuch as training in Oranim had only been in existence for a few years, most of the baby nurses were not trained professional people. They were about on a par with the average mother, though less anxious and less concerned. Usually the baby was taken care of by more than one metapelet as well as by the mothers, so that the baby was cared for by a number of people, as it might be in a large household. During the night the metapelet left, and a night watch, who looked in on the children about every half hour, made the rounds.

A certain amount of jealousy and competition existed between the mothers and the metapelet. Some mothers accepted advice and guidance from the metapelet; others were dissatisfied and critical about the way their babies were handled. This, of course, led to some contradictory handling of the babies. Nevertheless, the babies were physically well cared for. They were well fed and healthy; they went easily from one adult to the other. The picture changed, however, when the baby was weaned and when, according to plan, the mother spent less time with him.

Weaning is always a trying time and was even more so when coupled with longer periods of the mother's absence. Night crying generally increased. The children became more anxious at a time when they could not yet express their anxiety in words. Many people came to comfort the crying, anxious baby; but it was not always the person best known to the child, and apparently, the child did not always respond to just anyone. A number of sleeping difficulties and night anxieties reported to the Guidance Clinic could be traced back to these early years.

A little boy, 22 months old, woke up every night and stayed awake for at least two hours. He did this for about a year. First he used to cry, later on he talked and sang to himself. The complaint was that he did not wake up in the morning to get dressed together with the other children. He ate poorly and was aggressive toward the other children, hitting and pinching them. This picture changed when the parents were asked to sleep in the child's room for a few nights. Apparently, for this child, it was not sufficient to have a metapelet or a night watch talk to him. He wanted to have his father or mother.

When the babies' sleeping difficulties remain unmitigated for a long time, they may remain a disturbing symptom, into later years. Ely was ten years old when he was referred to therapy because of fears from which he had suffered since babyhood. He had cried excessively since the age of three weeks. He was nursed until he was seven months old. At the age of one year he was very anxious in the evenings when separating from his parents and it was reported that he cried at night. When he began to talk, he said he was afraid of wind and rain. His anxiety had a catastrophic character—he feared that the house would be blown away by the wind or that floods would come in. On stormy nights his mother had to sleep in the children's house to prevent him from running outside, through the kibbutz, to the parents' room. He was ashamed of his fears because of the other children and did not want his parents to sleep near him regularly. The mother, too, was ashamed of her child for behaving in this way. She herself had been raised in the kibbutz from infancy and strictly observed the rules of rearing her child. She nursed him as required, left him to the metapelet without question; yet, the child developed separation anxiety due to dependency on the mother, occurring in most children at the period of individuation and beginning independence. Some women, who were themselves raised in the kibbutz, remember the separation anxiety they suffered. They protest against having their babies raised in the same way and sometimes threaten to leave or actually leave the kibbutz. As mothers, they re-experience their own anxieties in those of their babies. Many of these women are still engaged in a constant fight with their own mothers. I have described this pathology elsewhere (Buxbaum, 1964a).

Observers of kibbutz children's groups remarked that the group which seemed the least satisfactory was the toddler group (Neubauer, ed., 1965). Anthony felt "that they were more at loose ends, less settled, more expectant and less lively" (p. 28); and Nagler (1963), who worked with kibbutzim for ten years, concurs with this observation when he states, "We are aware that this age group (second and third year) has been rather neglected in kibbutz education in practice and thinking" (p. 301).

Kaffman, in his 1957 investigation of the behavior of 403 kibbutz children in 1957 (quoted by Golan, 1959), found that 24 per cent of the children from two and a half to six years of age were enuretic. Rabin (1965) quotes Kaplan as saying "enuresis is endemic below the age of seven" (Neubauer, ed., 1965, p. 44). There were not enough professionally trained metapelets available for the infants, as I have mentioned before. This was equally true in the young children's houses, where no single person was responsible for the child's habit training, but a number of different people, who handled him in various ways. The children were diapered together at certain times, e.g. before going to sleep or when getting up; or they were put on the potty together when the metapelet thought it was time to do so. However, there was hardly time to pay attention to the individual needs of the child, to watch him when he needed to urinate or defecate, or when he was through and wanted to get off the pot. Suppositories were used freely, either for the relief of constipation, for medication, or for getting a child to sleep. The children were exposed to overstimulation of the anal region, while the achievement of sphincter control received little attention. Methods varied not only between nurses but also between parents and nurses.

As we know, parents base their ideas on education partly on their own backgrounds, partly on the theories to which they subscribe; so do the nurses. The conflict between the educators confuses the child and delays habit training. Moreover, since the children's constitutions, as well as their respective parents' constitutions, are different in many ways, they react differently to whatever habit training they are exposed to. In most of the cases brought to my attention, enuresis or encopresis had to be considered a sign of immaturity because the children had never achieved bladder or sphincter control. It was only rarely that we heard that control broke down at some point and the child developed enuresis or encopresis as a neurotic symptom. There were, however, a number of other symptoms which appeared in these children which we know to be related to fixations in the anal-urethral libidinal phase. Kaffman's study mentions the high incidence of temper tantrums and unrestrained aggression in children from one and a half to 12 years of age. I found their counterparts in extreme passivity and listlessness, stuttering and baby talk, extreme general dirtiness, and a high incidence of learning difficulties in school, which I consider related to the lack of concentration and expansion of effort as seen in children who have not learned sphincter control. Washing compulsions and constipation indicate the strength of reaction formations developed in order to defend against the original impulse which was allowed to go unchecked for such a long time. The removal of this phase of habit training from the parents has not been handled significantly more successfully by the educators of the kibbutz than by the parents of Western society.

DEVELOPMENTAL RETARDATION
AND DISTURBANCES

The oedipal conflict occurs when the child is between three and five. Kibbutz children spend these years in large part separated from their parents. What has been the result? Nagler (Neubauer, ed., 1965) says, "The early pioneers of collective education had very 'optimistic' ideas: they hoped that the removal of the child from the parents' room would cut the ground from under the Oedipus complex. . . . But these expectations have not come true as far as we can see from our experience. Even within the kibbutz structure, the parents of disturbed children definitely remain the basic and main object of the child's sexual and aggressive impulses, and its first object of identification" (p. 260). In the same book, Lewin points out that the Oedipus complex in kibbutz children seems to last longer than with children outside the kibbutz and has its highest point between the sixth and seventh year. He thinks the reason for this prolongation is that group life tolerates the freer expression of genital play, curiosity, and genital acting out. My own observations confirm that the Oedipus complex exists in kibbutz children just as much as in children who do not live in the kibbutz.

Kibbutz children spend a great deal of time with their parents and primal scene experiences are not entirely avoided. Although children ordinarily sleep in the children's houses, there are also occasions when they stay in the parents' room overnight. Sometimes they are sick or they spend holidays and vacations with their families, away from the kibbutz.

Occasionally, the children's houses might be used for kibbutz guests, and the children are sent to stay with their parents for the duration of the visit. These situations, because they are exceptional, impress the children and stand out in their minds.

That the Oedipus complex sets in somewhat later with kibbutz children may be attributed in part to the separation from their parents, however incomplete it may be. Also responsible is their retardation in general development up to the seventh year, as ascertained by Rabin (1965), and with it, retardation in libidinal development due to the anal fixation and diffuse object relations. The picture is similar to that of nonkibbutz children who are retarded in their phallic-genital development. This is always the case when pregenital strivings dominate the picture. Usually the genital phase is delayed under these circumstances. When the children enter the oedipal phase, their relations with their parents are colored by pregenital fantasies rather than genital ones. It is true, I think, that the oedipal conflict in kibbutz children continues in force longer than in non-kibbutz children, that the latency period is delayed, or perhaps in many cases is nonexistent. Rabin (1965) stated that he found less frustration anxiety and less guilt feelings in ten-year-old kibbutz children than in non-kibbutz children. Since the superego is, to a great extent, the result of the decline of the Oedipus complex, Rabin's statement fits the observation that these children have not yet arrived at the latency period.

The cases I am about to discuss were considered pathological by kibbutz parents and educators. The children suffered because they were maladapted to their environment. They were conspicuous among the children whose collective upbringing they shared. Their disturbances were exaggerations of behavior which occurred in some of the other children as well.

Hannah will serve as an example of the kibbutz's failure to detect a case of retarded development. She was referred to treatment when she was ten because of severe stuttering since the age of almost two. She was frightened at night and slept poorly. In order to make up for lost sleep, she was in the habit of resting longer than the other children at the habitual noontime siesta. In the kibbutz, there are usually three to four children sharing a bedroom. After the other children left, Hannah could masturbate undisturbed. She told the therapist that she masturbated by stuffing dirty rags between her legs in front and behind. She was upset and angry when a teacher found the rags and washed them, but did not dare say anything to the teacher. After a period of very severe stuttering, she managed to express her anger in speaking to her therapist, and her speech improved somewhat. Hannah also suffered from constipation. She had sado-masochistic fantasies while sitting on the toilet. She would imagine how painful defecating would be. She fantasied that she had to wash the floors and was beaten on the buttocks. She would be punished by the "black god." Cleaning ceremonials, which included the masturbatory activity with the rags, would invoke the "white god," who would forgive her and relieve her of her constipation.

Hannah was constantly angry with her mother who preferred a younger brother. She had little contact with her father who "was always busy." She admitted having fantasies about him but refused to talk about them. Her relations with the children in her group were extremely poor; they teased her and called her "dirty" names, which suggested that they knew about her anal preoccupations, although her appearance was meticulously neat and clean.

Hannah's compulsive masturbation was in the genital anal area. Her fantasies were anal-sadomasochistic. Her symptom, the stuttering, was oral-anal. All libidinal drives were equally strong so that dominance of the genital drive could not be achieved. Her object relations were poor, both to parents and to peers; she was isolated and withdrawn into her fantasies and masturbatory activities. Her parents brought her to treatment because they were embarrassed by her stuttering. They had no idea how unhappy their daughter was. Nor did the educators know how disturbed she was, since she was a good student and created no trouble in the children's house.

Golan's prediction that the cooperative spirit of the kibbutz would insure early detection of deviations and disturbances was obviously optimistic. However, the cases brought to the attention of the Child Guidance Clinic were taken care of, which is more than we can say about the American system of available child guidance clinics. Yet, the children's disturbed behavior was frequently not recognized or admitted for a long time, much as happens in schools and families everywhere, where parents and educators feel responsible and are afraid to be blamed for having failed in their duties. Disturbances were usually brought to the attention of the Clinic when the children were of school age, while the preschool child's problems were not "early discovered," as Golan hoped. Nevertheless, parents and educators, in fact the whole kibbutz, feel extremely responsible for the welfare of all of the children, as Golan said they would. The children are well cared for physically, and pathological and pathogenic maltreatment of children, which occurs in our society, does not exist. Physical punishment is generally frowned upon.

Another example may illustrate the effects on a kibbutz child of interpersonal conflicts between the parents, complicated by the conflicts between parents and educators. Zeev had been in treatment for two and a half years because of reading difficulties. He still could not read at the age of eleven, although he tested in the superior I.Q. range. He was described by the therapist as aggressive-depressed, dreamy, charming, insecure and unable to delay satisfactions or to concentrate. He wet and soiled.

The first metapelet, who stayed with him for three years, was his father's mistress. When their relationship broke up, she rejected the little boy along with his father. The second metapelet stayed with Zeev for four years, but his mother, herself a metapelet, criticized and competed with her. Both parents had extramarital relations, but kept up appearances for Zeev's sake—or so they said. Kibbutz parents, like non-kibbutz parents, have their marital difficulties. However, it is more or less a kibbutz rule that parents who have extramarital affairs meet with their children together, even though they may not live together, in an attempt to spare the children the disturbance caused by the conflicts of a troubled marriage. Actually, the children tend to be confused by such secretiveness.

Zeev's father had an important position in the kibbutz organization. Zeev admired him greatly, and so did the mother, despite their marital difficulties. She said that Zeev would never be able to measure up to his father. The father enjoyed his son's admiration. Zeev's sadly spoken comment, "My father is a great man; I'll never be like him," expressed the boy's feelings. On the other hand, both parents demanded and told Zeev that they wanted him to be "a thinker, creator, and a constructive person." Zeev was caught between their contradictory attitudes—he was to become a "great man" but could never "measure up"—as well as their conflicts with each other and with people around them who were significant in his life. Zeev reacted to the parents' confused living situation, their contradictory signals, and to the additional inconsistencies of kibbutz-training with developmental disturbances. Sphincter control was never achieved, and he never learned to exert himself constructively toward the achievement of a goal. His covering up his inability to read and write by bluffing, pretending, using big words and talking about inventions and big things he could not do were unsuccessful attempts at identifying with the father. At the same time, he pretended in the same way in which his parents did by pretending to love each other.

ADOLESCENCE

Among the cases referred to the Guidance Clinic were many adolescents. We are used to seeing disturbed adolescents in great number in our society too and are aware of the fact that adolescence is a troublesome time and a period of development in which the strengths and weaknesses of previous developmental phases are likely to come to the fore. The kibbutz adolescents who came to my attention in 1965 had been two-and-three-years old when they were first observed by Spiro (1951). In the new preface to *Kibbutz Venture in Utopia* (1963), he points out that "asceticism is no longer an ideal" (p. X), that the kibbutz has changed from its earlier ascetic tradition (p. XI). However, the adolescents of 1965 grew up in that ascetic heroic time and show its effects upon their development. Spiro described the situation at that time (1951) as follows:

> They often interact with no adult supervision. This means for one thing, that some of the children's physical needs remain unsatisfied. Children, for instance, often wear wet or soiled pants (before they are toilet-trained) for a long period before a nurse can change their clothes . . . aggression may go unsocialized because a nurse is not present. . . . A child who cries for comfort and/or protection because he has had an accident or has been the victim of aggression, may find that there is no one to care for or console him [p. 36].

Spiro adds, "This has perhaps a most important effect on the child's development." He points out that the period of toilet training is "the period in which training in the extinction of such responses as crying and aggression is begun while, on the other hand, there is a lack of concern for sexual training" (p. 43).

The description of adolescents in 1965 by Rabin seems to bear out what Spiro foresaw as an effect of the young children's training in 1951. Rabin's (1965) comparison of kibbutz and nonkibbutz adolescents revealed that: "Kibbutz adolescents more often fantasy being the victims of aggression or they direct aggression against themselves (suicide)" (p. 179). This is confirmed by Nagler (Neubauer, ed., 1965) who finds that "Children referred to us tend to have strong guilt feelings which may lead to self-punishment, mostly of an unconscious type. On the other hand, there are feelings of shame primed by highly developed pressure to conformity" (p. 84). These statements agree with my own impression that, among kibbutz adolescents severe masochistic fantasies and masochistic masturbatory practices are prevalent; needless to say, there is an equally strong sadistic underlay. Another related aspect is to be seen in the strength of their frequently conscious or near-conscious oedipal feelings. These strong sexual feelings toward parents are to some extent directly related to present living conditions of kibbutz adolescents.

Kibbutz education is co-educational from infancy to eighteen years of age. In early years, toilets and bathing facilities were shared. In the last ten years, kibbutz educators recognized the signs which the children gave in terms of shame and embarrassment and allowed and helped them to arrange privacy for these activities. However, sleeping arrangements remained the same, that is, usually two boys and two girls or one boy and two girls shared a bedroom.

Masturbation and mutual masturbation until the age of twelve remain unchecked. However, in high school, mutual sexual play and sex relations in the peer group are forbidden by the educators and by the group itself. This means that, during the time of increased sexual needs, the adolescents must suppress or repress sexual wishes despite exposure to constant sexual stimulation. The incest taboo is in full force toward the members of the peer group. Since they do not live with their parents, the danger of breaking through the incest barrier toward them is less than in the nonkibbutz family, and the suppression of actual incestuous wishes less necessary. However, conscious incestuous wishes toward the parents are accompanied by strong unconscious guilt feelings which are heightened by the lack of external restriction on the part of the parents. In the group situation, the prevalent feeling is one of shame and fear of being found out to have these forbidden feelings. What pertains to oedipal feelings is equally true for homosexual feelings. There are very few cases of overt homosexuality among the Clinic's cases; again, the repression is very strong and promotes homosexual fantasies and masturbatory activities. Failure to reach the genital level of development causes pre-oedipal libidinal strivings to become the vehicle for the expression of repressed genital drives. They are turned against the self in the form of masochistic fantasies and practices.

Among the adolescents coming to the Clinic was a fifteen-year-old boy who had come for help because he could not sleep and felt the urge to go near a girl and pet her. He tried to avoid the girls who slept in his room and found himself in the next room, touching a girl while she was sleeping. He was not discovered but confessed his difficulties to a man teacher who advised him to seek help at the Clinic. It seems paradoxical that people should consider it abnormal for a fifteen-year-old boy to want to touch a girl with whom he sleeps in the same room. Indeed, it would be extraordinary if he did not want to. Yet, this is what kibbutz educators expect and the children expect of themselves. They are not supposed to have these feelings, or if they have them, they are not supposed to act on them. Aggravating circumstances in this case were that the parents were divorced. Most of the time, the boy lived in his mother's kibbutz; he witnessed her promiscuity with young men who were not much older than he. She was openly seductive to him, would show herself to him in the nude, and then complain that he was fresh to her. He was so stimulated by her behavior that he could neither sleep nor concentrate on his studies. He was literally driven to distraction, and spent his time peeking and snooping and his energy in trying to control himself. In order to spare the girl he really liked, he displaced his need by touching girls he did not care for. He tried to extricate himself from the situation by moving to his father's kibbutz, but his difficulties continued there until it was arranged to have him sleep in a room with only boys. His state of continuous excitation lessened, and he was able to begin working on his problems.

Bennie, at seventeen, had been in treatment since he was twelve years old. He was unable to concentrate in school, where his work was very poor, and was lazy in doing his farm chores. He was constantly afraid that a man might attack him from behind. Bennie was born in a concentration camp and, at eight months of age, came into the infants' house of a kibbutz. When he was nine months old he contracted pneumonia. His mother took care of him in the parents' room. His father could not stand his crying and choked and beat him. He was referred to the children's house, where he was subjected to frequent changes of nurses. He was an unhappy child, beset by many fears. The other children made no secret of their contempt for him. He thought of himself as weak and feminine, and complained that this was why girls did not like him. He was poor in sports because he was afraid of being hurt. He remembered that he was severely beaten by his father when he was twelve years old. He considered his father weak, like himself.

Bennie had for years engaged in sex play with his sister who was six years younger. He had played "doctor" with her in the parents' room and had masturbated her. He wanted to expose himself in front of her but was afraid his penis would shrink if he did. He was afraid that he might get polio or cancer and his penis would fall off. In his room in the children's house, which he shared with two girls, he would watch them masturbate and would try to

touch them when they were asleep. On one occasion he returned to his room during school hours in order to masturbate, was caught by one of the girls, and feared that she
might tell others.

Bennie's struggle against his feminine strivings led him to
sexual acting out for which he punished and satisfied himself with homosexual fantasies. Heterosexual wishes served
mainly as a defense against homosexual ones. The constant
presence of the group kept him aroused and interfered with
repression of passive-feminine wishes. Because of his eagerness to secure the yearned-for respect of the group, his defense took the form of obsessive heterosexual fantasies, and
fantasies of masculine heroic deeds which were ego-syntonic.

Unprotected by adults, the youngest or weakest child in
the peer group of toddlers became the scapegoat. Unable to
protect himself or to fight, he accepted his debased position
and used it in a passive, masochistic way. He turned his aggression against himself because he was unable to vent it
against anybody else. What we see in the adolescent Bennie is the introjected process just described—what were the
persecuting children are now the fantasied people who tor-
ment him; the absence of a protective adult in the past
makes him unable to protect himself now in reality as well
as in fantasy. Consciously, he can only see himself as the
victim; his identification with the aggressor ends up, again,
being turned against himself.

There are adolescent boys who express their feminine
strivings openly. They talk about wanting to get rid of their
penises, masturbate in self-mutilating ways, and provoke
the children in the group to attack them. I heard of more
boys with this particular syndrome in the kibbutz than
in all my previous years of practice outside the kibbutz.
I am inclined to believe that group situations similar to
Bennie's are at least contributing factors to this phenomenon.

Although behavior we consider to be delinquent is not
reported as such, it occurs in connection with other symp-

toms. This was the case with George, a fifteen-year-old boy who was referred because of phobic fears. He was afraid to sit next to a strange man. He feared traveling by bus, lest the driver suddenly expel him from the bus and leave him stranded in the wilderness. In the parents' room, he would not stay alone with his father, but insisted that his mother or brother be present. In the peer group, George was a feared bully. For years he had stolen knives and tools from the workshop and stored them under his bed and mattress. None of the educators removed them or asked him to return them because they were community property. He also stole food from the community kitchen; this he shared with the children in his group. This was in no way because of hunger —children were always well fed, even when adults starved —but on a dare and as a means of making friends. Nobody intervened; food and kitchen belonged to everyone, although food was rationed.

One of the underlying causes for George's behavior was his ambivalent relationship with his older brother who bullied him when they were together in the parents' room. For instance, the brother would lie on top of him and force him to do what he wanted, even steal for him. However, the brother also acted as George's protector from the other children. When George was eight years old, the brother became so unmanagable that he had to be removed to an institution, and George was left to his own devices. It is at this point that he stopped wetting his bed, began stealing tools, and indulged in aggressive, delinquent behavior. In order to protect himself, he identified with his brother and imitated his behavior.

While George both feared and loved his brother, he only feared his father. His father never touched his children, either in a punishing or in an affectionate manner, on principle, because "he didn't believe in it." Apparently, the older brother's ambivalent behavior was less threatening to George than his father's remoteness. He could identify with the brother but not with father, who neither protected George from his brother nor liked the brother. When his brother was no longer available, the peer group became the focus of George's ambivalent feelings for him. When he took over the brother's role, the group had to do his bidding and he became their leader and bully. Yet, anytime he had to leave the kibbutz grounds, he was a helpless, scared little boy exposed to the dangerous and strange people like his father and brother. His counterphobic devices worked only in the protective environment of the kibbutz; and even there he did not feel secure without his arsenal of weapons, although he never used them in order to attack.

Adolescent girls too are troubled by their strong sexual wishes toward their peers and sleeping companions. Some girls say, "How can you want to make love with a guy with whom you have been sitting on the pot!" A girl who was becoming interested in one of the boys in her room said, "I thought I might like him, but then he farted loudly in the room—and that turned me off." Anal regression is more easily available to these adolescents than to others and helps them defend against their sexual wishes.

Randy, a seventeen-year-old girl, was referred because she was afraid she might go crazy. She was afraid her excessive masturbation had damaged her genitals. She fantasied observing a man beating, choking, and killing a woman. When she was with her parents, she incited them to quarrel. She said that they only fought and never had intercourse. When she stayed overnight in the parents' room, she insisted on sleeping in the same bed with the mother. She undressed in front of the father, asked him to help her with her dress, and when this was brought to her attention, said that was what she did in her room in front of the boys—which was true. She was constipated and would sit on the toilet for long periods of time fantasizing that she "produced fat pieces that fell out of me." She threw her bloody sanitary napkins out of the window. She said she was dirty and "attacked people with dirt." Her extremely disturbed behavior was in part an identification with an older, defective brother who had been institutionalized when Randy was seven years old. He had constantly masturbated in front of everyone and she thought he had gone crazy because of it. Her excessive masturbation and unruly behavior were patterned after his. She was jealous of him, reproaching her parents for caring more for him than for her. Her identification with him was aimed at punishing herself for wanting to dispose of him—in fact, she managed to have herself removed from home as he had been—and at punishing her parents for leaving her in the children's house and allowing him to remain with them until his institutionalization.

Randy never forgave her mother for letting other people take care of her. On one occasion she said to her mother, "I am not going to take care of you when you are old!" With all that, Randy was extremely dependent on her mother. She feared that she would die if mother died, and at the same time attacked her viciously whenever she was with her. Randy's ambivalent relationship with her mother is reminiscent of the love-hate relations of very young children described by Mahler (1952) and Mahler and Gosliner (1955). It may have been caused in part by separation from the mother at an unpropitious time, causing the child to experience too much anxiety. Spiro (1951) reports that, in the kibbutz, "almost every child has been separated for a varying period of time from one or both parents" (p. 51). Whatever the reasons for such absences, it was taken for granted that the parents would leave the child in the children's house for periods extending from one week to a year. While it is not known whether Randy was subjected to such absences, it is probable that she was, if we consider the overindulgent, guilt-laden parental attitudes: nothing was denied to her during her stays with the parents, not even sleeping in the same bed between them. By being too tolerant and by neglecting to make realistic demands upon her,

Randy's parents and educators did not help her to differentiate herself from the deficient brother. The children in her group made realistic demands on her in asking that she conform to their ways. Since she was not able to do so, they excluded and persecuted her by way of punishment.

Another seventeen-year-old girl, Lucy, was referred to a special educator for help at the age of ten because of her aggressive behavior toward the other children and her inability to do arithmetic. When she was twelve years old, she developed a severe washing compulsion and became withdrawn. She worked compulsively in school by copying her papers over for hours. She washed herself with four different soaps. She washed her genitals compulsively, fantasying that she would be beaten if she did not do so. She felt repelled by sex. She washed the floor of her room several times a day and, while on her knees, fantasied a woman was standing over her with a whip yelling, "more, more, faster, faster, more, more, faster, faster!" She was unable to go into the common dining room or to movies with others. Her plans for the future were either to work in a women's jail or with babies with whom "she could do what she wanted." When she was working in the babies' house, she was haunted by fears that one of the babies might die through her fault, while actually she worked well with the babies. In contrast, she thought that she was doing satisfactory work in school while, according to the teacher, she did not accomplish anything.

Lucy was brought up in a kibbutz where cleanliness training was early and strict. When she was with her parents, she was jealous of her younger sister, whom the father preferred. There had been a time when he preferred her and she remembered nostalgically that he took her with him into the men's shower. In her group, she shared a room with another girl and two boys. The girl left the kibbutz, and Lucy refused to have anyone else occupy the room in her stead. She kept the room exactly as it was when her friend was with her, but refused to visit her friend in town. When she finally developed a liking for another girl, who seemed as lonely as she, Lucy invited her to scrub the floor with her as a gesture of friendship.

The adolescents I have described had rather violent fantasies; the boys tended more toward masochistic persecution fantasies, the girls' punishment fantasies were more obsessive in character. Some of the fantasies were acted out, although, for the most part, they were directed against the self. The acting out that did occur was confined largely to the family, rarely extending to the peer group which exerted enormous pressure for conformity, under penalty of isolation, expulsion, punishment, or shame. This pressure was probably the strongest factor in forcing suppression of unrepressed oedipal wishes. The peer group served to supplement the superego, which is ordinarily responsible for repression but which, in these cases, had not developed satisfactorily.

Perhaps the masochistic fantasies and symptoms have their roots in the environment the kibbutz establishes for its children. During the period of habit formation, the child's world is divided between parents and metapelet—the one to providing satisfaction, the other, frustration. Anna Freud (1949, 1951) points out that libidinal feelings are not yet fused in the anal phase. I think that for the kibbutz children, whose frustrations and satisfactions are assigned to different people representing the good and bad mother, this fusion is delayed. The loving mother and frustrating, punishing metapelet are separated in reality, so that, in accordance with the kibbutz educator's plans, hate and love remain separate for the child. The results are not always in accordance with expectations. Sometimes, as with Randy, the parents reap the hatred. The multiple and weakened object relations which the children carry over from early childhood contribute to their splitting of object relations into good and bad, thus keeping their feelings separated. Sadistic-destructive tendencies pertaining to the anal phase remain unmitigated by libidinal strivings and, therefore, are too dangerous to express. Because they are not sufficiently warded off by the protective presence of the libido (Jacobson 1954), they are aimed at the self. The child, and later the adolescent, is afraid to destroy the elusive love object and thus lose it forever.

ROLE OF THE PEER GROUP

Golan (1959) views the peer group as one of the most important factors in the child's life. It "fosters a feeling of belongingness." This may be of particular importance when his parents fail him. For instance, kibbutz children with one psychotic parent are not necessarily as disturbed as children who grow up in a family where a parent is psychotic. The effect of the parent's illness is to some degree mitigated by other educators, but particularly by the group. It is also true that in cases of divorce or death in the family, the children are protected from the disruption of home life by living away from the parental home. However, the parents are of great importance when the group fails the child. Both the parents and the peer group are the most consistent factors in the child's life.

In contrast to the changing metapelet and teachers, the child's group remains the same from the first days of life until he finishes high school at the age of seventeen or eighteen. The children comfort each other when they are anxious, and punish each other when they are "bad." Whereas the adults are not always available, the children are always there to lend support or exercise controls. When a child is anxious at night, another child reassures and calms him; however, if his behavior creates a commotion, and his crying becomes disturbing to the group, they become angry with him. The group exerts pressure on its members, demanding suppression of anxiety. Reaction formations and counterphobic behavior are the consequences.

Children who suffer from sleeping disturbances or who are ill are occasionally taken into the parents' room overnight. After a short time, they display an eagerness to get back to the other children. I think that, mixed with their desire for company and their love for the other children, there is also fear of censure by the group. Upon their return from the parents' room, the children are greeted with contempt, heavily tinged with jealousy, and are made to pay the penalty for evoking these feelings. There is a high premium on performance. From an early age, the children do a certain amount of work on their farm or garden; beginning at around ten years of age, they perform certain services on the adults' farm. To shirk one's duty in this regard is looked on very critically by the community of children. In any kind of performance, be it in the area of school or work, endurance and leadership are highly valued by the group. While nonacceptance by one's peers is a rather serious matter for nonkibbutz children too, they do have recourse to other people and other groups. This is not so for kibbutz children. They remain with their own group without being able to make any changes. They do not have the opportunity of being accepted by an older or younger group or to play with the children around their homes rather than with the children in the school, so that once they are shunned by their own group, their situation is rather miserable.

Lack of privacy forces children to stay with their group for better or for worse. In the children's houses, boys and girls live and sleep and use the bathrooms together. Masturbation, as well as mutual exploration and sexual play, goes on in all children's houses. They are unrestricted until they get into high school, at which time the educators let them know that sexual relations are not desirable and the children themselves erect a shame barrier which up to this time has not seemed to exist. The girls do not want to be seen by the boys when they dress and undress, and they avoid the common bathroom when the boys are there. The group is highly critical of boys and girls of the same group who are sexually interested in each other. Sexual urges in adolescence are heavily suppressed and repressed and pregenital strivings come to the fore. Exhibitionism, voyeurism, and masturbation—the last heavily tinged with anal connotation—are common. Compulsions are relatively frequent. The fear of being caught doing something wrong is rather high and so is the feeling of shame in being apprehended. It would seem that those feelings which we regard as precursors of the superego are more in evidence than what we would call superego proper in terms of internalization of prohibitions stemming from libidinal objects.

For the kibbutz children, the group constitutes one of the chief sources of security, and of demands and prohibitions. It offers them social standards and values. It is instrumental in curbing their aggression, and frequently forces them to turn that aggression inward. It offers the child relative security should his parents desert him. The child's dependence is shifted from the parents, particularly the mother, to the group. The group represents the sum total of kibbutz educators: parents, metapelets, and teachers, who have, in turn, been influencing it.

Kibbutzim pathology suggests that early training under the metapelet does not spare the children from conflicts with their parents or reduce intrapsychic conflicts. Oedipal feelings set in later and continue in full force into adolescence. The symptoms presented by kibbutz children seem to be very much like those met with in nonkibbutz communities. Insofar as these children were only partially separated from their parents, many of their difficulties could be traced back to parental influences. Nagler (1963), who for many years worked in the same place in Oranim where I worked, makes this point convincingly. Rapaport (1958) wondered whether "the behavior problems reported are the natural price (i.e., attributable to developmental crises) that the education for this type of society exacts, or are they pathological symptoms indicating that collective upbringing violates human nature?" (p. 596).

Among the severely disturbed children, no autistic child came to my attention, nor did extreme pathology usually attributed to severe deprivation and neglect in infancy and early childhood. This is the more surprising since many kibbutz parents suffered from the effects of Nazi persecution and concentration camps. These people, who had been exposed to the most inhumane treatment, were not always entirely in control of themselves. The removal of children from such severely disturbed parents was, in many instances, the lesser evil.

In my opinion, kibbutz education has been most successful in rearing children of parents who were psychologically damaged through Nazi persecution and who, in nonkibbutz societies, were hurting their children unwittingly. This result had not been foreseen by kibbutz educators because nobody anticipated a persecution of such dimensions. What the kibbutz offered was the best that could be done for the children without removing them completely from the parents who were unable to give them the kind of care which they needed, particularly mothering. I hold the opinion that, where it is available, individual mothering is preferable to the uncertainties of group upbringing.

KIBBUTZ GROUPS AS COMPARED TO OTHERS

In the sense that kibbutz children live in groups of necessity and not from choice, they may be compared with children who live in boarding schools and other institutions. The latter develop a certain *esprit de corps;* they are loyal to each other and, for the most part, helpful. Those who do not fit into the group are the exception and are lonely and unhappy. What goes on in the group in sexual and pregenital activities and relations is very similar to what goes on in the kibbutz group.

I found that the relations to the individual educators in a kibbutz were not as important as in institutional settings. The children do not feel as dependent as they do in institutions where individual relationships are encouraged. The leader-follower relationship seems to be centered in the group with the educator remaining on the periphery. Whereas in an institution or boarding school the group frequently focuses on an educator in either adoration or contempt, I have not noticed any such formation in the kibbutz. The kibbutz group sems to be oriented more toward the fulfillment of the kibbutz ideal. Institutions or boarding schools isolate the children from the community and create an artificial atmosphere in which relationships, particularly to the adults, become transference relationships. In contrast, the kibbutz group is a part of the community, and frequent changes of educators as well as continued contact with parents prevent strong attachments or transference relationships from developing. The group is indoctrinated by all the adults with whom it is in contact. The ever-present danger of enemy attack unites the group in civil defense drills and, from early adolescence, in military exercises. Kibbutz youth, many of them in positions of leadership, were conspicuous for their bravery in the wars of 1956 and 1967. In addition to the loyalty which all Israelis feel for their country, adults and children of the kibbutzim feel particularly attached to their kibbutz, which is their home. Indeed, any attack on their territory is an attack upon their life and they defend themselves accordingly.

Kibbutzim are not only agricultural, but also military settlements. The kibbutz farmer at the border farms drives an armored tractor and risks being shot at. Kibbutz youth are trained for warfare long before they enter the armed services for a two-year tour of duty. All of this surely contributes to their heroism in war. However, kibbutz soldiers have no monopoly on heroism, so that it cannot be said with certainty whether group education is the principal factor responsible, or whether other circumstances determine their courageous behavior and solidarity.

Kibbutz society is presented to its youth as the good life. Those who do not agree with the kibbutz ideal may leave, and some do. However, in order to remain in the youth group, this ideal must be accepted.

Another comparison can be made between the adolescent groups in the kibbutz with groups which adolescents join by choice. Adolescents in general have a strong desire for group membership. Deutsch (1967) calls it their need to feel and speak in terms of "we" rather than "I." They find strength in the group which they do not find in themselves. They use the group as a haven and a way-station between the security and dependence of childhood and the desired and feared independence of adulthood. They use it to gain independence from their parents—which gives such youth groups their particular flavor of rebellion. The choice of group, be it as a leader or a member, is voluntary; they can take it or leave as they choose. It is indeed the aspect of freedom of choice which gives the group its flavor and value for the adolescent.

This aspect is missing in the kibbutz youth groups. There is no need for a rebellious youth group within the kibbutz. The rebellion remains the act of an individual adolescent and is directed against the peer group rather than against parents and the community. The group is a source of strength for the individual as it is in other youth groups, but it is not particularly helpful in leading to individual independence. When the adolescents leave the kibbutz in order to enter military service or a university, many of them suffer the pangs of separation anxiety. They miss the group, the kibbutz and their parents—in that order.

HUTTERIAN COMMUNES AS COMPARED TO KIBBUTZIM

There are a number of communal societies in existence today besides the kibbutzim. One of them, that of the Hutterites, has been described by Bennett (1967), who studied and compared six Hutterian colonies in Saskatchewan with the Israeli kibbutzim in 1966. According to Bennett, a specific kind of education is an essential part of the Hutterite society. The children are educated so that they fit into it and stay in it.

The Hutterites are a religious group, Anabaptists, who refuse to participate in military service and who live as an endogenous communal society. The first such community was established in 1533 in Tyrol. The Hutterites were much persecuted and moved from country to country seeking a peaceful place to live under the protection of a benevolent government. They were sometimes forced to give up communal living, but managed to reestablish their communes wherever circumstances were favorable. In 1965, there were approximately 18,000 Hutterites in Canada and the United States, organized in 164 colonies.

Their commune serves the purpose of assuring the Hutterites the possibility of living according to their religious principles and beliefs and to educate their children accordingly. The children live at home until the age of three. After that, they go to school all day until they are fifteen. During that period they sleep and breakfast at home; lunch and dinner are provided by the school. According to Bennett, they are thoroughly indoctrinated by the age of twelve. They have few toys but are encouraged to play and experiment with the tools and machines of the farm. At the age of ten, they are assigned work in the fields and with the farm animals. This work is part of their education and is, at the same time, valuable to the community. In their schooling, achievement through skills and intelligence is minimized and competition is discouraged. On the contrary, "the Hutterites take enormous pains to train their children and themselves in egalitarian patterns, and in the repression of self-seeking and individualizing tendencies" (p. 244). "They largely substitute moral training and bureaucratically supervised conformity for dependence on the individual conscience" (p. 247). Their children are graduated in the eighth grade; "if they were to educate their young men beyond the eighth grade level, they would be forced to send them to town high schools, thus precipitating a general exodus from the colonies" (p. 192). As it is, the men leaving the colony discover that, "their training and education . . . and their socialization in the Hutterian system has not provided them with the highly competitive and outgoing personality needed to get along outside" (p. 253). Because of this, the Hutterites have a high rate of return to their colonies. In his comparison of Hutterite communes and Israeli kibbutzim, Bennett states:

. . . Hutterites seek to maximize the colony world and to minimize the individual world [p. 254]. Their belief system makes no allowance for the personal sphere whatsoever—although there is the latent feeling among members that it exists. The Israeli kibbutz offers a sharp contrast: here the development of the personal world is encouraged to a large extent. The individual is expected to have his own hobbies and intellectual interests, and he is permitted to participate in the larger society and culture to a considerable extent. Consequently, the kibbutz experiences considerable difficulty with loss of ideological and social commitment, and its regular loss of members and whole families results in a static or declining overall population. The kibbutz seeks to reward its disaffected member with creature comforts and other inducements to remain—a measure that is also practiced in the colonies, but not to any great extent, since the colony socialization system is most effective in impressing communal ideals and austerity. . . . The "repressive" social system of the colony is a means of protection and gratification; in the kibbutz these functions appear to be out of balance [p. 253].

However, Bennett goes on to say that the efficiency of the Hutterite economy is limited by their level of education. He agrees with Sorokin (1954) who states that the Hutterite culture is truly altruistic, but believes that "the price paid for the Brethren's achievement can be viewed as much too high for the majority of humans" (p. 246n).

The Hutterite and kibbutz organization of education show many similarities. The children are educated apart from their families—with the Israeli, in some cases from birth. The formal education of Hutterite children begins at the age of three and ends in the eighth grade. The Israeli educate their children through high school, until they are approximately eighteen years old. However, they do not receive a certificate equivalent to that of city high schools which would facilitate professional training. The kibbutz people, like the Hutterites, do not want the children to leave the settlement, and they limit their education for that reason. The Hutterites discourage competition and minimize individual achievement. Many kibbutzim use the project method in teaching, which allows every child to work at his own speed and ability. They too discourage competition —not by forbidding it, but by preventing it. Since everybody works more or less by himself and no grades are given, the opportunities for comparing one's work with another's are not easily available.

Despite the above-mentioned similarities, there are numerous differences between the Hutterite and kibbutz education. In both societies, the educators are aware of a lack of drive and interest in learning. However, this is probably more true of the Hutterites, who want no traffic with the outside world whereas the kibbutz population works in Israel at large and abroad. The children are encouraged to stay within the kibbutz and discouraged from working outside. However, if they do leave, they are still welcome to return. Also, a man may marry a nonkibbutz member and bring her to the kibbutz to live. The Hutterite who leaves the colony has lost his home and his family; he cannot bring in a wife from outside the colony; he can only return as a penitent son.

The Hutterites and the kibbutz people have different reasons for wanting to keep in the colony. For the Hutterites, communal life is prescribed by their religion. They are firm in their conviction that theirs is the only right way of living. The kibbutzim, on the other hand, serve other purposes besides the religious. Those who live in them not only accept as a fact that theirs is not a way of life suited for everyone, but are constantly in search of new ideas. They are dedicated to the future and want the younger generation to carry on their work. To this end, they proselytize for the kibbutz throughout the world, and this brings them in constant contact with people outside the kibbutz.

Because kibbutz life is not the only life they and their children know, the pull toward the world outside is ever-present and makes for conflicts. These are expressed in the educational system of the kibbutz which is designed, on the one hand, to train the child so as to keep him there and, on the other hand, to develop his abilities to their full potential. Scientific and artistic interests are encouraged. However, when the adolescent wants to leave to pursue these interests on the outside, difficulties are put in his way. The Hutterites are much more consistent; they suppress such interests from the beginning because they are in disagreement with their religion. Consequently, their children are inhibited and limited in their development, and the majority stay in the colony. The kibbutz adolescents who are strong enough may leave. Since all adolescents of eighteen, girls as well as boys, serve in the military for two years in Israel, all adolescents leave the kibbutz temporarily at that time. All are exposed to experience in the outside world and may decide whether or not they want to return. In these respects, the kibbutz youngster has a great deal more freedom than the

Hutterite, except for the limitations which kibbutz education has built into him.

The period of upbringing in which kibbutz education
differs not only from that of the Hutterites, but from Western education generally is from birth to the third year, particularly in the kibbutz groups of Shomer Hazair, where the
babies are removed from their parents at birth. According
to Golan, the goal is to create a new society based on justice,
cooperation and equality. Since parents themselves are a
product of the capitalist society which should be left behind, they cannot be entrusted with the upbringing of their
children. This radical theoretical point of view was soon
abandoned in practice, however, and parents were entrusted
with a great deal of their children's upbringing.

The Hutterites do not wish to create a new society; they
want to preserve their old one, which they have had for
400 years and which walls them off from the world as much
as possible. The parents, as carriers of this tradition, are
the logical ones to communicate it to their children. The
kibbutz is, of course, much younger than the Hutterite
colonies. Although the first kibbutz was established in 1910,
the great increase in kibbutz population came only in the
thirties under the pressure of the Nazi persecution. The
socialist ideas and ideals which they wished to implement
were not within the traditional upbringing of these refugees.
The problems which they encountered were described by
Bernfeld (1925b), who pointed out that educators brought
up in a society of a certain kind fall back into old ways of
handling children, however hard they may try to do otherwise. Consciously, they may reject their own upbringing,
but unconsciously, they remain under its influence.

The comparison of kibbutz education with that of the
Hutterites suggests that children can be effectively indoctrinated when they live with their parents. I have pointed
out that the Hutterite parents are themselves more convinced of their's being the right way of living than are the

kibbutz parents. Removal of the children from home, however, does not remove them from the parental influence in that respect nor does it spare them the interpersonal and intrapersonal conflicts as Golan and the kibbutz educators had planned and hoped.

THREE GREAT PSYCHOANALYTIC
EDUCATORS

———•·•———

Between 1925 and 1930 three books appeared which dealt with the then unfamiliar subject of the importance of psychoanalytic theory to the field of education: Siegfried Bernfeld's *Sisyphus or the Limits of Education* (1925b), August Aichhorn's *Wayward Youth* (1925), and Anna Freud's *Psychoanalysis for Teachers and Parents* (1930).

I see a significance in these major works of psychoanalytically oriented educators coming out when they did. I assume the stimulus came from Freud's recently published *Group Psychology and the Analysis of the Ego* (1921) and *The Ego and the Id* (1923), two books which reach beyond individual psychoanalysis to explore the problems of society and its influence on the individual. *Group Psychology and the Analysis of the Ego* considers the interactions between leaders and groups, with emphasis on identification as the process responsible for group loyalty to its leader. In *The Ego and the Id*, Freud deals with the development of superego and ego ideal, pointing out that both derive from the parents as representatives of society. Freud's emphasis here shifted to ego psychology and the problems of adaptation. Bernfeld, Aichhorn, and Anna Freud were the first to realize

———

This paper was published originally in the *Reiss-Davis Clinic Bulletin*, 3:5-13, 1966.

that Freud had given them the tools for education in addition to those for therapy.

I had the good fortune of being acquainted with and learning from Bernfeld, Aichhorn, and Anna Freud. I might add that knowing them had a decisive influence on my choice of career.

Siegfried Bernfeld was a socialist, a social worker, who studied biology and psychology before turning to psychoanalysis. He worked with all kinds of youth groups: in institutions, in the socialist youth movement, as well as with teachers and students in the promotion of the revolutionary and controversial student self-government. He was a charismatic leader—a fascinating man who cast a spell on young and old alike. Bernfeld's particular strength lay in his brilliant, inescapable logic.

The analytic approach, his natural way of thinking, attracted him to Marx as well as to Freud. He maintained that reading the works of these two great men sufficed for everybody. I met Bernfeld during a period of social revolution when everybody took a keen interest in politics. He was a socialist, but a skeptical one. He questioned the ideas and hopes of socialism as much as he questioned those of any other system or ideology.

In *Sisyphus or the Limits of Education,* Bernfeld showed not only the limitations of a socialist education but also the limitations of education in any society where the educators are a part of the society which employs them. He viewed education as a function of society, and analyzed society's goals and means of reaching them as reflected in its educational system. Society, he said, has used education as a means of perpetuating the status quo. Its primary concern has been to keep the children of the ruling class in their position of superiority. The method by which they are being educated, he said, was not important. He has Machiavelli address a secret meeting of top educational administrators, exhorting them, in a fictitious speech, to keep a firm hand on their educational organization inasmuch as their educational methods are of no consequence.

Bernfeld's book was published in 1925. His views were in sharp contrast to those of German and Austrian Socialists who were optimistically assuming that the world was getting closer to the realization of their ideals of equality of educational opportunities for all. Living in Germany, he saw the development of National Socialism under which only the master race was allowed to partake of the benefits of education. The Hitler youth fulfilled his Machiavellian speech to a T. Of course, this now seems a minor issue in view of the total destruction to which non-Nazis were condemned. Yet, it is interesting to see that National Socialism used education as a tool for power, as a means of accepting one part of the population and rejecting the rest.

Bernfeld conceived of all education as "being conservatively organized in relation to the society who educates," and saw "changes in educational systems always as consequences of political happenings" (p. 126). Erikson (1950) expressed similar views when he described the impact of early training upon the formation of the individual. The practices of child rearing are a social tradition which is never questioned; it automatically prepares the child to become like other members of the society to which he belongs. Through these traditions he is being adapted to it. To use Bernfeld-Machiavelli's words, Erikson too saw the function of education as the "conservation of the bio-psychological, socio-economic and cultural-spiritual structure of society."

Much as educators may want to play a part in shaping the future society through their disciples, they are nevertheless products of that society themselves, unable to rid themselves of the limitations which society imposes on them. Bernfeld saw an alternative to this self-perpetuating state of affairs. He believed psychoanalysis made a scientific investigation of human development possible. Such a study would reveal which conditions were favorable, which detrimental, to producing an integrated personality. A precondition to such an undertaking would be the analyses of educators who then, like psychoanalysts, would be able to understand the working of mind and body scientifically, without being swayed like weathervanes by political and other ideologies and the prejudices of society. Or, rather, one should say that educators would at least be aware of their own frailties and the societal influences under which they work and have the capacity to resist them. Once these ideal conditions were approximated, there would exist a real basis for devising educational methods.

This scientific approach to child development is an important departure from the moralistic approach which prevailed up to that time. It is a break with the idea that a child has to obey the rules of society, be a "good" child, whatever it may cost in loss of abilities and creativity; it opens the way to the best possible realization of human functioning. The educator's role is projected not so much as a conservator of society but as a scientist who promotes human development, which in turn may point toward a changing society. A kinship exists between these ideas and Freud's thinking, as expressed in *The Future of an Illusion* (1927b) and in *Civilization and Its Discontents* (1930). Bernfeld knew it was impossible to put education on a scientific basis before a scientific body of information on child development was evolved. Some of his work was concerned directly with this endeavor. He wrote the first psychoanalytically oriented book on infancy, *Psychology of the Infant* (1925a), as well as a number of books on adolescence. Other of his publications are concerned with questions of methodology, which he considered a necessary theoretical preliminary to establishing a science.

After emigrating from Germany, Bernfeld left the field of education entirely. It was impossible for him to continue with his work in Germany under Hitler, and by the time he arrived in America he had become disillusioned with socialism. Apparently he felt that there was no reward at the time in attempting to influence youth or education. Perhaps he agreed with Freud (1925), who said that "the three impossible professions are teaching, healing and governing." Like Freud, he felt that in devoting himself to clinical and theoretical work, he was doing all he could to serve education in the future.

August Aichhorn was quite the opposite of Bernfeld, the disappointed idealist. Aichhorn remained an educator throughout his life, despite political upheaval and change. He was a realist, accepting society as it was, and making the best of it. He looked upon education as a means of adapting a child to the existing society. In his introduction to *Wayward Youth,* he said, "Life forces [man] to conform to reality; education enables him to achieve culture" (p. 7). The forms and institutions of society are part of its culture, and man has to accept them in order to live. Aichhorn looked upon educational work as "an art, in which intuition is of primary importance" (p. 10).

A personal friend of Freud, a partner in his *Tarockpartie—* the card game Freud liked so well—he valued psychoanalysis highly. He considered a personal analysis indispensable for remedial educators. When I talked to him about my intention of working with disturbed children, his response was: "Well then, you just have to get yourself an analysis first, and then I'll talk to you again." Yet Aichhorn was aware of the dangers of undue emphasis and warned educators not to "overvalue the significance of psychology for remedial training. For well-rounded work he must take into consideration many other factors, psychiatric, sociologic and cultural" (p. 10).

He also thought that educators must start with a capacity for this work. Although they may "learn a great deal through observation, experience and earnest study of the problems

. . . [one] cannot make an educator out of every personality."
He said, somewhat impatiently perhaps, "I can give you no
general directions how to proceed; every educator must work
out the details of his own techniques." In his introduction
to Aichhorn's book, Freud agreed: "Psychoanalysis could
teach him little that was new to him in a practical way, but
it offered him a clear theoretical insight into the justification
of his treatment and enabled him to explain his method to
others in this field" (p. 6).

Aichhorn's book originated in a series of lectures. He was
an excellent lecturer who held his audience spellbound. He
talked about the way he dealt with parents, children, educators; he described them with a few words so vividly that
his listeners could see and hear them. He explained why
he had proceeded the way he had—justifying his procedure
with theoretical, analytical insight—but, as he said, he could
not teach anyone how to do it in another case, because no
two cases were the same.

The way he worked was an art, and as such it was un-
teachable. He did many things that were anathema to correct analytic procedure at one time and eventually became
fashionable at another. He used all the maneuvers which
are now honored by the term "parameter"—which does not
mean that they have become altogether teachable. He saw
his patients alone or with their families; he visited them in
their homes or met them on the street. He saw them at the
appointed time or deliberately kept them waiting; he saw
them for one hour or for five minutes. He gave and accepted
presents. Sometimes it seems it just happened that he did
this or that; yet he was able to put to use all that occurred.

He considered it most important to assess a patient and a
situation in the first interview and to proceed accordingly. It
is only rarely that one can consciously consider all the
factors in such a short time—psychiatric, sociological, cultural; I know that I cannot do it. In a situation where time
is of the essence, as it is with delinquents, one can only

work with one's unconscious, which is what intuition really is, but it is not teachable. I don't think any student of Aichhorn's was able to work as he did. He remains a unique phenomenon among educators. He worked with his personality—which is what everybody in this field does more or less—but his was more effective than most. He said, "Specific educational methods are far less important than an attitude which brings the child in contact with reality." To acquire such an attitude, to be able to make use of what intuition one had, was his reason for advocating analysis for educators. With analysis, they would know themselves, be aware of their impulses, good and bad, acceptable and forbidden, and understand the other person empathically. Aichhorn had this understanding even prior to analysis. Being acquainted with Freud personally, hearing him talk about his ideas, and getting some on-the-spot analytic advice and interpretations confirmed what he already knew and was.

Where Bernfeld impressed with dazzling brilliance and intellect and Aichhorn with his magic and personality, Anna Freud impressed with her clarity of thinking and lucid simplicity, a simplicity which, however, is most deceptive. Her early book, *Psychoanalysis for Teachers and Parents* (1930), shows this characteristic as much as one of her latest, *Normality and Pathology in Childhood* (1965). Her simplicity delighted and captivated her audiences in lectures and discussions in the past as much as it does today. One of her most striking features is her voice, which is as sweetly musical today as it was when I first met her forty years ago. It is easy to imagine how children react to her: they immediately feel that here is a friend who understands, in whom they can confide. This was not the case with Bernfeld or Aichhorn. With Bernfeld, the adolescents felt a certain distance and awe; only gradually was this superseded by the feeling that the beloved leader was very much interested in their lives and experiences, that he wanted to know; only when they felt this, could they talk. Aichhorn, on the other hand, seemed so completely the authority, the parental figure, that the children were completely thrown off balance when this big impressive man burst out with a quite unexpected insight and empathy into their most hidden and secret feelings. With Anna Freud, it seemed only natural that she should understand and that one could trust her. Everything followed from this.

Anna Freud's reader or listener is in a situation somewhat similar to that of the child patient. It is easy to follow her thinking; it sounds as if we had known it all along anyway. Her presentation reminds us somehow of Freud's writing; there is the easy contact with the reader, the imagined dialogue, the anticipation of objections and resistances. When she finally comes out with her conclusions they are so well prepared that we accept them without reservations. And if, at this point, we feel a bit overwhelmed, we can only blame ourselves.

In her lectures to teachers and parents in 1930, Anna Freud said, "The universal aim of education is always to make out of the child a grown-up person who shall not be very different from the grown-up world around him. It regards as childlike behavior everything in which the child differs from the adult . . . education struggles with the nature of the child or—as the grownup usually calls it—naughtiness" (p. 43). Anna Freud began by assuring the readers or listeners that she, like them, is against childish behavior and naughtiness. She continued by subtly leading her audience first to accept naughtiness as normal links in a predetermined chain of development, then to recognize certain traits whose origins are in the past but which are still present in adults in only slightly changed forms—like greediness and love of sweets; and, finally, to appreciate naughtiness as the possible beginnings of valuable activities, that is, painting and sculpture. In the third lecture she summarized the theoretical knowledge which she had imparted to her listeners during the first two lectures: "You have become acquainted with a number of the most important fundamental ideas of psychoanalysis and with its customary terminology. You have met with the idea of the unconscious, repression, reaction formation, sublimation, transference, the Oedipus complex and the castration complex, the libido, and the theory of infantile sexuality" (p. 70). This is indeed a great deal to have given in two lectures to a rather unsophisticated audience, which absorbed it easily without realizing that they were being introduced to extremely complicated analytic theory. However, the reader-listener is never left in doubt that he has really just been given a taste of knowledge, enough to whet his appetite for more without satisfying him.

Anna Freud, like Bernfeld, thought that it was necessary to arrange systematically the phenomena facing the educator and to trace them to their original source. She has done just that in her recent book, *Normality and Pathology in Childhood* (1965). She has collected and classified a tremendous catalogue of human behavior and put it at the disposal of educators, researchers, and psychoanalysts. Years ago, however, she warned, "such classification requires special knowledge" (1930, p. 11). She now says that "without exploration during analysis, these forms of behavior remain therefore inconclusive" (1965, p. 22).

She has repeatedly stressed that observers need to be analytically trained. In 1930 she maintained that "psychoanalysis is well qualified to offer a criticism of existing educational methods" (p. 104), but that "no analytical pedagogy exists . . . it will be a long time before theory and practice are complete and can be recommended for general use" (p. 103). In 1965 she described certain areas within which the psychoanalytic theories can be applied profitably to preventive work. Preventive work in psychiatry is generally considered mental hygiene; insofar as it concerns children it is an area close to education. Although Anna Freud does not offer an educational system, she considers herself an educator, particularly an educator of educators. She is able to impart knowledge about the forms of human behavior and a method of understanding and influencing it.

Aichhorn, who worked mainly with his intuition, left rather stranded the educator who was less gifted in that way. Anna Freud's book, *Normality and Pathology*, gives the educator a large amount of material which he may store within himself, so that he may draw on memory rather than intuition for his understanding and reactions. However, only the analyzed educator will be able to make full use of this book.

REFERENCES

Aichhorn, A. (1925), *Wayward Youth*. New York: Viking Press, 1935.
Allen, F. H. (1942), *Psychotherapy with Children*. New York: Norton.
Alpert, A. (1941), The latency period. *Amer. J. Orthopsychiat.*, 11:126-133.
——— (1949), Sublimation and sexualization. A case report. *The Psychoanalytic Study of the Child*, 3/4:271-278. New York: International Universities Press.
Balint, A. (1936), Versagen und Gewähren in der Erziehung. *Ztschr. psychoanal. Pädogogik*, 10:75-83.
Bender, L.; Keiser, S.; & Schilder, P. (1936), Studies in aggressiveness, from Bellevue Hospital Psychiatric Division and the Medical College of New York University. *Genetic Psychol., Monogr.*, 18:357-564.
——— (1953), *Aggression, Hostility and Anxiety in Children*. Springfield, Ill.: Charles C Thomas.
Bennett, J. W. (1967), *The Hutterian Brothers*. Stanford, Calif.: Stanford University Press.
Beres, D. (1952), Clinical notes on aggression in childhood. *The Psychoanalytic Study of the Child*, 7:241-263. New York: International Universities Press.
Bergman, P. & Escalona, S. K. (1949), Unusual sensitivities in very young children. *The Psychoanalytic Study of the Child*, 3/4:333-352. New York: International Universities Press.
Bernfeld, S. (1922), *Vom Gemeinschaftsleben der Jugend. Beiträge zur Jugendforschung*. Leipzig: Internationaler psychoanalytischer Verlag.
——— (1925a), *The Psychology of the Infant*. New York: Brentano, 1929.
——— (1925b), *Sisyphos, oder die Grenzen der Erziehung*. Leipzig: Internationaler psychoanalytischer Verlag, 1928.
——— (1934), The psychoanalytic psychology of the young child. *Psychoanal. Quart.*, 4:3-14, 1935.

318   REFERENCES

Bettelheim, B. & Sylvester, E. (1949), Delinquency and morality. *The Psychoanalytic Study of the Child*, 5:329-342. New York: International Universities Press.

Bibring-Lehner, G. (1947), Psychiatry and social work. *J. Soc. Casework*, 28:203-211.

Bonnard, A. (1950), The mother as a therapist in a case of obsessional neurosis. *The Psychoanalytic Study of the Child*, 5:391-408. New York: International Universities Press.

Bornstein, B. (1931), Phobia in a two-and-a-half-year-old child. *Psychoanal. Quart.*, 4:93-119, 1935.

———— (1936), Ein Beispiel für die Leugnung durch die Phantasie. *Ztschr. psychoanal. Pädagogik*, 10:269-275.

Bornstein, S. (1933), A child analysis. *Psychoanal. Quart.*, 4:190-225, 1935.

———— (1937), Missverständnisse in der psychoanalytischen Pädagogik. *Ztschr. psychoanal. Pädagogik*, 11:81-90.

Bühler, C. (1933), Social behavior of children. In: Murchison, C. A., *Handbook of Child Psychology*. Worcester, Mass.: Clark University Press.

Burlingham, D. T. (1951), Present trends in handling the mother-child relationship during the therapeutic process. *The Psychoanalytic Study of the Child*, 6:31-37. New York: International Universities Press.

Buxbaum, E. (1935), Exhibitionistic onanism in a ten-year-old boy. *This Volume*, pp. 149-175.

———— (1936), Massenpsychologie und Probleme in der Schulklasse. *Ztschr. psychoanal. Pädagogik*, 10:215-240.

———— (1941), The role of detective stories in the analysis of a twelve-year-old boy. *This Volume*, pp. 196-205.

———— (1945), Transference and group formation in children and adolescents. *This Volume*, pp. 243-258.

———— (1946), Psychotherapy and psychoanalysis in the treatment of children. *This Volume*, pp. 133-146.

———— (1947), Activity and aggression in children. *This Volume*, pp. 37-44.

———— (1949a), The role of a second language in the formation of ego and superego. *This Volume*, pp. 230-240.

———— (1949b), *Your Child Makes Sense*. New York: International Universities Press.

———— (1950), A contribution to the psychoanalytic knowledge of the latency period. *This Volume*, pp. 206-229.

———— (1954), Technique of child therapy. A critical evaluation. *This Volume*, pp. 88-132.

———— (1955), The problem of separation and the feeling of identity. *This Volume*, pp. 23-36.

———— (1959), Psychosexual development. *This Volume*, pp. 7-22.

—— (1960), Hair pulling and fetishism. *This Volume*, pp. 176-195.

—— (1964a), The parents' role in the etiology of learning disabilities. *This Volume*, pp. 60-87.

—— (1964b), Aggression und die Bedeutng der Gruppe für die Adoleszenz. *Bishierher und nicht weiter*, ed: Mitscherlich, A. Munich: R. Piper and Co.

—— (1966), Three great psychoanalytic educators. *This Volume*, pp. 306-315.

Deutsch, H. (1944), *Psychology of Women*, Vols. 1 & 2. New York: Grune & Stratton.

—— (1967), *Selected Problems of Adolescence*. [Psychoanalytic Study of the Child, Monogr. 3]. New York: International Universities Press.

Dollard, J.; Miller, N. E.; Doob, L. W.; Mowrer, O. H.; & Sears, R. R. (1939), *Frustration and Aggression*. New Haven: Yale University Press.

Dostoevsky, F. (1879-1880), *The Brothers Karamazov*. New York: New American Library, 1957.

Eissler, K. R. (1953), The effect of structure of the ego on psychoanalytic technique. *J. Amer. Psychoanal. Assn.*, 1:104-143.

—— (1959), Notes on the environment of a genius. *The Psychoanalytic Study of the Child*, 14:267-313. New York: International Universities Press.

Ekstein, R. & Matto, R. (1964), Psychoanalysis and education. *Reiss-Davis Clin. Bull.*, 11:7-25.

Erikson, E. H. (1946), Ego development and historical change. *The Psychoanalytic Study of the Child*, 2:359-396. New York: International Universities Press.

—— (1950), *Childhood and Society*. New York: Norton.

—— (1956), The problem of ego identity. *J. Amer. Psychoanal. Assn.*, 4:56-121.

—— (1958), *Young Man Luther. A Study in Psychoanalysis and History*. New York: Norton.

Escalona, S. K. & Leitch, M. (1954), Emotional development in the first year of life. In: *Problems of Infancy and Childhood*, ed. Senn, M. J. New York: Josiah Macy, Jr. Foundation.

Fenichel, O. (1945), *The Psychoanalytic Theory of Neurosis*. New York: Norton.

Ferenczi, S. (1911), Obscene words. Contribution to the psychology of the latent period. In: *Sex in Psychoanalysis*. New York: Basic Books, 1950, pp. 132-153.

Finley, M. H.; Gerard, M. W.; Liss, E.; Markey, O. B.; Zachry, C. B. & Levy, D. J. (1943), Orthopsychiatry and the profession of education. *Amer. J. Orthopsychiat.*, 13:266-283.

Fishman, J. R. & Solomon, F. (1963), Youth and social action. *Amer. J. Orthopsychiat.*, 33:872-883.

Fraiberg, S. (1950), On the sleep disturbances of early childhood. *The Psychoanalytic Study of the Child*, 5:285-309. New York: International Universities Press.

—— (1952), A critical neurosis in a two-and-a-half-year-old girl. *The Psychoanalytic Study of the Child*, 7:173-215. New York: International Universities Press.

Freud, A. (1926), Introduction to the technique of the analysis of children. In: *The Psychoanalytical Treatment of Children*. New York: International Universities Press, 1946.

—— (1927), Theory of children's analysis. In: *The Psychoanalytical Treatment of Children*. New York: International Universities Press, 1946, pp. 55-64.

—— (1930), *Psychoanalysis for Teachers and Parents*. New York: Emerson Books, 1935.

—— (1936), *The Ego and the Mechanisms of Defense* (Revised Edition). New York: International Universities Press, 1966.

—— & Burlingham, D. (1943a), *Infants without Families: the Case for and against Residential Nurseries*. New York: International Universities Press, 1944.

—— & —— (1943b), *War and Children*. New York: International Universities Press, 1944.

—— (1945), Indications for child analysis. In: *The Psychoanalytical Treatment of Children*. New York: International Universities Press, 1946, pp. 67-93.

—— (1946a), *The Psychoanalytical Treatment of Children*. New York: International Universities Press.

—— (1946b), Psychoanalytic study of infantile feeding disturbances. *The Psychoanalytic Study of the Child*, 2:119-132. New York: International Universities Press.

—— (1949), Aggression in relation to emotional development: normal and pathological. *The Psychoanalytic Study of the Child*, 3/4:37-42. New York: International Universities Press.

—— (1951), Observations on child development. *The Psychoanalytic Study of the Child*, 6:18-30. New York: International Universities Press.

—— (1952), The mutual influences in the development of ego and id. *The Psychoanalytic Study of the Child*, 7:42-50. New York: International Universities Press.

—— (1954a), Problems of infantile neurosis: a discussion. *The Psychoanalytic Study of the Child*, 9:25-31. New York: International Universities Press.

—— (1954b), Psychoanalysis and education. *The Psychoanalytic Study of the Child*, 9:9-15. New York: International Universities Press.

—— (1954c), Safeguarding the emotional health of our children. An inquiry into the concept of the rejecting mother. *Casework*

Papers from the National Conference of Social Work. New York: Family Serv. Assn. Amer., 1955, pp. 5-17.

——— (1958a), Adolescence. *The Psychoanalytic Study of the Child,* 13:255-278. New York: International Universities Press.

——— (1958b), Child observation and prediction of development: *The Psychoanalytic Study of the Child,* 13:92-116. New York: International Universities Press.

——— (1960), Introduction to Kata Levy's paper. *The Psychoanalytic Study of the Child,* 15:378-380.

——— (1965), *Normality and Pathology in Childhood. Assessments of Development.* New York: International Universities Press.

Freud, S. (1901), The psychopathology of everyday life. *Standard Edition,* 6. London: Hogarth Press, 1960.

——— (1905), Three essays on the theory of sexuality. *Standard Edition,* 7:125-243. London: Hogarth Press, 1953.

——— (1911), Formulations on the two principles of mental functioning. *Standard Edition,* 12:218-226. London: Hogarth Press, 1958.

——— (1915), Instincts and their vicissitudes. *Standard Edition,* 14:111-140. London: Hogarth Press, 1955.

——— (1916), Some character-types met with in psycho-analytic work. *Standard Edition,* 14:316-331. London: Hogarth Press, 1957.

——— (1920), Beyond the pleasure principle. *Standard Edition,* 18:7-64. London: Hogarth Press, 1961.

——— (1921), Group psychology and the analysis of the ego. *Standard Edition,* 18:69-143. London: Hogarth Press, 1955.

——— (1923), The ego and the id. *Standard Edition,* 19:19-27. London: Hogarth Press, 1961.

——— (1924), The dissolution of the oedipus complex. *Standard Edition,* 19:173-179. London: Hogarth Press, 1961.

——— (1925), Preface to Aichhorn's *Wayward Youth. Standard Edition,* 19:273-275. London: Hogarth Press, 1961.

——— (1927a), Fetishism. *Standard Edition,* 21:149-157. London: Hogarth Press, 1961.

——— (1927b), The future of an illusion. *Standard Edition,* 21:3-56. London: Hogarth Press, 1961.

——— (1930), Civilization and its discontents. *Standard Edition,* 21:59-145. London: Hogarth Press, 1961.

——— (1933), Why war? *Standard Edition,* 22:197-215. London: Hogarth Press, 1964.

Fries, M. (1946), The child's ego development and the training of adults in his environment. *The Psychoanalytic Study of the Child,* 2:85-112. New York: International Universities Press.

Giovacchini, P. L. (1963), Integrative aspects of object relationships. *Psychoanal. Quart.,* 32:393-407.

Golan, S. (1959), Collective education in the kibbutz. *Psychiat.*, 22:167-177.

Greenacre, P. (1944), Infant reactions to restraint: problems in the fate of infantile aggression. *Amer. J. Orthopsychiat.*, 14:204-218.

—— (1953), Certain relationships between fetishism and the faulty development of body image. *The Psychoanalytic Study of the Child*, 8:79-98. New York: International Universities Press.

—— (1955a), Further considerations regarding fetishism. *The Psychoanalytic Study of the Child*, 10:187-194. New York: International Universities Press.

—— (1955b), *Swift and Carroll: Psychoanalytic Study of Two Lives.* New York: International Universities Press.

Grunebaum, M. G.; Hurwitz, I.; Prentice, N. M. & Sperry, B. M. (1962), Fathers of sons with primary neurotic learning inhibitions. *Amer. J. Orthopsychiat.*, 32:462-472.

Harlow, H. F. (1959), Love in infant monkeys. *Sci. Amer.*, 200 (6):68-74.

Hartmann, H. (1939), *Ego Psychology and the Problem of Adaptation.* New York: International Universities Press, 1958.

—— (1946), Comments on the formation of psychic structure. *The Psychoanalytic Study of the Child*, 2:11-38. New York: International Universities Press.

—— Kris, E.; & Loewenstein, R. M. (1949), Notes on the theory of aggression. *The Psychoanalytic Study of the Child*, 3/4:9-36. New York: International Universities Press.

Hellman, I. (1954), Some observations on mothers of children with intellectual inhibitions. *The Psychoanalytic Study of the Child*, 9:258-273. New York: International Universities Press.

Hoffer, W. (1949), Mouth, hand and ego integration. *The Psychoanalytic Study of the Child*, 3/4:49-56. New York: International Universities Press.

—— (1950), Development of the body ego. *The Psychoanalytic Study of the Child*, 5:18-23. New York: International Universities Press.

Jacobson, E. (1954), The self and the object world: vicissitudes of their infantile cathexes and their influence on ideational and affective development. *The Psychoanalytic Study of the Child*, 9:75-127. New York: International Universities Press.

Johnson, A. M. & Szurek, S. A. (1952), The genesis of antisocial acting out in children and adults. *Psychoanal. Quart.*, 21:323-343.

Katan, A. (1950), Structural aspects of a case of schizophrenia. *The Psychoanalytic Study of the Child*, 5:175-211. New York: International Universities Press.

—— (1959), The nursery school as a diagnostic help to the child guidance clinic. *The Psychoanalytic Study of the Child*, 14:250-264. New York: International Universities Press.

Kaufman, I. C. (1960), Some ethological studies of social relationships and conflict situations. *J. Amer. Psychoanal. Assn.*, 8:671-685.

Kiell, N. (1964), *The Universal Experience of Adolescence.* New York: International Universities Press.

Klein, M. (1932), *The Psychoanalysis of Children.* New York: Grove Press, 1960.

Koff, R. H. (1961), Learning difficulties in childhood (Panel Report). *J. Amer. Psychoanal. Assn.*, 9:125-134.

Kris, E. (1943), Some problems of war propaganda. *Psychoanal. Quart.*, 12:381-395.

——— (1948), On psychoanalysis and education. *Amer. J. Orthopsychiat.*, 18:622-635.

——— (1955), Neutralization and sublimation: observations on young children. *The Psychoanalytic Study of the Child*, 10:30-46. New York: International Universities Press.

——— (1962), Decline and recovery in the life of a three-year-old or data in psychoanalytic perspective on the mother-child relationship. *The Psychoanalytic Study of the Child*, 17:175-215. New York: International Universities Press.

Levy, D. M. (1944), On the problem of movement restraint. *Amer. J. Orthopsychiat.*, 14:644-671.

Levy, K. (1960), Simultaneous analysis of a mother and her adolescent daughter. *The Psychoanalytic Study of the Child*, 15:380-391. New York: International Universities Press.

Lorenz, K. (1963), *On Aggression.* New York: Harcourt, Brace & World, 1966.

Lowrey, L. G. et al. (1943), The treatment of aggression. *Amer. J. Orthopsychiat.*, 13:384-441.

Mahler, M. S. (1952), On child psychosis and schizophrenia: autistic and symbiotic infantile psychosis. *The Psychoanalytic Study of the Child*, 7:286-305. New York: International Universities Press.

——— & Gosliner, B. J. (1955), On symbiotic child psychosis: genetic, dynamic, and restitutive aspects. *The Psychoanalytic Study of the Child*, 10:195-212. New York: International Universities Press.

Mittelman, B. (1955), Motor patterns and genital behavior: fetishism. *The Psychoanalytic Study of the Child*, 10:241-263. New York: International Universities Press.

Nagler, S. (1963), Clinical observations on kibbutz children. *Israel Annals Psychiat. & Related Disciplines*, 1:201-216.

Neubauer, P. B., (ed.) (1965), *Children in Collectives.* Springfield, Ill.: Charles C Thomas.

Nunberg, H. (1932), *Principles of Psychoanalysis. Their Application to the Neuroses.* New York: International Universities Press, 1956.

Pearson, G. H. J. (1958), *Adolescence and the Conflict of Generations.* New York: Norton.

Peller, L. (1946), Incentives to development and means of early education. *The Psychoanalytic Study of the Child*, 2:397-415. New York: International Universities Press.

Piaget, J. (1926), *The Language and Thought of the Child*. New York: Harcourt, Brace.

Rabin, A. I. (1965), *Growing Up in the Kibbutz*. New York: Springer.

Rambert, M. L. (1949), *Children in Conflict*. New York: International Universities Press.

Rank, B. & MacNaughton, D. (1950), A clinical contribution to early ego development. *The Psychoanalytic Study of the Child*, 5:53-65. New York: International Universities Press.

Rank, O. (1909), *The Myth of the Birth of the Hero*. New York: Robert Brunner, 1952.

Rapaport, D. (1958), The study of kibbutz education and its bearing on the theory of development. *Amer. J. Orthopsychiat.*, 28:587-597.

Redl, F. (1942), Group emotion and leadership. *Psychiat.*, 5:573-596.

——— & Wineman, D. (1951), *Children Who Hate*. Glencoe, Ill.; Free Press.

——— & ——— (1952), *Controls from Within*. Glencoe, Ill.: Free Press.

Reich, W. (1927), Zur Technik der Deutung und der Widerstandsanalyse. Über die gesetzmässige Entwicklung der Übertragungsneurose. *Internat. Ztschr. ärztl. Psychoanal.*, 13:142-159.

——— (1928), On character analysis. In: *Psychoanalytic Reader*, ed. Fliess, R. New York: International Universities Press, pp. 129-147.

Ribble, M. A. (1943), *The Rights of Infants*. New York: Columbia University Press.

Rickman, J., (ed.) (1936), *On the Bringing Up of Children*. London: Kegan, Paul.

Robertson, J. (1962), Mothering as an influence on early development: a study of well baby records. *The Psychoanalytic Study of the Child*, 17:245-264. New York: International Universities Press.

Romm, M. E. (1949), Some dynamics in fetishism. *Psychoanal. Quart.*, 18:137-153.

Ross, H. (1943), Psychology of pre-adolescent children in war time. II. Emotional forces in children as influenced by current events. *Amer. J. Orthopsychiat.*, 13:502-504.

Safran, N. (1963), *The United States and Israel*. Cambridge: Harvard University Press.

Salk, L. (1952), Mother's heartbeat as an imprinting stimulus. *Trans. N. Y. Acad. Sci.*, 24:753-763.

Schwarz, H. (1950), The mother in the consulting room: notes on the psychoanalytic treatment of two young children. *The Psychoanalytic Study of the Child*, 5:343-357. New York: International Universities Press.

Silverberg, W. V. (1952), *Childhood Experience and Personal Destiny*. New York: Springer.

Sorokin, P. A. (1956), The Hutterites of the U. S. A. In: *The Ways of Power and Love*. Boston: Beacon Press.

Sperling, M. (1949), Analysis of a case of recurrent ulcer of the leg. *The Psychoanalytic Study of the Child*, 3/4:391-408. New York: International Universities Press.

——— (1950), Children's interpretation and reaction to the unconscious of their mothers. *Internat. J. Psychoanal.*, 31:36-41.

Spiro, M. E. (1951), *Children of the Kibbutz*. New York: Schocken Books.

——— (1963), *Kibbutz Venture in Utopia*. New York: Schocken Books.

Spitz, R. A. (1945), Hospitalism: an inquiry into the genesis of psychiatric conditions in early childhood. *The Psychoanalytic Study of the Child*, 1:53-74. New York: International Universities Press.

——— (1946a), Hospitalism: a follow-up report. *The Psychoanalytic Study of the Child*, 2:113-117. New York: International Universities Press.

——— (1946b), Anaclitic depression: an inquiry into the genesis of psychiatric conditions in early childhood. *The Psychoanalytic Study of the Child*, 2:313-342. New York: International Universities Press.

——— (1951), The psychogenic diseases in infancy: an attempt at their etiologic classification. *The Psychoanalytic Study of the Child*, 6:255-275. New York: International Universities Press.

——— (1959), *A Genetic Field Theory of Ego Formation*. New York: International Universities Press.

——— & Wolf, K. M. (1946), The smiling response. *Genet. Psychol. Monogr.*, 34:57-125.

Sprince, M. P. (1962), The development of a preoedipal partnership between an adolescent girl and her mother. *The Psychoanalytic Study of the Child*, 17:418-450. New York: International Universities Press.

Stevenson, O. (1954), The first treasured possession: a study of the part played by specially loved objects and toys in the life of certain children. *The Psychoanalytic Study of the Child*, 9:199-217. New York: International Universities Press.

Sylvester, E. (1945a), Psychotherapy for children (Symposium). *Amer. J. Orthopsychiat.*, 15:30-32.

——— (1945b), Analysis of psychogenic anorexia in a four-year-old. *The Psychoanalytic Study of the Child*, 1:167-188. New York: International Universities Press.

326 REFERENCES

Szurek, S. A. (1951), The family and the staff in hospital psychiatric therapy of children. *Amer. J. Orthopsychiat.*, 21:597-611.

Thomas, D. S. (1929), *Some New Techniques for Studying Social Behavior.* New York: Columbia University Press.

Thrasher, F. M. (1927), *Gang: A Study of 1,313 Gangs in Chicago.* Chicago: University of Chicago Press, 1963.

Waelder, R. (1933), The psychoanalytic theory of play. *Psychoanal. Quart.*, 2:208-224.

Waelder, R. (1937), The problem of the genesis of psychical conflict in earliest infancy. *Int. J. Psychoanal.*, 18:406-473.

Winnicott, D. W. (1953), Transitional objects and transitional phenomena: a study of the first not-me possession. *Int. J. Psychoanal.*, 34:89-97.

Witmer, H. L., (ed.) (1946), *Psychiatric Interviews with Children.* New York: Commonwealth Fund.

Wulff, M. (1946), Fetishism and object-choice in early childhood. *Psychoanal. Quart.*, 15:450-471.

—— (1951), The problem of neurotic manifestations in children of preoedipal age. *The Psychoanalytic Study of the Child*, 6:169-179. New York: International Universities Press.

Zulliger, H. (1930), Psychoanalyse und Führerschaft in der Schule. *Imago*, 16-39-50.

—— (1933), Der Abenteurer Schundroman. *Ztschr. psychoanal. Pädagogik*, 7:357-377.

INDEX